Uneasy Allies?

Uneasy Allies?

Evangelical and Jewish Relations

Edited by Alan Mittleman, Byron Johnson, and Nancy Isserman

LEXINGTON BOOKS

A division of
ROWMAN & LITTLEFIELD PUBLISHERS, INC.
Lanham • Boulder • New York • Toronto • Plymouth, UK

LEXINGTON BOOKS

A division of Rowman & Littlefield Publishers, Inc.
A wholly owned subsidiary of
The Rowman & Littlefield Publishing Group, Inc.
4501 Forbes Boulevard, Suite 200
Lanham, MD 20706

Estover Road
Plymouth PL6 7PY
United Kingdom

British Library Cataloguing in Publication Information Available

Library of Congress Cataloging-in-Publication Data
Uneasy allies? : Evangelical and Jewish relations / edited by Alan Mittleman,
Byron Johnson, and Nancy Isserman.
    p. cm.
Includes bibliographical references.
ISBN-13: 978-0-7391-1965-5 (cloth : alk. paper)
ISBN-10: 0-7391-1965-6 (cloth : alk. paper)
ISBN-13: 978-0-7391-1966-2 (pbk. : alk. paper)
ISBN-10: 0-7391-1966-4 (pbk. : alk. paper)
  1. Evangelicalism—Relations—Judaism. 2. Judaism—Relations—
Evangelicalism. 3. Christianity and other religions—Judaism—
4. Judaism—Relations—Christianity—1945– . 5. Evangelicalism—United
States. 6. Judaism—United States. I. Mittleman, Alan, 1953– . II. Johnson,
Byron, 1955– . III. Isserman, Nancy, 1951– .
  BR1641.J83U54 2007
  261.2'6—dc22   2007016699

Printed in the United States of America.

©™ The paper used in this publication meets the minimum requirements of
American National Standard for Information Sciences—Permanence of Paper
for Printed Library Materials, ANSI/NISO Z39.48-1992.

$ 30.05

Contents

Foreword

Nancy Isserman

Several years ago, the late Murray Friedman, the founder and first director of the Myer and Rosaline Feinstein Center for American Jewish History, Temple University, expressed a concern about the shift of the Left
from a position of support for the State of Israel to one of opposition. At
the same time he observed the increasing support for Israel from conservative groups and the Right. Friedman wrote in an article online for *Front
Page* on February 12, 2004, "Even as mainline Protestant groups began to
shift ground following the Six-Day War, Israel's victory dramatically in-
tensified its positive image among many evangelical leaders." He noted
that as early as the 1980s some Jewish organizations, including The
American Jewish Committee, began reaching out to Evangelicals. Friedman continued, "In what has been perhaps the most astonishing development, in the last two or three years, we have witnessed a significant
shift by Jewish leaders in their response to the Christian Right. Just a few
years ago they had attacked it as anti-Semitic and criticized it for engaging in missionary activity among Jews." But starting in 2002 Jewish organizations such as the Zionist Organization of America and the Anti-
Defamation League honored Christian Evangelical activists for their
support of Israel. It is these dramatic changes that fueled Friedman's desire to convene a forum to focus on Evangelical-Jewish relations.

Together with Alan Mittleman, a former colleague of Friedman's at
the American Jewish Committee, and now the director of the Louis
Finkelstein Institute for Religious and Social Studies of The Jewish
Theological Seminary, and Byron Johnson, director of The Baylor Institute for Studies of Religion, Baylor University, Friedman advocated for

a conference of scholars who would interact with Evangelical and Jewish activists to examine the current and historical state of Evangelical-Jewish relations.

In 2004, planning for the conference began among these institutions and their staffs. These organizations have been at the forefront of exploring interfaith issues in the academic arena. Since 1938, the Louis Finkelstein Institute for Religious and Social Studies has maintained an innovative interfaith and intergroup relations program that emphasizes conversation among diverse communities about matters of public significance. The Institute sponsors conferences on the theoretical, political, and theological dimensions of the controversial role of religion in liberal democracies, both in the United States and abroad.

The Baylor Institute for Studies of Religion (ISR) seeks to approach the study of religion from multiple disciplines and to offer collaborative research opportunities for religion scholars across the disciplines, both at Baylor and nationally. ISR exists to involve scholars in creative efforts to grasp the complexities and interconnections of religion in the life of individuals and societies.

The third participating institution in the conference and book that followed is Murray Friedman's own institution, the Myer and Rosaline Feinstein Center for American Jewish History, Temple University. The Feinstein Center serves to inspire public awareness and scholarly research related to the American Jewish experience. It designs and develops unique lectures, conferences, publications, and fellowships in order to promote discussion regarding the place of Jews in American life.

The three institutions and their staffs envisioned a conference with the goals of exploring and beginning to document the relationship between Evangelicals and Jews; providing an understanding of changes taking place in the relationship between the two groups; and then using this understanding to help activists in the field develop better programming and foster stronger ties between Evangelicals and Jews. The conference was held at The Jewish Theological Seminary in November 2005. This book is an outgrowth of that conference, containing papers from many of the presenters at the 2005 event. Unfortunately for all of us, Murray Friedman passed away six months before the conference. But the conference and this book are the product of his vision, his insight and scholarship, and his uncanny ability to detect what would be the crucial policy issues facing the Jewish and other religious communities when they were still minor blips on the public policy agenda.

This book is dedicated to Murray Friedman, Visionary, Activist and Scholar, 1926–2005.

Introduction

Alan Mittleman

This book attempts to understand the evolving relationship between American Jews and Evangelical Christians. As such, it tries to break a new path. There is very little in the way of scholarly literature or opinion research surveys from which the contributors to this volume could draw. The relationship of American Jews with Mainline Protestants or with Catholics is well documented. Those ongoing encounters have produced much documentation and there are also many scholarly studies dedicated to interpreting it. The relationship with Evangelicals, however, is in its infancy. Both documentation stemming from the encounter of the two groups and scholarly evaluations of that encounter are scarce.

What is actually out there? There are two books that grew out of conferences conducted by the American Jewish Committee in the 1970s and 1980s. These represent a first attempt to explain basic features of each community to the other and to enter into dialogue about salient theological differences and purported similarities.[1] There are also books that try sympathetically to interpret Jews and Judaism to an Evangelical audience and to do likewise for a Jewish one.[2] The Jewish books have a neoconservative provenance and advocate closer relations based on Evangelical support for Israel or for traditional social values attractive to Jewish neoconservatives.[3] There seem to be no studies that merely explore the relationship without either the bias of advocacy or of criticism.

The reasons for this relative dearth of literature are not hard to find. Although the traditions that feed into contemporary Evangelicalism have been active in American religious life since colonial times, what we call Evangelicalism today is a rather recent phenomenon. As several of the contributors to this volume explain, Evangelicalism in its present incarnation is largely a postwar movement among traditional Protestants to shed the sectarianism of fundamentalism, itself a turn-of-the-century reaction, and reengage American culture in a positive way. Contemporary Evangelicalism traces its lineage to preachers such as Billy Graham, theologically conservative intellectuals such as Carl Henry, and the organizers of the National Association of Evangelicals, founded in 1942.

At the very moment when Evangelicalism was finding its modern orientation, Jews were struggling to secure the conditions that have led, over the past half-century, to their full acceptance into American society and their rise to a high status group. The postwar Jewish effort was, first and foremost, the fight against institutional anti-Semitism. Jews associated institutional, as opposed to free-floating personal anti-Semitism, with the residue of semi-official Protestantism in American society. By this they meant Sunday closing laws, school-sponsored prayer and Bible reading, public nativity displays, religious instruction during the school day, etc. What conservative Christians took to be normal signs of moral and political health, Jews found exclusionary and backward.[4] In somewhat of an ironic twist, Jewish agencies would not have been able to mount successful challenges to these long-standing practices had they not had the support of liberal Protestants. Liberal Protestantism was in its heyday in the postwar period and Jews, long suspicious of traditional, orthodox Christianity of all stripes as a potent source of anti-Semitic inclinations, found in it an ally of sorts. Although liberal Protestant leaders did not embrace the State of Israel, they did seem to stand for the progressive, civil and human rights commitments, and social reforms which the largely liberal Jewish community found essential for its own survival and deeply compatible with its own values. In the 1950s and 1960s, Jews thought that their own Jewish Orthodoxy would pass away, a dying remnant of the Old World, and that a liberal Protestantism, more Deweyan than divine, would inherit the future. The opening up of Catholicism to more democratic and humanistic impulses in Vatican Council II (1962–1965) seemed to confirm this confidence in the world-conquering imperative of religious liberalism. Against such a worldview, Evangelicalism could only seem like a throwback to an earlier fundamentalism that many adherents were anxious to shed.

To their credit, Jewish agencies such as the American Jewish Committee and the Anti-Defamation League had begun, by the late 1960s, to notice that the cultural and demographic map of American Christianity was changing and that it was in the Jewish interest to make contact with leaders of the new Evangelicalism. The silence of the Mainline Churches before the 1967 war, in which Jews feared a second Holocaust would take place, the liberal criticism afterwards, compared to some Evangelical affirmations of Israel's right to the conquered territories, did not escape Jewish notice. Although Evangelicals were already emerging as allies of Israel and potential dialogue partners for American Jews, suspicion on the Jewish side still remained strong. Evangelicalism is typically about evangelism. Whereas the Mainline Churches and Catholicism were moving both morally and theologically in the direction of a pluralism that affirmed the dignity of Judaism, Evangelicalism seemed to undermine the legitimacy of Judaism at every turn. Not only did (and does) the Evangelical insistence on acceptance of Jesus as one's personal savior seem to undercut any ongoing role for Judaism, but the general tendency to dichotomize the world into saved and damned, good and evil, etc., seems intellectually non-kosher to Jews. American Jews are devoted, by and large, to social inclusion, minority and civil rights, multiculturalism—to strategies of expanding boundaries and embracing differences. A Manichaean mentality that is comfortable with bright lines and hard edges is alien to the (non-Orthodox) majority of Jews and threatening to its epistemic style, so to speak.

Another reason that the Evangelical-Jewish relationship has had such difficulty getting off the ground and sustaining momentum has to do with the relative secularity of the Jewish community vis-à-vis Evangelicalism, a community constituted by religion alone. Even Jews who claim Judaism as their religion hold social, economic, moral and political views often indistinguishable from those of the non-religious. Jews, given their propensity toward a secular orientation, tend to view America as a secular nation with a "godless" Constitution. They see governmental institutions as ideally neutral or, more precisely, as religion-free zones. The Establishment clause tends to loom larger in their collective civil imagination than the Free Exercise clause. They view the Founders as Enlightenment humanists or deists, rather than as convinced Christians. Their root image of America is as a nation of immigrants with no heritage to defend other than enlightened traditions of human and civil rights. Evangelicals, by contrast, are more likely to hold religiously inflected images of

America as a nation whose ideals are rooted in Scripture and whose scriptural heritage is deserving of special attention and protection. In addition to discrepant constructions of the civil space both groups inhabit, the mere fact of taking religion seriously—very seriously in the case of Evangelicals—strikes Jews as odd. Whether as an artifact of high levels of education or as an aspect of their affirmation of modernity, Jews are more skeptical of the claims of traditional religion than other contemporary groups.

The essays that follow explore these themes in greater depth. The volume begins with a chapter by Yaakov Ariel, an Israeli scholar of American religion. In the tradition of foreign observers, beginning with Alexis de Tocqueville, who locate the salient values and traits of America in its religious heritage, Ariel underlines the ways in which America remains a Christian nation. In his view, attempts to see America as fully multicultural and multireligious, such as Diana Eck's or as significantly post-Protestant, such as E. J. Dionne's, are exaggerated. Ariel's essay describes the religious and cultural context in which the Jewish-Evangelical encounter occurs. He offers a corrective, in a sense, to the overly secularized or neutral image of America tacitly endorsed by many American Jews. If America remains a nation deeply etched by Protestant values and habits of mind and if Evangelicals represent some of these constitutive American values, then the encounter with Evangelicals is not arcane or exotic; it is an encounter with the heart and soul of America.

The next two chapters, by leading scholars of Evangelical and Jewish opinion, John Green and Barry Kosmin, try to determine what the two groups think of one another. Green's study of Evangelical opinions and attitudes toward Jews is facilitated by the many studies of Evangelicals he has conducted. In Kosmin's case, however, there are no direct data. Because Jews are a negligible percentage of the adult population of the United States (less than 3 percent) they do not show up in sufficient numbers on opinion research surveys for credible results. What we know of Jewish opinion comes primarily from expensive surveys undertaken periodically by national and local Jewish bodies. Questions about views toward Evangelicals, for example, would be considered a luxury and not pursued. In the absence of data that directly address what Jews think about Evangelicals, Kosmin's strategy is to compare Evangelical and Jewish responses on a host of values and policy questions and so determine how far the groups are from one another in attitudes. His general conclusion is that the socioeconomic gap is not great but the demographic and cultural one remains large. Similarly, John Green shows that Evangelicals themselves do not perceive a significant socioeconomic gap between Jews and other Americans, themselves included. They have, as do other Americans, largely positive views of Jews. Nonetheless, there are large cultural-attitudinal differences between the two groups.

The fourth chapter, by the authoritative historian of Jewish communal affairs, Lawrence Grossman, is a detailed look at the organized Jewish community's interaction with Evangelical elites. Grossman surveys the many ups and downs of the evolving relationship up to late 2005. Despite the fact that Evangelicals were the most steadfast supporters of Israel during the dark days of the second *Intifada*, prominent Jewish leaders in 2005 voiced their discomfort with the alleged "Christianizing" of America perpetrated by these same Evangelical elites. This opened a rift within the Jewish community over how to relate to this important constituency—what matters more, its domestic agenda (not monolithic, to be sure) or its Israel-friendly activism? The open criticism by Jewish leaders also stung Evangelicals, as well, leading to questions on their part over whether they want or expect a quid pro quo.

The fifth and sixth chapters are by Evangelical and Jewish activists, writing out of the midst of the troubled context described by Grossman. In chapter 5, Evangelical leader, George Mamo, assesses the history offered by Grossman from an Evangelical point of view. Mamo expresses a sense of hurt at the tensions that continue to characterize relations between the two communities. He calls for a sober, mature alliance based on what Jews and Evangelicals can agree on. The disagreements need not impede mutual commitments to Israel's security. But why are so many Evangelicals interested in, let alone committed to, the State of Israel? Is it because, as most Jews fear, they endorse—from a Jewish point of view—weird beliefs about the end times in which Israel has an apocalyptic role to play? Based on survey data commissioned by his organization, George Mamo argues that a predominant reason is less theological than political: Evangelicals believe that Israel and America share the same values. And where theology is pertinent, the predominant theological reason has nothing to do with eschatology. It has to do with God's promise to Abraham in Genesis, chapter 12 ("I will bless those that bless you and I will curse those that curse you"). Even on this delicate theological ground, is there not more of a bridge here than a divide, Mamo wonders.

In chapter 6, Ethan Felson, associate executive director of the Jewish Council for Public Affairs, who is centrally involved with Evangelical-Jewish relations, details the state of those relations from the perspective of the community relations practitioners who pursue them. From a local perspective, the picture of tense, "uneasy allies" offered by Grossman and other contributors is mitigated somewhat. The chapter offers a fascinating look at divisions within the Jewish community—even within the same local community—over whether or how to relate to Evangelicals.

The survey alluded to by George Mamo and others notwithstanding, some Evangelicals do, of course, believe in supporting Israel for eschatological reasons. The long history of Christian Zionism, paralleling the rise of Zionism itself, has had an eschatological component. Investigating this strand, both historically and in terms of its contemporary impact, Gary Dorrien outlines the theology of dispensationalism and its peregrination from a theological curiosity to a kind of fundamentalist dogma. He evaluates the influence of dispensationalist views on the Christian Right's attitudes toward Israel. Dorrien draws distinctions between fundamentalists and Evangelicals and sees the Christian Right more dominated by the former than the latter. He also sees Evangelicals gaining a less fundamentalist, more pragmatic political voice and speculates about what this will mean for future relations with Israel and the Jewish community.

Gerald McDermott reaches farther back into the past and offers a thorough review of the Christian theological sources on Israel from which Evangelicals draw. He too distinguishes strongly between fundamentalists and Evangelicals and explores the similarities and differences in the relationship of these two groups to Zionism and to the modern State of Israel. Both Dorrien and McDermott show the pluralism within the Evangelical community and give evidence for why some Evangelicals hold highly critical views of Israel, similar to what Jews have long found among the Mainline Protestants. Together, these two chapters offer a thorough, synoptic understanding of the crucial topic of Evangelical approaches to the modern State of Israel.

In the ninth chapter, Yehiel Poupko offers a Jewish, theologically grounded response to the Evangelical eschatology outlined in the previous chapters. Poupko, a Jewish veteran of years of dialogue with Evangelicals in the heartland, speaks to how Jews and Evangelicals relate differently to scripture, to prophecy, and to messianism. He assesses what impact, if any, fundamental differences in religious phenomenology should make to inter-group relations, dialogue and coalition building. Poupko foresees a future in which Evangelical-Jewish relations might come to resemble Catholic-Jewish relations in normality, "comfort level," and respectful appreciation of ineradicable and constitutive differences.

In chapter 10, Carl Schrag takes a more political approach to the questions addressed by Yehiel Poupko. He analyzes how different elements within the Jewish community weight the reality of Evangelical support for Israel. How do they construe the salience of eschatological anticipation among Evangelicals? What weight, if any, should it have as a determinant of Jewish cooperation with Evangelicals? Does the Evangelical-Jewish relationship in some way stand outside of the normal parameters of intergroup cooperation, where allies agree on some things and disagree on others yet remain allies? Why, for some Jews, do Evangelicals remain uniquely inassimilable to this norm of community relations practice?

Two assessments of where we stand today conclude the volume. The first, by a Jewish scholar of contemporary American culture and religion, Mark Silk, reckons with the fact that Evangelicals have, for the first time, real power. Any Jewish assessment of how to relate to them must take their political clout into consideration, as well as the unabashedly partisan style of Evangelical politics. Given the moral and political distance between the groups, Silk does not see the prospect of a "new entente, heartfelt or merely pragmatic." Silk believes that relations will be good on the playground and in the PTA. But in the policy making bodies of the Jewish community, he does not see much space for a broader opening to, as he characterizes it, an increasingly politicized and assertive Evangelicalism.

By contrast, David Neff distinguishes sharply between the Christian Right or Religious Right and rank-and-file Evangelicals, whom he finds far more tolerant and affirmative of pluralism than some of their politicized "leadership." He understands the Jewish fixation on the threat posed by the most politicized factions within the Evangelical spectrum but urges Jews to assume a more nuanced perspective. Responding to five questions Jews typically ask of Evangelicals, Neff's answers provide valuable insights for Jewish activists seeking to understand contemporary Evangelicalism. They also reveal the acute sensitivity Evangelical intellectuals can show to Jewish concerns.

Taken together these essays depict a rapidly evolving, multifaceted and promising relationship between Evangelicals and Jews. Although rooted in a common concern for the safety and well-being of Israel, Evangelical-Jewish relations have the potential to aim at a larger common good. There are tasks that both groups, defined in unique ways as communities of biblical faith, can share. Those shared tasks—care for the environment, concern for the most vulnerable among us, for the well-being of the family and the institutions of civil society, and for religious liberty abroad and at home—may increasingly enrich the relationship between these "uneasy allies" and redound to the benefit of both.

NOTES

1. Marc H. Tanenbaum, A. James Rudin and Marvin Wilson, *Evangelicals and Jews in Conversation: Scripture, Theology and History* (Grand Rapids, MI: Baker Book House, 1978) and A. James Rudin and Marvin R. Wilson, eds., *A Time to Speak: The Evangelical-Jewish Encounter* (Center for Judaic-Christian Studies, 1987).

2. David Rausch, *Building Bridges: Understanding Jews and Judaism* (Chicago: Moody Press, 1988); David Rausch, *Communities in Conflict: Evangelicals and Jews* (Philadelphia, PA: Trinity Press International, 1991); David Rausch, *Friends, Colleagues and Neighbors: Jewish Contributions to American History* (Grand Rapids, MI: Baker Publishing Group, 1996).

3. Elliot Abrams, *Faith or Fear: How Jews can Survive in a Christian America* (New York: Free Press, 1997); David Brog, *Standing with Israel: Why Christians Support the Jewish State* (Frontline, 2006). Zev Chafetz, *A Match Made in Heaven* (New York: Harper Collins, 2007).

4. For a thorough accounting, see Gregg Ivers, *To Build a Wall: American Jews and the Separation of Church and State* (Charlottesville: University of Virginia Press, 1995).

Is America Christian?

Religion in America at the Turn of the Twentieth Century

Yaakov Ariel

At the turn of the new millennium, a professor of religion published a book in which she advocated the opinion, popular among scholars of religion at the time, that non-Western religious communities, such as Islam, Hinduism and Buddhism, had acquired the same place in American life as Christianity had historically occupied, and that in fact this was already the nature of the religious and cultural scene in the United States.[1] At the turn of the twenty-first century, a number of scholars and public leaders have cast doubt on the role of Christianity in America history and life. Wishing to view American civic space as religiously neutral or as religiously diverse they portray all religious groups as standing on equal ground within the American polity. Christianity, according to this view, has either completed its historical course in America or is just one religion among the many on America's religious and public map.

This essay comes to counter such claims and to state, what to the author seems obvious, that Christianity, especially in its Protestant form, has had a deep and long lasting impact on shaping America's civic institutions and national agenda, as well as the country's values and morality. I maintain that Christianity has been and still remains the nation's most influential religion, towering above all other faiths in America. The Christian character of America has played a decisive role in shaping American attitudes toward Jews and Israel.

It is doubtful whether the aforementioned book would have received the same welcome had it been published in 2002. The reactions to the attacks on the World Trade Center made it clear that Christianity was still the majority religion in America, while Islam, Hinduism and Buddhism were the faiths of small albeit growing minorities. While America's religious landscape at the beginning of the twenty-first century is more diverse than ever before, non-Christian faiths do not hold the same status in American society as Christianity does, and Christianity still informs the imagery and spirit of the nation as a whole.

NEW PERCEPTIONS

Until the 1980s, few historians had doubted that Protestant Christianity had played a central role in shaping the values and agenda of the American nation. In the last generation, scholars of religion have made considerable efforts to present American religious life in an inclusive manner. They have given voice to an ever-growing number of religious groups and have often refrained from pointing to participants in the history of religion in America as major or marginal, giving equal voices to all of them.[2] Many historians have given up on constructing an historical narrative of American religion altogether and have become contented instead with offering snapshots of specific communities or congregations. For example, the most acclaimed book in the field of religion in America in the 1990s–2000s has been Robert Orsi's *The Madonna of 115 Street*, which tells the story of an Italian Catholic congregation in Harlem.

Other successful choices have been the depiction of the contemporary American religious scene by themes, such as architecture, pilgrimage, or religion and consumer culture. These have been new and exciting means of studying religion in America, offering enlarged and enriched perspectives. There have been, however, serious drawbacks. One of them is the anthological, quiltlike nature of the new studies whose authors relate to all religious groups on the American scene as equal participants in the larger drama of religion and culture in America. Unfortunately, such an approach does not offer a compelling interpretation of the relationship between faith and communal values in America. Themes such as the Protestant ethic and the spirit and agenda of the American republic have been abandoned and forgotten or condemned to ridicule. Instead, historians have moved to portray the course of American religious history as being multireligious and non-distinctly Protestant already in the colonial period. While such attempts represent an inclusive and tolerant vision of contemporary

America and as such are commendable, such studies are more eschatological than historical. They represent the writers' hopes more than a sound and empirical observation of American life. If one of the aims of studying history is to understand the impact of the past on the present, to examine the roots and origins of the social and cultural world in which we live, such histories, as well-meaning as they may be, are not very helpful. The revision and reorientation of the research and the teaching of history of religion in America, during the 1990s–2000s, has been so swift and so radical that scholars have often thrown away the baby with the bathwater. Protestantism was given a marginal role in the new panoramic kaleidoscope, if even that.[3] Classical studies by twentieth-century historians, such as Perry Miller, H. Richard Niebuhr, Sidney Mead, Robert Handy, Martin Marty, and William Hutchinson, have been cast aside, either forgotten or used as examples of historians who had privileged in their work the groups to which they had happened to belong.

However, something is terribly wrong, I argue, if scholars of religion in America present Buddhism as standing on the same ground with Christianity in American history and life. A casual look would suffice to see the gross inaccuracy of such a claim. One can compare, for example, the number of Buddhists and Christians in nationally influential positions. Who have been and still are the presidents, vice presidents and congressmen of the United States, the state governors and members of the states' legislatures, the Supreme Court justices, the generals in the American armed forces and the CEOs of America's corporations? Christians or Buddhists? No less important, what perceptions of the divine and its relation to the American Republic are promoted by America's civic institutions? For example, what does the printing on American currency of "In God We Trust" come to tell us? If Buddhists or Hindus were as influential as Christians, the inscription would read very differently.[4] It seems that scholars of religions in America have been carried away and while one should appreciate their contributions, I believe that it is time to correct some of their assessments and set the record straight.

Although the United States has no official religion and takes pride in its non-sponsorship of churches, America is, as a whole, a Christian nation, which adheres to Christian Protestant values and is run on Christian Protestant principles. While in its first generation the ruling elite of America was almost exclusively Protestant, in recent generations members of other Christian groups, such as Roman Catholics or Mormons, have come to exercise much influence too. Other religious groups are also making an impact on America's public and private life.

These do include Buddhists, Muslems, and Hindus.[5] Their numbers and influence lag far behind those of Christians, who have made a strong impact on the American mind and public discourse for generations, and are presently the larger group.

Proponents of the idea that America's public sphere should become devoid of religious components point to the nation's alleged secular constitution as a proof that America is in essence a secular commonwealth. Thus, by definition it is not a Christian country.[6] Such an outlook views attempts to influence national policies and legislation as a breach of proper civic conduct and a violation of the principles on which America had been built.[7] While one may respect the values and agendas of such thinkers and activists, their claims are devoid of a sense of reality. America has organized the relationship between church and state differently from other Christian nations. Perhaps, because of its seemingly more neutral stand, America has maintained a strong Christian character, stronger than in Christian nations that have not disengaged the church from the state, such as Britain or Sweden (and lately Spain!). While non-Christian religious communities have, especially since the 1960s, found a comfortable home in America, the constitutional system benefited Christian Protestant groups more than anyone else. In fact, the American arrangement created an open market of religions that has forced Protestant Christianity to maintain an energetic spirit, evangelize aggressively, and ultimately continue to shape the spirit and character of American society at large.[8]

A CHRISTIAN NATION FROM THE BEGINNING

The British colonies that eventually formed the American Republic began as Christian commonwealths. This does not come to say that all residents in the British colonies lived their lives in perfect harmony with Christian ideals, or that all of them even took their faith seriously. But the principles of the societies that they had created were Christian, and Christianity, in different forms and divisions, was the religion officially practiced in the colonies. Moreover, the wish to build a Christian society, and a more perfect one than in Europe, stood at the ideological center of the American colonial experience, shaping both communal and political agendas. Especially in New England, the founders of the colonies wished to establish a "city built upon a hill," an exemplary Christian commonwealth, that would serve as an inspiration for other parts of the world. The Puritan founders of the New

England colonies understood their experiences in biblical terms as a society in covenant with God, and this perception made its impact on the American national ethos.[9] Classical historians of religions in America, such as Perry Miller and H. Richard Niebuhr, have pointed to such Protestant ideals as playing a role in shaping the spirit of the American nation, as well as in directing the global policies of the United States.[10] Niebuhr attributed much of America's foreign policy and the manner in which Americans had wished to think of such policies, to the nation's sense of mission, and its self-image as a God-blessed commonwealth that served as a light unto the nations. While such an analysis idealizes American motives and does not mesh well with the more cynical post-colonial view of America as promoting, first and foremost, its own interest, it can well explain some of the current American global policies, including the latest (not necessarily successful) American attempts to export American ways and standards to nations that had never run their affairs on such principles.[11]

In contrast to Niebuhr, historians and political scientists have often pointed to the American political and civic systems, which were created at the turn of the nineteenth century, as influenced by the ideas of the European Enlightenment. From that perspective, the American Constitution and its early amendments had been based on abstract ideas rather than resulting from the interests of the nation's ruling elites or from struggles between conflicting agendas of different segments of the new nation.[12] While the United States decided not to have an official state church, there was no doubt that religious tradition inspired and instructed the American elite and the nation as a whole.[13] The decision in favor of religious disestablishment took place within a Christian cultural context. Ideas originating in the European Enlightenment certainly influenced the writers of the American Constitution, but their (non-orthodox) private faiths were Christian, even if influenced by the French and English Enlightenment.[14] The Enlightenment did not turn Christians into non-Christians, although it altered their faith and their perceptions of civic institutions.

Demands for liberty on the part of new or underprivileged Christian groups played an important part in bringing about the early constitutional changes. In essence, the American elite was allowing for more room and opportunity for Christian groups that had previously not been part of the civic and religious establishment. The amendment to the American Constitution did not really envision religious pluralism of the kind America has come to practice today. It aimed at the more limited goal of not providing any particular Protestant church with a privileged position within the American polity, and forbade Congress to pass a law that would require people to subscribe to a particular Christian creed in order to obtain a position in the American government.[15] The Founding Fathers were opening the gates for Christian, mostly Protestant, pluralism. Thomas Jefferson's rationale for the policy of religious disengagement should be understood in that light. When he spoke about the prospect of many religions coming along on the American scene, he envisioned Christian ones.[16] Significantly, the ultimate result of the American constitutional amendment has been a growth in Christian life and commitment, as new Christian movements have periodically increased their influence, and numerous new Christian groups have come on the scene.

One should bear in mind that the new Republic had no "Church of America" at its disposal and different Protestant denominations reigned in different colonies. The religious disengagement was, among other things, a practical move, and reflected the interests of Christian groups, the established ones as well as the underprivileged.[17] Only from the perspective of later generations can one make the claim that this constitutional reform had served as a stepping stone toward the creation of a society that has allowed for freedom of religious activity for all groups, old and new, no matter what they advocate and where they come from.

For long decades after the enactment of the constitutional amendment, Protestant Christianity ruled over the civic scene in America. From prayers in official public ceremonies to the commissions offered to military chaplains, American public life was almost completely Christian, and mostly Protestant. Only during the Civil War did the Union army allow the Jewish community to provide its soldiers with a chaplain, the salary for whom Jews paid from their own pockets.[18] Even this experiment was not entirely successful. The Union Army was a Christian institution with Protestant evangelizing agencies, such as the Christian Commission, being an integral part of the military organization. Jewish chaplains were the first non-Christian clergymen to officiate in the American armed forces and would remain the only non-Christians for decades to come. Alongside Roman Catholicism, and a number of new nineteenth-century Christian religious movements, such as Adventists or Jehovah's Witnesses, Judaism would remain the most visible minority faith in America well into the 1960s. This does not imply that other religious traditions, such as Islam or Buddhism, did not have representatives in America before that time.[19] Their presence, however, was considered almost a curiosity and for the most part such "alien" or "exotic" communities lived their lives outside the public eye and interest. As late as 1960, the sociologist Will Herberg pointed to the growing acceptance of Catholics and Jews in America as a novelty. He hardly took notice of the presence of religious groups in America that were not Protestant, Catholic or Jewish.[20]

Well into the twentieth century, religious pluralism in America meant mostly the ability of new or marginal Christian groups to grow in numbers and gain more power and space. The religious disestablishment at the turn of the nineteenth century created an open market for Christian churches, where new, small or previously disadvantaged Christian groups could compete with more established churches on more favorable terms than before. Relatively new groups, such as Methodists and Baptists, began an energetic campaign of evangelism, increasing their numbers and their influence. Within a few decades they moved from the margins to the center of the American polity, providing America with many of its leaders. The new constitutional arrangements promoted an entrepreneurial attitude toward religion, with religious groups competing with each other over their share of the spiritual market.[21] In the first half of the nineteenth century, America witnessed an unprecedented growth in Protestant Christian evangelism, as well as in the rise of Christian messianic movements, some of which predicted dates for the arrival of the Lord.[22] The American religious system proved particularly hospitable to Pietist communities, including Evangelical, Adventist, Baptist, Holiness, Pentecostal, and Mormon groups who, while struggling at first, eventually thrived and prevailed.

At the same time, the first half of the nineteenth century saw the crystallization of an American brand of Christianity. While denominations differed in their organization and in their liturgy, they came to share a great deal in common. As a rule, churches became voluntary, entrepreneurial, more democratic, and centered on the spiritual and emotional well-being of the lay members. Most new American churches were Pietistic or Evangelical in their interpretation of the Christian sacred scriptures and the personal morality they advocated, as well as in their demand that their members establish a personal relationship with Jesus Christ.[23] Churches could not rely anymore on privileged positions within society or on state support. Priests, pastors, and ministers had to try harder and cater to the needs and aspirations of the congregants. Religious groups that grew and thrived were therefore those that best expressed the more democratic spirit of America and the wishes of its people. Nineteenth-century revivalism went hand in hand with the process of democratization of American society and culture. New types of ministers came about on the American scene: employees of their congregations rather than members of privileged religious hierarchies. Donald Miller has pointed out that the process of democratization has been an ongoing one, and has pursued its course even during the latter decades of the twentieth century.[24]

The churches that participated in the revivals of the early nineteenth century either were or became Evangelical. Inspired in part by the Pietist movement of the seventeenth and eighteenth centuries in Central Europe and by British Evangelicalism of the eighteenth century, Evangelicals have viewed the Bible, both the Old and New Testaments, as the authoritative source for living a Christian life on both the individual and communal levels. They insisted on the obligation of every human being to undergo a personal experience of conversion and accept Jesus as Lord and Savior in order to be "saved," and ensure his or her eternity. Conversion or regeneration became a necessary rite of passage into the communities of practicing Christians, and members of Protestant Evangelical churches become committed to spreading the Christian message and the demand that everyone undergo conversion experiences. Awakenings, revivals and Crusades became important American cultural institutions. Revivalists set out to bring large numbers of people to undergo conversions, as a means of enlarging the ranks of the Christian believers. Inner religious experiences, which in Puritan and Pietist circles were exclusivist and private, turned in America into mass productions with preaching and evangelism carried out on an unprecedented scale.

Democracy and revivalism, two major American institutions, have had a lot in common. Both are based on a similar perception of the relationship between individuals and the larger community. In the democratic religious paradigm, individuals are not conscripted or coerced, but they are also not ignored. They are offered a sense of freedom and the notion that they are masters of their own domains. It is up to them to decide about their own spiritual well-being and by extension that of the community at large. Within this worldview each person counts and each person's soul is important. One creates large and influential religious communities the same way one wins an election, by struggling to win the souls of as many individuals as possible. Revivalists have made it their business to convert large numbers of people, utilizing the most effective means of mass communication and commercial techniques, skillfully articulating the reality of sin and the prospect of redemption. Between these two existential realities stands the experience of conversion, which comes to transform individuals' souls and transport them from one spiritual stage to the other.

While millions of Americans, including many newly arrived immigrants, remained loyal to their ancestral faiths or denominational affiliations, millions of others took advantage of the new freedom to choose their own churches based on their spiritual needs and communal preferences. In the nineteenth century, "conversion" became a major spiritual and psychological American category as evident in William James's seminal work, *The Varieties of Religious Experience*, which appeared at the beginning of the twentieth century.[25]

By the mid-nineteenth century, differences between Christian Evangelical groups became less doctrinal than liturgical and organizational, and joining churches turned into a matter of choice, rather than conviction. Protestant activists created a series of interdenominational institutions that gave expression to the values and agendas of Protestant America as a whole. Among the more well known ones are the YMCA, the Young Men's Christian Association, which started as an inner-city missionary organization, and the ABCFM, the American Board of Commissioners of Foreign Missions, an international missionary group. Other organizations were extensions of societies that started in Britain, such as the Bible and Tract Society. Groups that came to promote specific issues, such as temperance, were also interdenominational. By the second half of the nineteenth century revivals became generic in nature. Leading Evangelists, such as Dwight Moody, would not advocate a specific brand of Protestant Christianity, promoting instead the obligation to undergo conversion in principle and, following that transforming experience, the need to join a Protestant church of one's choice.

This is not to say that Protestants always agreed with each other. An issue on which Protestants differed at the mid-nineteenth century was slavery. Before the Civil War, Evangelical Christianity in the North was a progressive political force, advocating a series of social reforms, and a number of northern Evangelical Christians militated against slavery. Southern preachers, on the other hand, came to accept slavery and even found justifications for it. In the years preceding the Civil War, a number of Protestant churches split and the slaveholding South and the antislavery North created separate churches. After the Civil War, new divisions plagued American Protestantism, mainly disagreement between liberals and conservatives over the proper manner of reading the Bible. While moderately liberal forms of Christianity gained influence during the 1930s-1960s, more conservative modes of the Protestant tradition would have the upper hand in the later decades of the twentieth century and the beginning of the twenty-first century. However, while Protestant churches underwent inner struggles and a series of secessions, Protestantism as a whole thrived even while its thinkers and leaders attacked one another. And while major Protestant churches were undergoing a crisis of identity, groups that seceded from the Protestant mainstream, such as Mormons or Adventists, were also gaining ground, enlarging their constituencies and influence. Their strong presence on the American scene would strengthen Protestant values and modes of thinking.

PROTESTANTISM AND AMERICAN VALUES

One cannot overlook the close proximity between Protestant ideals and American values. The Evangelical Protestant understanding of redemption and the American perception of good citizenship mesh well together, if not intertwine completely. In the Evangelical Christian view, undergoing conversion and joining the ranks of the true Christian believers entails more than a spiritual transformation on the road to redemption. In Evangelical or Pietist understanding, as well as that of Mormons and Adventists, Christians are better members of their families and communities. They are good spouses, parents and neighbors, and better citizens of the American polity. Protestant spiritual messages have thus meshed well with American middle-class values. One can point, for example, to the Protestant differentiation between the sinner and the saved as the basis of the American dualistic division between good and bad, which is so prominent in American popular culture. That paradigm, which is featured daily in American TV shows, as well as in films, cartoons, and popular novels, leaves no room for ambiguity. Human beings are not complex, neurotic beings, a mixture of strong and weak qualities. Nor are they characterized by good intentions hampered by bad decisions. In fact, humans are not a mixture of good and bad; they are either good or bad.

Especially in Pietist and Evangelical theology, each and every human being can become fully moral by establishing a personal relationship with Jesus Christ. Those who have adopted Jesus as their Savior are thus removed from Satan and his devastating influence. By definition, they act morally on all fronts: they obey the laws, show impeccable loyalty to their country, and prove themselves to be good spouses, parents, and neighbors, as well as employers or employees. They would neither cheat on their wives nor lie to their colleagues. They would shun all "illicit" sex, and abhor pornography and gambling. Whether or not all Protestants, including Pietists, Evangelicals,

Adventists, and Pentecostals, truly fulfill such expectations and live such exemplary lives, is immaterial. These are the public American norms and citizens are expected to abide by them, at least superficially. In the mid-1990s, European observers of American life looked with disbelief when the "improper" sexual life of the president of the United States became a subject for public debates and official investigations, offering the president's political enemies an axe to grind him with. Such a commotion would have been unfathomable in France, for example, where it is assumed as a matter of course that the presidents of the Republic have active and spicy sexual lives.

Many "illicit" human vices or pleasures go underground in America. While pornography is extremely popular in the United States, and an extensive pornographic industry prospers in America, it operates in a semi-underground manner. Mainstream American movies, whether in the cinemas or on television, would not show nudity, not to mention explicit sexuality. In American movies, couples make love with both men and women's private parts and most of their bodies covered. Newspapers and public billboards also refrain from featuring nudity, at the same time that a multibillion-dollar industry of pornography enjoys the patronage of millions of Americans. Non-Americans are also amazed by the pious manner in which Americans cover their bodies.[26] In America even one- or two-year-old infants have to be dressed modestly and not roam around naked, as they do almost everywhere else on Earth.

Another very central realm in which Christian Protestant values reign high in America is the workplace, as well as in the ethics of work. It would not be an exaggeration to attribute America's work ethics and its entrepreneurial spirit to Protestant perceptions. When visiting America at the turn of the twentieth century, the German sociologist Max Weber was impressed, like others before and after him, by the energetic entrepreneurial atmosphere of a country where ambition, thrift and material success were seen as demonstrations of good moral character. He came out with a grand theory on the relationship between Protestant ethics and the Spirit of Capitalism.[27] I believe that Weber hit on something very real. American Christians expect all good citizens, and especially true Christians, to be hardworking, law-abiding individuals. Protestant ethics has become the moral code of Americans as a whole, and Protestant attitudes and qualities are expected from all good citizens.

No less significant is the manner in which Americans relate to poverty, neediness, homelessness, and unemployment. It is no coincidence that no other postindustrial nation has been as disinclined as America to carry out welfare programs. In line with Christian Pietist

ethics of thrift and prudence, helplessness, joblessness, and homelessness are viewed as unavoidable results of weak and unreformed char-
acters. True Christians do not let themselves reach such a low level.
Good people work hard and are rewarded, often in modest ways.
Protestant ethics meshes well with the American dream, according to
which it is inconceivable that industrious and frugal citizens would
find themselves homeless. Many Protestant preachers advocate a
"gospel of success." True Christians are lavishly rewarded and are entitled to enjoy the fruits of their hard work. In principle, Americans
view their earnings as entirely their own, and are not keen on high tax-
ation, except for the sake of national security, including the maintenance of a strong military infrastructure and the financing of wars.
Taking care of the poor is not the responsibility of responsible citizens.
The poor should have taken care of themselves. In fact the poor can
still do so, provided that they transform themselves spiritually and
morally.[28] Significantly, Protestant values of thrift and self-reliance
have remained predominant in America while they lost much of their
appeal in increasingly less Christian Britain.

While American public norms work for providing ambitious and
hard-working people with wonderful opportunities, they are less gra-
cious when it comes to those who do not do well. Americans offer little compassion to the poor or the needy as well as to those who get in
trouble with the law. In line with Protestant dualistic morality, American society shows little patience for bad citizenship. "Zero tolerance"
for criminals on all levels has come to characterize American society,
with non-Protestants adjusting themselves to the majority's norms.
Dualistic morality has come to inform American legislation and the
nation's penal systems. To outsiders some American laws and regulations seem bizarre. The United States is currently the only Western
nation that exercises the death penalty as well as the only nation to
sentence people to life in prison without parole. No less significant is
the American "Three Strikes" law, according to which felons convicted for the third time are sent to prison for life, even if each of their
crimes separately is a relatively minor one. Likewise, convicted felons,
even after completing their prison terms, lose their citizenship and
have no say anymore in decisions made by their society.[29] Such harsh
attitudes are not accidental. They reflect a moral understanding that is
totally dualistic. According to that conviction, criminals, even petty
ones, who have not committed murders, rapes, or physical assaults,
are negative people who should be locked away. Their bad deeds reflect
unreformed personalities, very different from those of good citizens,
who are entitled to have such bad weeds removed from their yards.

At the turn of the twenty-first century, the harsh American penal system has created the largest prison population since the dissolution of Stalin's gulags in the 1950s. Writers and journalists rarely criticize America's penal system, and tellingly, the harsh and extensive internal penal colonies have not stirred movements of reform or even protest. As a rule such measures have gained the nation's approval. The opinions of Zen Buddhists, who are liberals, do not count very much when such laws are legislated and put into effect. Such regulations enjoy popular support as they reflect the most basic American principles, first and foremost among them being a dualistic understanding of human nature, and a belief in the devastating consequences inflicted on those who chose the wrong path.

American dualistic perfectionism also accounts for the wish to root out the oldest human profession. Only in the United States, and a number of other English-speaking nations, is prostitution outlawed and patrons of the oldest vice prosecuted. In their turn, Americans are shocked when discovering how openly permissive other societies are in their relation to that uncommendable trade. America, like all other countries, has its own, not necessarily small, constituency of prostitutes and their patrons. But in American public morality, prostitution has no place. It is not an unfortunate reality that human societies have always come to terms with, but a moral failure which society needs to struggle against at all costs.

For the most part, twenty-first-century Americans do not divide people into good or bad according to racial or ethnic affiliations. Such notions have been known in the past, but in the last decades have gone out of fashion. Open pronunciations of divides based on racial differences place religious groups outside the mainstream of American Christianity.[30] Instead, Evangelical and Pietist Christian groups have adopted a "color-blind" attitude. Conversion, which results in constructive behavior, is all that people of all races or ethnicities need. They have come to recognize members of all races and colors as positive members of society when such people share their faith and cultural norms, and they no longer see reasons to differentiate between brothers and sisters in Christ.

NON-PROTESTANTS IN A CHRISTIAN LAND

It would be a gross generalization to assert, as many non-Americans do, that in America members of all religious groups are in essence Protestant. But there would be more than a grain of truth in such an observation. Already during the nineteenth century, non-Protestants, and occasionally non-Christians too, had gone through a process of Protestantization, as part of their efforts to adjust to America.[31] Non-Protestant religious groups were not always willing to adapt their doctrines and liturgy as quickly as they had reconfigured and amended the relationships between the hierarchies and the laypersons within their ecclesiastical structures and acquired the decorum of Protestant churches. As individuals, non-Protestants had to adjust their perceptions of private and public morality to that of the Protestant majority in order to survive and thrive in America. To feel at home in that culture they had to change their work ethic completely. This does not say that Protestants always work better than non-Protestants, or that non-Protestants are lazier. It does say that Protestants and Americans in general view work as much more than a means of making a livelihood. For them performance at work and professional achievements reflect their worth as human beings. This also is not to say that non-Protestants have not found a convenient home in America.

Restructuring the relationship between church and state, America offered nonconformist religious groups, such as Jews and Mennonites, almost unprecedented freedoms. Members of such groups could congregate without fear of harassment or persecution. But unlike in Europe, their communities enjoyed no legal status and had no authority anymore over their congregants. And so Judaism in America became a voluntary based, congregationally structured, religious community. With no legally sanctioned *kehila* to impose taxes on its members, Jewish congregations became autonomous bodies, governed by the laity in every community. As there was no one state-sanctioned form of Judaism and no regional or national Jewish governing body, Jews, like Protestants, had greater freedom to reinterpret their tradition, and split and organize separately when facing internal disagreements. The Protestant cultural atmosphere encouraged religious innovations and the creation of new churches and denominations, and Jews took full advantage of the new freedoms. Consequently, America became a center for Jewish life and thought, encouraging the creation of new Jewish forms and expressions.

Jews fared well in America. Being a small minority they posed little threat to Protestant hegemony, and they were happy to acculturate and learn from their Protestant neighbors. Some Jews have attributed their finding a home in America to the allegedly religiously neutral nature of American society and the alleged separation of church and state.[32] This outlook has demonstrated a naïve understanding of the dynamics by which societies govern themselves. Jews have fared better in

America than in almost all non-English-speaking countries because the dominating religion and culture in America, English-speaking Protestant Christianity, mostly Reform, mostly Pietist or Evangelical, have treated them more tolerantly and benevolently.

The history of Catholicism in America has been somewhat different. As the largest and most influential minority, the Catholic saga tells us a great deal about the Protestant nature of the American polity. Protestants saw in a strong Catholic presence a threat to their hegemony and to the kind of Christian commonwealth they were trying to build. At times they organized politically to combat Catholic influence. In fact, one of the major complaints of the Founding Fathers against the British had been the benevolent manner in which the British treated the French Canadians, offering them home rule in 1774. Such antagonistic notions have persisted well into the mid-twentieth century. Many Protestants, for example, took exception to the bid for the presidency of the Catholic candidate Al Smith in 1928. America was not ready then to vote for a Catholic president. Only at the turn of the twenty-first century would Roman Catholicism stop being an issue for most American Protestants.

As a vulnerable group, with somewhat different values and priorities than Protestants, Catholics were also suspicious of the Protestant establishment and many of them judged the American public sphere to be in essence Protestant. For example, they were afraid that they would lose the loyalty of their potential constituencies if Catholic children would study in America's public schools. In the second half of the nineteenth century, the Catholic hierarchy set out to create an alternative Catholic educational system that came to ensure the future of the Catholic faith. During the heyday of the Immigrant Church, from the post–Civil War era to World War II, millions of Roman Catholics lived in ethnic neighborhoods in American cities, viewing their loyalty to their faith as a matter of identity.[33] While living in a semi-separate social structure, Catholics acculturated into an English-speaking Protestant nation, absorbed Protestant values and competed with Protestants for their standing in the American polity and for their share of the national pie. In a moderate way, they have also Protestantized their church, their ecclesiastical and educational institutions moving more and more to be under lay supervision.

A move into the Protestant faith is popular among immigrants to America. The documentary movie "Blue Color and Buddha" shows the interaction, in the 1980s, between Laotian immigrants and the Christian white majority in a small town in Illinois. Hundreds of Laotians have left the Buddhist community, converted to Christianity and moved into an Evangelical church as a means of assuring their acceptance in the larger community and their acculturation into their new American environment. The documentary *Mine Eyes Have Seen the Glory* similarly depicts immigrants from Latin America who join Pentecostal churches as a means of adjusting to America. Immigrants also join such quintessential American churches as the Seventh-Day Adventists or the Church of Jesus Christ of Latter-day Saints as a means of becoming Americans.

CONCLUSION

In the last analysis, America is a Christian country, governed by Christians, on the basis of Christian Protestant principles. It is at the same time a nation that has gradually opened its doors to members of all religious communities to live and practice their faiths in freedom and security. America has created a constitutional system that offers freedom of worship to members of all faiths and protects churches from one another, guaranteeing an open market of religions. One should therefore look at the historical religious disengagement of the turn of the nineteenth century and the partial separation of church and state that followed, as policies advocated by Christians, for the sake of Christians, although other groups benefited from them as well. At the same time, the ruling Protestant elite attempted openly or covertly to Protestantize members of other communities and bring them to accept the values of the majority faith.

Ultimately, America has come to promote its own brand of Christianity, which represents American values, including emphasis on thrift and proper civil conduct. This American brand shows respect for individual choices within a framework of mass culture. Religion in America has become both a matter of choice and a social convention. It offers a great variety of communities that advocate similar values and norms. In their many forms and guises, Pietist churches have captured the souls of Americans and, to a large extent captured the soul of the nation as a whole. The reason, I would claim, that Evangelical, Adventist, Mormon, and Pentecostal forms of Christianity have become so successful in our time is because they represent American values, no less than they have helped to shape them. Protestant Christianity has had such a profound influence on American thinking that non-Protestants, from Jews to Zen Buddhists, have gone, in one way or another, through a process of Protestantization, altering their manners and values as they make room for themselves in American society. American culture is so thoroughly Protestant that one wonders how anyone could suggest it is equally Buddhist. That is, unless one reaches the conclusion that in America, Buddhism is Protestant, too.

NOTES

1. Diana L. Eck, *A New Religious America: How A "Christian Country" Has Become the World's Most Religiously Diverse Nation* (San Francisco: Harper San Francisco, 2001). On the mood among scholars of religion at the time see William Hutchison, *Religious Pluralism in America: the Continuing History of a Founding Ideal* (New Haven, CT: Yale University Press, 2003).

2. See also Thomas A. Tweed, ed., *Revisioning Religion in America* (Berkley: University of California, 1996).

3. Hutchison, *Religious Pluralism in America*.

4. On the close relationship between Protestant norms and American civil religion, see Catherine L. Albanese, *America: Religions and Religion* (Belmont, CA: Wadsworth Publishing Company, 1999), 396–461.

5. See Conrad Cherry, Betty A. Deberg, and Amanda Fosterfield, *Religion On Campus* (Chapel Hill: University of North Carolina Press, 2001).

6. Tom W. Smith and Seokho Kim, "The Vanishing Protestant Majority," *Journal for the Scientific Study of Religion*, Vol. 44, No 2 (June 2005): 211–23. The authors, who assert that Protestants are still the majority, take a rather minimalist count of Protestants. Most independent churches in America are Protestant.

7. For example, James Rudin, *The Baptizing of America* (New York: Thunder Mouth Press, 2006).

8. See Mark A. Noll, *The Work We Have to Do: The History of Protestants in America* (New York: Oxford University Press, 2000).

9. Conrad Cherry, ed., *God's New Israel: Religious Interpretations of American Destiny* (Chapel Hill: University of North Carolina Press, 1998).

10. Perry Miller, *Errands Into the Wilderness* (Cambridge, MA: Harvard University Press, 1956); H. Richard Niebuhr, *The Kingdom of God in America* (New York: Harper and Row, 1937).

11. See Paul D. Carrington, *Spreading America's Word: Stories of its Lawyer-Missionaries* (New York: Twelve Tables Press, 2005).

12. Complaints of such activists as James Rudin are based on that perception.

13. See Jon Meacham, *American Gospel: God, the Founding Fathers, and the Making of a Nation* (New York: Random House, 2006).

14. Michael Novak and Jana Novak, *Washington's God: Religion, Liberty, and the Father of Our Country* (New York: Basic Books, 2006); David L. Holmes, *The Faith of the Founding Fathers* (New York: Oxford University Press, 2006). Novak and Holmes hold very different perceptions on the faith of George Washington and by extension the Founding Fathers in general.

15. Edwin S. Gaustad, *Proclaim Liberty Throughout All the Land: A History of Church and State in America* (New York: Oxford University Press, 2003).

16. On the constitutional amendment, see John M. Murrin, "Religion and Politics in America from the First Settlement to the Civil War" in *Religion and American Politics*, edited by Mark A. Noll (New York: Oxford University Press, 1990).

17. See Jon Butler, "Religion in Colonial America" in Jon Butler, Grant Wacher and Randall Balmer, *Religion in American Life* (New York: Oxford, 2003), 1–164.

18. On Judaism in America and America's civic institutions, see Will Herberg, *Protestant, Catholic, Jew* (Garden City, New York: 1960).

19. See Thomas A. Tweed, *The American Encounter with Buddhism, 1844–1912: Culture and the Limit of Dissent* (Bloomington: Indiana University Press, 1992).

20. Herberg, *Protestant, Catholic, Jew.*

21. Roger Finke and Rodney Stark, *The Churching of America, 1776–2005: Winners and Losers in Our Religious Economy* (New Brunswick: Rutgers University Press, 2005).

22. See for example, Ronald L. Number and Jonathan M. Butler, *The Disappointed: Millerism and Millenarianism in the Nineteenth Century* (Bloomington and Indianapolis: Indiana University Press, 1987).

23. Nathan Hatch, *The Democratization of American Christianity* (New Haven, CT: Yale University Press, 1983).

24. Donald Miller, *Reinventing American Protestantism* (Berkeley: University of California Press, 2000).

25. William James, *The Variety of Religious Experiences* (New York: Random House, 1902).

26. Somerset Maugham, *His Majesty's Agent* (London: 1928).

27. Max Weber, *The Protestant Ethic and the Spirit of Capitalism*, translated by Talcott Parsons (London: Unwin Paperbacks, 1985).

28. See Franklin Graham, *It's Who You Know: The One Relationship That Makes All the Difference* (Nashville, TN: Nelson Books, 2002).

29. Elizabeth A. Hull, *The Disenfranchisement of Ex-Felons* (Philadelphia: Temple University Press, 2006).

30. See Michael Brakun, *Religion and the Racist Right* (Chapel Hill: University of North Carolina Press, 1997).

31. See Nathan Glazer, *American Judaism* (Chicago: University of Chicago Press, 1957); Herberg, *Protestant, Catholic, Jew.*

32. See Rudin above. Only recently have a number of Jewish leaders and thinkers come to look upon the Jewish relationship with the Protestant majority in more realistic terms.

33. Jay Dollan, *The American Catholic Experience* (Garden City, NJ: Image, 1985).

❷

Evangelical Protestants and Jews

A View from the Polls

John C. Green

Evangelical Protestants and Jews have an ambivalent relationship at the beginning of the twenty-first century. On the one hand, the two communities often disagree over religious and political matters, and their interaction is clouded by the broader history of Christian-Jewish relations. But on the other hand, they have some important things in common, including support for the State of Israel. This ambivalence is complicated by mutual misunderstanding of each other's perspectives and opinions.

This essay seeks to improve this situation by describing the attitudes of Evangelical Protestants toward Jews on a range of issues important to both groups. To this end, it uses a variety of public opinion surveys on a number of topics. The majority of the surveys employed come from the last decade (1996 to 2005), but some data are presented from 1964 to provide some historical perspective.[1] Most of this information is presented in simple percentage tables that include the views of Evangelicals[2] and of the American public at large. The tables also report Jewish opinion, but these results must be viewed with great caution because the number of Jews in the surveys is typically quite small.[3]

This information leads to three conclusions. First, Evangelical Protestants have generally positive views of Jews and their views have become more positive over the last forty years. Second, major disagreements remain between Evangelicals and Jews on religious matters, the proper role of religion in public affairs, and social issues.

Third, religion is a motivating factor for Evangelicals' positions on many issues, including support for Israel.

WHAT DO EVANGELICALS THINK OF JEWS?

A good place to begin is with Evangelicals' attitudes toward Jews in the present day. The first entry in table 2.1 shows that Evangelicals have positive views, with three-quarters reporting "very favorable" or "mostly favorable" opinions of Jews. And just 7 percent of Evangelicals have "very unfavorable" or "mostly unfavorable" views of Jews (with the remaining one-fifth reporting "neutral" views or no opinion). These figures are almost identical to the public at large.

The second entry in table 2.1 reports Evangelicals' average "thermometer" rating of Jews. This measure asks respondents to rate their feelings on a scale rating from "100 degrees" (very warm) to "0 degrees"

Table 2.1.   Evangelical Protestants and Jews: General Evaluations

	Evangelicals	All Adults	Jews
ALL AMERICANS			
Favorability Toward Jews (2005)[1]			
Very Favorable	25	23	72
Mostly Favorable	50	54	7
Neutral, No Opinion	18	16	21
Mostly Unfavorable	4	5	0
Very Unfavorable	3	2	0
	100%	100%	100%
Average "Thermometer" Rating (2004)[2]	68°	67°	89°
WEEKLY WORSHIP ATTENDERS			
Favorability Toward Jews (2005)[1]			
Very Favorable	32	27	78
Mostly Favorable	51	53	0
Neutral, No Opinion	12	14	22
Mostly Unfavorable	4	4	0
Very Unfavorable	1	2	0
	100%	100%	100%
Average "Thermometer" Rating (2004)[2]	70°	70°	93°

Sources:
1. Pew Forum on Religion and Public Life, July 2005 (N=2200)
2. 2004 National Election Study (N=1212)

(very cold). In 2004, the Evangelical rating of Jews was a fairly warm 68 degrees, essentially the same as the public as a whole. Not surprisingly, Jews have even more positive views of themselves on both the "favorability" and "thermometer" questions (79 percent "very" or "mostly favorable" and 89 degrees, respectively).

The final two entries in table 2.1 repeat this analysis, but only for respondents who reported attending worship once a week or more. Note that weekly worshipers had even more positive views of Jews than the less frequent worshipers. For example, almost one-third of weekly attending Evangelicals reported a "very favorable" view of Jews, compared to one-quarter of Evangelicals as a whole. Indeed, more than four-fifths of weekly attending Evangelicals had "very favorable" or "mostly favorable" views of Jews. The thermometer ratings show a modest increase as well.

This evidence on weekly worship attendees holds more generally: Evangelicals with higher levels of religious commitment tend to have more positive views of Jews than their coreligionists with lower levels of commitment. This pattern is so consistent that weekly attendees will not be broken out in the subsequent tables for ease of presentation.

It is possible that Evangelicals' positive attitudes are less about Jews than about Judaism. Indeed, a recent survey found only one-half of Evangelicals reported knowing any Jews personally, markedly fewer than Mainline Protestants (67 percent) or Roman Catholics (65 percent).[4] Indeed, much of what Evangelicals know about Jews may come from their own religious instruction rather than from personal experience.

SOCIAL IMAGES

Whatever its source, Evangelicals' positive view of Jews is widespread, as can be seen in table 2.2, which contains questions about social images of Jews. The first entry in the table asks if Jews are "pretty similar to other Americans" and nearly nine of ten Evangelicals agreed, while less than one-tenth disagreed. Thus, few Evangelicals perceive Jews as distant from American society, a factor often associated with prejudice.

The second entry asks if Jews are more "willing to use shady practices to get what they want." Only about one-tenth of Evangelicals agreed with this statement and almost three-quarters disagreed. The third item is closely related to the second, asking if Jews choose

Table 2.2.   Evangelical Protestants and Jews: Social Images and Stereotypes

	Evangelicals	All Adults	Jews
Despite Their Special Customs and Beliefs, Jews are Really Pretty Similar to Other Americans (1996)[1]			
Agree	89	92	82
Neutral, No Opinion	4	4	9
Disagree	7	4	9
	100%	100%	100%
Jews Are More Willing to Use Shady Practices to Get What They Want (1996)[1]			
Agree	11	12	10
Neutral, No Opinion	16	18	0
Disagree	73	70	90
	100%	100%	100%
When it Comes to Choosing Between People and Money, Jews Will Choose Money (1996)[1]			
Agree	24	23	0
Neutral, No Opinion	23	18	0
Disagree	53	59	100
	100%	100%	100%

Source:
1. American Jewish Committee, "Survey of the Religious Right," 1996 (N=572)

"money over people." Here about one-quarter of Evangelicals agreed and more than one-half disagreed. These patterns suggest that only a minority of Evangelicals hold traditional stereotypes of Jewish economic behavior. With regard to these social images, Evangelicals closely resembled the public as a whole.

RELIGIOUS IMAGES

What about religious images of Jews based in Christian beliefs? Table 2.3 considers several items on this subject. The first two entries concern one of the most negative images of Jews among Christians. The first question asks if Jews were responsible for the death of Christ. Here less than one-third of Evangelicals agreed and more than one-half disagreed. The public as a whole was a little less likely to agree with this statement than Evangelicals. This question can be read as an empirical one: a casual reading of key passages in the New Testament might lead one to agree that this statement is part of the Passion narrative.

The next table entry covers the same topic but explicitly addresses an implication sometimes drawn from the Passion narrative: "Now as in the past Jews must answer for killing Christ." Here just one-sixth of Evangelicals agreed with this statement, about one-half the level of agreement with the previous empirical question. Moreover, three-quarters of Evangelicals disagreed with the statement. Here Evangelicals resemble the public as a whole. Taken together, these results suggest that only a minority of Evangelicals hold these religious images of Jews, and even fewer hold the most pejorative version.

Not all religious images are negative toward Jews. A casual reading of the Old Testament might lead one to agree with the final entry in table 2.3: "Now as in the past Jews remain God's chosen people."

Table 2.3.   Evangelical Protestants and Jews: Religious Images and Stereotypes

	Evangelicals	All Adults	Jews
Were the Jews Responsible for Christ's Death? (2004)[1]			
Yes	30	26	2
No Opinion	14	14	4
No	56	60	94
	100%	100%	100%
Jews Must Answer for Killing Christ (1996)[2]			
Agree	15	12	0
Neutral, No Opinion	10	14	0
Disagree	75	74	100
	100%	100%	100%
Now as in the Past, Jews Remain God's Chosen People (1996)[2]			
Agree	46	32	64
Neutral, No Opinion	9	15	0
Disagree	45	53	36
	100%	100%	100%

Sources:
1. Pew Research Center and Pew Forum, March 2005 (N=1703)
2. American Jewish Committee, "Survey of the Religious Right," 1996 (N=572)

Evangelicals are divided on this question, with almost equal numbers agreeing and disagreeing about the special relationship of Jews to God. In this regard, Evangelicals differ from the public as a whole, which is less likely to see Jews as God's chosen people.

POLITICAL IMAGES

Table 2.4 reports on political images of Jews. The first entry asks a standard question about influence in public affairs, asking if Jews have "too much" influence, "too little" influence, or if their influence is "about right." A little less than one-sixth of Evangelicals said Jews had

Table 2.4.   Evangelical Protestants and Jews: Political Images and Stereotypes

	Evangelicals	All Adults	Jews
Influence of Jews in Public Affairs (2000)[1]			
Too Much	14	13	9
About Right	66	65	73
Too Little	20	22	18
	100%	100%	100%
Jews are the Main Backers of Left-Wing Causes in the United States (1996)[2]			
Agree	9	12	18
Neutral, No Opinion	20	20	0
Disagree	71	68	82
	100%	100%	100%
Jewish Liberals are to Blame for Much of What Is Wrong with America (1996)[2]			
Agree	9	8	20
Neutral, No Opinion	15	13	0
Disagree	76	79	80
	100%	100%	100%
If a Qualified Jew Ran for President: (2003)[3]			
Would Vote for	84%	85%	100%
No Reason to Vote Against	72%	80%	80%

Sources:
1. PSRA Newsweek Poll, August 2000 (N=914)
2. American Jewish Committee, "Survey of the Religious Right," 1996 (N=572)
3. Pew Research Center and Pew Forum, March 2003 (N=2002)

"too much" influence in public affairs. But interestingly enough, one-fifth said Jews had *too little* influence. Like the public as a whole, the overwhelming majority of Evangelicals said that Jewish influence in public affairs was "about right." Thus, it appears unlikely that many Evangelicals believe that Jews wield the vast power alleged in some "conspiracy" theories on politics.

The next two items address the connections between Jews and liberalism in American politics. One item asks if "Jews are the main backers of left-wing causes in the United States," and the other asks if "Jewish liberals are to blame for much of what is wrong with America." Less than one-tenth of Evangelicals agreed with these statements, while better than seven of ten disagreed. These numbers suggest the absence of a negative stereotype of Jews as liberals, a term that carries a negative stigma for many Evangelicals, who tend to be politically conservative.

The final entries in table 2.4 report on prospective presidential voting and Jewish candidates. Because of the great symbolic significance of the American presidency, such questions are a useful means of assessing the political images of social and religious groups. The survey employed asked two different questions on this topic. One option was: "If your party nominated a generally well-qualified person for president who happened to be Jewish, would you vote for that person?" When asked this way, 84 percent of Evangelicals said they would vote for a qualified Jewish candidate nominated by their party. This figure is about the same as the public as a whole.

The other option was: "Are there any reasons why you might not vote for a Jew for president if he or she were nominated by the party you usually prefer?" When asked this way, only 72 percent of Evangelicals could think of "no reason to vote against" a Jewish candidate. This result was 12 percentage points lower than the first version of the question, and lower than the public as a whole. Note, however, that the level of support for the second question declined for all categories in the table.

Taken together, these questions suggest that a large majority of Evangelicals do not have a negative image of Jewish politicians, but a small minority may, ranging between one-sixth and one-quarter of the Evangelical public. In fact, a glance back at the items in tables 2.2 and 2.3 reveals small minorities of Evangelicals with negative attitudes within the same range. The existence of small groups of Evangelicals with such negative views can be quite problematic, of course. However, it should not obscure the overall positive attitudes that most Evangelicals have toward Jews.

CHANGE IN EVANGELICAL ATTITUDES TOWARD JEWS

Have these generally positive attitudes of Evangelicals toward Jews increased in recent times? Some evidence suggests this may be the case. Table 2.5 compares Evangelical attitudes in 1964 to the present period on questions with similar wording. The first entry reports the average thermometer ratings from 1964 and 2004 (from table 2.1). These data show an increase of ten "degrees" for Evangelicals over this forty-year period, from 58 degrees to 68 degrees.

The second entry concerns the question of whether Jews are like other Americans (from table 2.2). Here Evangelicals posted a significant increase, from 67 percent agreement to 89 percent between 1964 and 1996. Next, agreement with the stereotype of Jews using "shady practices" (also from table 2.2) declined for Evangelicals, from 38 to 11 percent. Then, on the question of whether Jews were responsible for Christ's death (the empirical question from table 3), the level of agreement among Evangelicals was nearly cut in half, falling from 56 percent

TABLE 2.5.   Change in Evangelical Protestant Attitudes toward Jews

	Evangelicals	All Adults	Jews
Average "Thermometer" Ratings			
2004	68°	67°	89°
1964	58°	60°	75°
Jews are Like Other Americans			
Agree 1996	89%	92%	82%
Agree 1964	67%	74%	96%
Jews Use Shady Practices			
Agree 1996	11%	12%	10%
Agree 1964	38%	34%	9%
Were the Jews Responsible for Christ's Death?			
Yes 2004	30%	26%	2%
Yes 1964	56%	51%	5%
If a Qualified Jew Ran For President:			
No Reason to Vote Against 2003	72%	80%	80%
No Reason to Vote Against 1964	57%	78%	100%

Sources:
1964 Thermometer ratings 1964 National Election Study; all other 1964 items from anti-Semitism study; all contemporary items as listed in previous tables.

to 30 percent. Finally, between 1964 and 2004, there was a 15 percentage point increase in the number of Evangelicals who reported "no reason to vote against" a qualified Jewish presidential candidate nominated by their party. Overall, the level of change for Evangelicals was about the same as for the entire public over this period of time.

Because the survey questions employed in the over-time comparison were not worded exactly the same way, these findings must be viewed with some caution. However, the changes since 1964 are large enough that they are unlikely to have resulted entirely from modest differences in the wording of the questions. In addition, the direction of change is the same for all the items, and the change for Evangelicals paralleled the public as a whole. And these patterns are certainly consistent with studies that reveal an increase in tolerance and a decline in anti-Semitism over the last two generations.[5] Indeed, even the 1964 figures were positive enough to suggest that by the mid-1960s the trend toward greater tolerance was already well under way.

In sum, Evangelicals have generally positive attitudes toward Jews and these attitudes have become more positive over time.

RELIGIOUS BELIEFS AND PRACTICES

Although Evangelicals have generally positive views of Jews, there are nonetheless important religious differences between the two communities. Table 2.6 reports some religious views that have often generated tensions between Evangelicals and Jews. The first entry is a central belief of Evangelicalism: Salvation is achieved only by faith in Jesus Christ. Nearly nine of ten Evangelicals affirmed this belief and just one-eighth did not, saying there are other ways to salvation. As one might expect, these figures are higher than for the public as a whole. This belief can be expressed in a way that excludes non-Christians and raises questions about the legitimacy of other faiths.

The second entry in table 2.6 concerns the potentially exclusive quality of Evangelical beliefs by asking if "people who have not accepted Jesus can go to heaven." Only about one-quarter of Evangelicals agreed with this idea and some two-thirds disagreed, a pattern that follows logically from the first question in the table. In contrast, the public at large was evenly divided on this matter.

The third item in table 2.6 reveals some nuance in these beliefs. It asks if "Jews can go to heaven." This survey item is one of the few in existence that asks this question specifically about Jews. Interestingly, four-fifths of Evangelicals agreed that Jews can go to heaven and less

Table 2.6.   Evangelical Protestants and Jews: Christian Exclusivity

	Evangelicals	All Adults	Jews
Salvation Only by Faith in Jesus Christ (2004)[1]			
Yes	86	62	na
No Opinion	2	6	na
No, There are Other Ways	12	32	na
	100%	100%	
People Who Do Not Accept Jesus as Their Savior Can Still Go to Heaven (1996)[2]			
Agree	26	45	73
Neutral, No Opinion	8	10	27
Disagree	66	45	0
	100%	100%	100%
Can Jews Go to Heaven (2004)[3] (of respondents who believe in Heaven)			
Yes	80	87	100
No Opinion	12	9	0
No	8	4	0
	100%	100%	100%
God Hears the Prayers of All People, Not Only Christians (1996)[2]			
Agree	90	93	100
Neutral, No Opinion	1	2	0
Disagree	9	5	0
	100%	100%	100%

Sources:
1. *Religion and Ethics Newsweekly*, April 2004 (N=1610)
2. American Jewish Committee, "Survey of the Religious Right," 1996 (N=572)
3. PSRA/Newsweek Poll, May 2004, (N=1010)

than one-tenth disagreed, figures that are comparable to the public at large. These results may reflect the view that Jews have their own special relationship with God or perhaps that Jews can reach heaven if they convert to Christianity (a point discussed below).

The fourth entry in table 2.6 asks if "God hears the prayers of all people, not only Christians." Nine of ten Evangelicals agreed with this statement, much like the public at large. Taken together, these data suggest that many Evangelicals do not necessarily hold with the most exclusive rendering of their basic beliefs.

PROSELYTIZING AND CONVERSION

The Evangelical emphasis on proselytizing and making converts or "evangelizing" has long been a source on tension with Jews. Indeed, some Evangelical denominations and ministries have made a special effort to convert Jews in recent times. Table 2.7 reports on attitudes in this regard. The first entry asks about the importance of converting

Table 2.7.   Evangelical Protestants and Jews: Conversion and Proselytizing

	Evangelicals	All Adult	Jews
It Is Important to Convert Others to My Faith (2004)[1]			
Agree	81	8	52
Neutral, No Opinion	3	0	3
Disagree	16	92	45
	100%	100%	100%
Jews Do Not Need to be Converted to Christianity (1996)[2]			
Agree	45	91	61
Neutral, No Opinion	12	9	12
Disagree	43	0	27
	100%	100%	100%
Have You Ever Tried to Convert Others? (2004)[1]			
Yes	72	51	na
No Opinion	1	1	na
No	27	48	na
	100%	100%	
Deeply Religious People: (2004)[3]			
Should Spread the Word of God Whenever They Can	64	18	41
Should be Very Careful about Doing So That They Do Not Offend	31	27	37
Should Keep Their Faith as a Private Matter Altogether	5	55	22
	100%	100%	100%

Sources:
1. Religion and Ethics Newsweekly, April 2004 (N=1610)
2. American Jewish Committee, "Survey of the Religious Right," 1996 (N=572)
3. Public Agenda, Religion and Public Life, August 2004 (N=1004)

others to one's faith. Some four-fifths of Evangelicals agreed with this imperative and only one-sixth disagreed. On this matter, Evangelicals differed substantially from the public at large, where less than 10 percent agreed.

The second entry in table 2.7 takes this idea a step further, asking if "Jews do not need to be converted to Christianity." On this question, Evangelicals were almost evenly divided, with 45 percent agreeing and 43 percent disagreeing with the statement. Here, too, Evangelicals are sharply different from the public as a whole, where over 90 percent agreed that Jews need not be converted.

The third item in table 2.7 is reported proselytizing. Almost three-quarters of Evangelicals claimed to have tried to convert someone to their faith at one time or another, just over one-half of the public at large that reported similar activity. Even if these reports are exaggerated, they do suggest that Evangelicals are likely to follow the imperatives of their faith, which can have both positive and negative consequences.

The final entry explores the process of proselytizing and some of its negative consequences. This question offers three options for "deeply religious people": spread the word of God whenever possible; do so carefully lest it offend others; or keep one's faith as a private matter. Nearly two-thirds of Evangelicals picked the first option, to share one's faith whenever possible. Another one-third agreed that proselytizing should be done carefully, and very few agreed that faith was a private matter. The public at large had a different distribution of opinion: just under one-fifth favored sharing one's faith whenever possible and just over one-fourth supported careful proselytizing. The remaining one-half saw faith as a private matter.

Taken together, these data reveal some significant religious differences between Evangelicals and Jews, especially on proselytizing. These differences are likely to remain a source of tension between the two communities. There is, however, some nuance in Evangelical beliefs and behaviors in this regard. More importantly, these religious views and practices are not associated with negative attitudes toward Jews.

RELIGION AND PUBLIC LIFE

Evangelicals' focus on proselytizing raises special concerns about the role of religion in public life. After all, a direct connection between religion and public policy may appear to favor one faith over others.

Table 2.8.   Evangelical Protestants and Jews: Religion and Public Life

	Evangelicals	All Adults	Jews
Pass a Constitutional Amendment Permitting Prayers to be Spoken in Public Schools (1996)[1]			
Favor	77	69	36
No Opinion	8	8	0
Oppose	15	23	64
	100%	100%	100%
Allow Ten Commandments to be Posted in Public Buildings (1996)[2]			
Agree	84	65	35
No Opinion	8	14	8
Disagree	8	21	57
	100%	100%	100%
Public Funding Should be Available for Houses of Worship to Provide Social Services (2004)[2]			
Agree	59	51	39
No Opinion	15	15	4
Disagree	26	34	57
	100%	100%	100%
Pass a Constitutional Amendment Declaring the U.S. a Christian Nation (1996)[1]			
Agree	43	27	0
Neutral, No Opinion	12	10	0
Disagree	45	63	100
	100%	100%	100%

Sources:
1. American Jewish Committee, "Survey of the Religious Right," 1996 (N=572)
2. University of Akron, Fourth National Survey of Religion and Politics, 2004 (N=4000)

Table 2.8 reports on a number of questions regarding policies which directly involve religion in governmental policy. The first three entries are actual policy controversies; the fourth is a hypothetical one.

The initial entry in table 2.8 asks about an amendment to the U.S. Constitution that would allow spoken prayer in public school, a practice ruled illegal by the Supreme Court in the 1960s. Evangelicals were quite supportive of this idea, with more than three-quarters in favor and just one-sixth opposed. And the public as a whole was also strongly supportive of such an amendment, but at a lower rate than Evangelicals.

The next entry asks about posting the Ten Commandments in public buildings, a matter on which the Supreme Court has recently issued ambiguous rulings. Here better than four-fifths of Evangelicals agreed with the policy and less than one-tenth disagreed. Here too, the public at large strongly agreed with the policy, but less so than Evangelicals.

The third entry asks if public funds should be allowed for houses of worship to provide social services. This idea is at the center of President Bush's faith-based initiative. Almost three-fifths of Evangelicals agreed with this policy and roughly one-quarter opposed. Here the public as a whole was less supportive, mustering just a bare majority in agreement.

Some advocates of these policies argue that the majority ought to rule on such matters, and they often point to survey data showing that a large majority of Americans believe that the United States is a "Christian nation." Such poll results regularly cause alarm in other quarters. But such data must be read with great caution because they reflect the simple fact that Christians (but not Evangelical Protestants) actually do make up a majority of Americans. Such data should not be read as demonstrating that most Americans want Christianity to be given legal sanction.[6]

The final entry in table 2.8 addresses this normative concern with a hypothetical question, asking if there should be an amendment to the U.S. Constitution declaring the country a "Christian nation." No one has seriously proposed such an amendment, let alone advocated for it, and so opinions about it must be viewed with some skepticism. On this hypothetical question, Evangelicals were evenly divided, with 43 percent agreeing and 45 percent disagreeing with the idea. However unlike the other policies in table 2.8, the public at large was solidly opposed to such a proclamation.

RELIGION AND POLITICS

Table 2.9 explores more abstract views of the role of religion in public affairs. The first entry asks about the government's role with regard to religion. Here better than three-fifths of Evangelicals agreed that the government "should take special steps to protect our religious heritage," and one-third disagreed, believing that there "should be a strict

Table 2.9.   Evangelical Protestants and Jews: Religion and Public Life

	Evangelicals	All Adults	Jews
Government Should: (2000)[1]			
Protect Our Religious Heritage	63	48	13
Have a Strict Separation of Church/State	32	48	83
No Opinion	5	4	4
	100%	100%	100%
Religion and Public Life: (2000)[1]			
Play a bigger role	74	50	38
Stay the same	21	32	12
Play a smaller role	3	14	50
No Opinion	2	4	0
	100%	100%	100%
Organized Religious Groups of all Kinds Should Stay Out of Politics (2004)[2]			
Agree	34	46	56
No Opinion	2	2	0
Disagree	64	52	44
	100%	100%	100%
Favorability Toward Christian Conservative Movement (2005)[3]			
Very Favorable	21	11	17
Mostly Favorable	48	32	11
Neutral, No Opinion	15	24	11
Mostly Unfavorable	14	21	12
Very Unfavorable	2	12	49
	100%	100%	100%

Source:
1. University of Akron, Third National Survey of Religion and Politics, 2000 (N=6000)
2. University of Akron, Fourth National Survey of Religion and Politics, 2004 (N=4000)
3. Pew Research Center and Pew Forum, March 2005 (N=1703)

separation of church and state." Interestingly, the public as a whole was evenly divided on this question.

The second entry asks if religion should have a bigger or smaller role in American public life. Almost three-quarters of Evangelicals favored a bigger role for religion, and just three percent wanted a smaller role; the remaining one-fifth preferred the status quo. However, just one-half of the public as a whole wanted a bigger role for religion in public life, while one-sixth believed it should be smaller.

The third table entry turns to politics directly, asking if "religious groups of all kinds should stay out of politics." About one-third of Evangelicals agreed with this prohibition, but almost two-thirds disagreed. The public as a whole was more divided, with a slight majority disagreeing with a prohibition against religious groups in politics.

The final entry here deals with the most visible example of Evangelicals in politics, the "Christian conservative movement," often called the "Christian Right" or "Religious Right." About one-fifth of Evangelicals felt "very favorable" toward the Christian Right and almost one-half were "mostly favorable." Thus, better than two-thirds of Evangelicals had a favorable view of this movement. Meanwhile, about one-sixth had unfavorable views, and nearly as many felt neutral or had no opinion. Here, the public as a whole was much more divided, with more than two-fifths holding "very" or "mostly favorable" views, and one-third "very" or "mostly unfavorable" evaluations, with the remaining one-quarter neutral or lacking an opinion.

In sum, Evangelicals, like many other Americans, favor some direct connections between religion and public policy, and agree with a broader involvement of religion in public life. Unlike the public as a whole, however, Evangelicals are stronger advocates of political activity by religious groups, including the Christian Right. However, these attitudes on religion and public life are not associated with negative views of Jews.

ISSUES POSITIONS

As with many religious communities, Evangelicals' religious beliefs influence their issue positions. Table 2.10 reports on several issues that are closely tied to Evangelicals' beliefs. The first entry asks if "The main cause of America's problems is moral decay." More than 90 percent of Evangelicals agreed with this statement and very few disagreed. But note that nearly four-fifths of the public as a whole also agreed that the decline of morals was a cause of the nation's problems. Such attitudes are the basis of the much discussed "moral values" voters, although the relative importance of moral questions varies from election to election.

The second entry in the table pertains to abortion. Evangelicals tend to oppose abortion, with 18 percent favoring making abortions illegal and another 48 percent for allowing abortions only under restricted circumstances. Thus, two-thirds of Evangelicals hold a pro-life

Table 2.10. Evangelical Protestants and Jews: Issues Positions

	Evangelicals	All Adults	Jews
The Main Cause of America's Problems Is Moral Decay (1996)[1]			
Agree	92	79	42
Neutral, No Opinion	1	7	0
Disagree	7	14	58
	100%	100%	100%
View of Abortion: (2005)[2]			
Generally Available	18	36	88
Available But Under Stricter Limits	16	21	12
Permitted Only in Rare Cases	48	32	0
Not Permitted at All	18	11	0
	100%	100%	100%
Has the U.S. Enjoyed Special Protection from God? (2002)[3]			
Special Protection	69	48	32
No Opinion	8	12	13
No Special Protection	23	40	55
	100%	100%	100%
In the Dispute Between Israel and the Palestinians, Who Do You Sympathize with More: (2003)[4]			
Israel	55	41	85
Palestinians	6	13	0
Neither, Both, No Opinion	39	46	15
	100%	100%	100%
Do You Sympathize with Israel Because: (2003)[4]			
God Gave Israel to the Jews	84%	58%	59%
Of Biblical Prophecy	75%	49%	20%

Sources:
1. American Jewish Committee, "Survey of the Religious Right," 1996 (N=572)
2. Pew Research Center and Pew Forum, March 2005 (N=1703)
3. Pew Research Center and Pew Forum, 2002 (N=2002)
4. Pew Research Center and Pew Forum, March 2003 (N=2002)

position of one kind or another, and one-third hold pro-choice positions. The public as a whole is more liberal on abortion, with almost three-fifths holding pro-choice positions on abortion. In many ways abortion is the emblem for the application of religion to politics among Evangelicals.

The next entry asks if the United States has enjoyed "special protection from God." Evangelicals strongly endorsed this providential view of the nation, with seven out of ten in agreement with the statement. Less than one-quarter of Evangelicals disagreed with this view of the country's relationship with God. The public as a whole was more divided on this question, with just under one-half seeing the hand of Providence in American history and two-fifths disagreeing with this perspective. More than most other Americans, Evangelicals tend to interpret foreign policy in religious terms.

The final entries in table 2.9 concern support for Israel. The first question asks "In the dispute between Israel and the Palestinians, who do you sympathize with most?" Overall, 55 percent of Evangelicals reported sympathizing with Israel and 6 percent with the Palestinians. The remaining 39 percent had no sympathies or no opinion, a pattern not often found on foreign policy questions. However, if one considers only Evangelicals with an opinion on this question, the margin in favor of Israel is quite large: 90 percent favor Israel and just 10 percent the Palestinians.

The public at large has similar sympathies: 41 percent favored Israel and 13 percent the Palestinians (and 46 percent with no opinion). In terms of respondents with an opinion, some 75 percent favored Israel. Of course, the entire public also includes Evangelicals, which helps mask Christian groups that are much less sympathetic to Israel. Other survey evidence shows that Evangelicals' support is quite intense, and many Evangelical leaders are especially vocal in supporting Israel.

The final entry in table 2.10 concerns religious reasons for sympathy toward Israel. Overall, 84 percent of Evangelicals who sympathized with Israel said it was because "God gave Israel to the Jews." Meanwhile, 75 percent of Evangelicals who sympathized with Israel said it was because of biblical prophecy, mostly concerning the End Times. Obviously, there was considerable overlap of these two responses. In fact, two-thirds of Evangelicals sympathized with Israel for *both* reasons. Here the entire public provides a contrast: just 58 percent of those who sympathize with Israel listed God's gift to the Jews, and 49 percent listed biblical prophecy (and 39 percent listed both).

DISCUSSION

Three conclusions can be drawn from the foregoing analysis. First, Evangelical Protestants have generally positive views of Jews and these views have become more positive over the last forty years. Second, major disagreements remain between Evangelicals and Jews on religious matters, the proper role of religion in public affairs, and social issues. Third, religion is a motivating factor in the opinions of Evangelicals on many issues, including support for Israel.

Given the broader history of Christian-Jewish relations, Evangelicals' positive views toward Jews are worthy of attention. Evangelicals do not perceive social distance between Jews and American society as a whole, and by and large they do not hold negative social, religious, and political images of Jews. Furthermore, these positive attitudes toward Jews have increased over the last forty years. In regard to these issues, Evangelicals closely resemble the population as a whole. To be sure, there are minorities of Evangelicals who do hold negative attitudes and such minorities can be quite problematic. But such minorities should not obscure the fact that a majority of Evangelicals have positive views of the Jewish community. Indeed, critics of Evangelical Protestants should not be too quick to assume that this large and diverse religious community harbors hostility to Jews and other minority faiths.

Evangelicals and Jews have significant disagreements, however, and these are likely to continue to be a source of tension between the communities. Particularly problematic is the Evangelical imperative to proselytize. It is worth noting, however, that there are some nuances in Evangelical beliefs in this regard. Similarly, Evangelicals and Jews have important differences on the proper role of religion in public affairs. On some of these matters, Evangelicals share the views of a majority of Americans, but on others they hold a distinctly minority position. All of these matters can be problematic, but it is worth noting that neither Evangelicals' religious beliefs nor their views on religion in public life are associated with negative attitudes toward Jews.

Evangelicals' religious beliefs are closely associated with their positions on many issues, especially "moral" questions and foreign policy. A good example of this influence is Evangelicals' views on Israel. Interestingly enough, Evangelicals are more likely to support Israel because of the belief that God gave Israel to the Jews rather than because of biblical prophecy, although both perspectives are important. Thus, the very religious beliefs that lead Evangelicals to conservative positions on many domestic issues also lead them to be among the strongest supporters of Israel in the United States.

NOTES

1. The author wishes to acknowledge the use of survey data from the Roper Center at the University of Connecticut, the Interuniversity Center for Political and Social Research, the National Opinion Research Corporation and the Pew Research Center. All interpretations of the data are the responsibility of the author, who can provide additional details of the analysis upon request.

2. Measuring Evangelical Protestants in survey research is often problematic because surveys do not use the same religion items. Here Evangelicals are defined as white, born-again Protestants, except when the born-again question is absent, in which case the group is defined by denominational affiliation.

3. In the surveys used, Jews make up between two and three percent of the sample. This means that in the largest surveys used, there are between eighty and one hundred Jewish respondents, and in the smaller samples, a few dozen. Valid inferences are problematic with so few respondents.

4. These data come from the 2004 General Social Survey.

5. See Tom W. Smith, *Anti-Semitism in Contemporary America* (New York: American Jewish Committee, 1994).

6. For example, a 2004 Pew Research Center survey found that 71 percent of the public at large believed the United States was a "Christian nation;" 77 percent of Evangelicals agreed, but so did 66 percent of Jews.

3

How Wide is the Social Distance Between Jews and Evangelicals?

Barry Kosmin

The evolution of this chapter throws some light on the wider issue of the relationship between the two communities here under discussion. This chapter was originally intended to parallel the prior one by John Greene and so to answer the question as to what Jews think about Evangelicals. Unfortunately, the answer to that is very short—we really don't know. This situation reflects a major lacuna in the social science literature on American Jews, which reflects the infinitesimal amount of attention and time that the plethora of American Jewish communal organizations has invested in investigating Jewish social attitudes toward "the other" rather than outsiders' attitudes toward Jews. A trawl of the various local and national studies of Jewish populations reveals that Jewish social attitudes regarding prejudices and social distance are a "black hole."

Faced by a lack of material, I then investigated what Jews today might be taught about Evangelical Christians in the myriad of educational institutions the community sponsors—colleges, day schools, seminaries, adult educational courses, etc. Yet again, I found very little evidence of a concern to educate rabbis, school children, or the general Jewish public about Evangelical Christianity or even of an attempt to try to understand the nature of this important sector of the American religious scene and large segment of the national population. In fact, there seemed a dearth of educational activity under Jewish auspices generally focusing on the theological differences, doctrinal positions, and concerns of the various Christian churches and denominations.

Aside from the Catholic Church and black Christians, Jews individually and institutionally seem to be much more interested in learning about and dialoguing with Buddhists and Muslims.

My next step was a rather quick and inadequate piece of qualitative research among the Jewish elites—a small sample of rabbis, academics and communal professionals. This revealed a great deal of confusion and ignorance about distinctions between Evangelicals and fundamentalists and only a general recognition of Evangelical Christian support for the State of Israel, which they felt rather embarrassed about and tried to explain using a vague version of pre-millennialist theology. When pressed further, they tended to respond to me with talk about, in their opinion, the Evangelical Christians' unacceptable missionary impulse to convert Jews and the problems posed to the Jewish community by Jews for Jesus, Hebrew Christians, and Messianic Jews. However, the overall impression I gained of the situation as regards intellectual knowledge and engagement and dialogue between these religious traditions is that Jews and Evangelicals are like ships passing in the night. And so, if ignorance and lack of education lead to prejudice and negative stereotypes as the Jewish defense organizations have long maintained, then we should expect American Jews to be prejudiced about Evangelicals.

I leave to others the task of dealing in more detail with this blind spot in contemporary Jewish education and the Jewish communal and public disinterest in engagement and particularly grassroots dialogue. Instead, here I shall try to account in structural terms for why studies are not undertaken and conversations are not held. To do this, I shall provide contemporary social data and analysis on how sections of the two communities compare on a variety of religious and social indicators. I hope these profiles will in a small way better inform each community about the other and so furnish them with a greater knowledge of the social reality of the United States in the twenty-first century. Hopefully, this may go some way to dispel some of the myths that linger on from fifty or seventy years ago, especially among those who dwell in the isolationist Jewish bubble.

My first task is to state that both the Evangelical community and the Jewish community are imprecise entities with unfixed boundaries. As John Green has acknowledged, the definition of who is an Evangelical is nearly as open to question as who is a Jew. Moreover, in neither case is there an acknowledged person or entity that is recognized or authorized to decide the matter. As a result, counting both populations is an imprecise science and the size of both communities is much debated and various estimates are bandied about. Yet if Evangelicals are a community of faith while Jews are a community of fate, Evangelicals as a strictly associational group of individuals based on belief should in some ways be easier to determine. In contrast, the Jews are a population based on a mixture of descent, religion and culture. The inevitable dissensus this involves leads to nonrecognition or nonacceptance between various religious streams. The result is that American Jews are a "problematic" community: they are really a series of communities difficult to fix in space and time.

However, in order to avoid controversy I shall slice the sociological Gordian knot by resorting to a democratic principle and define as Jews and Evangelicals only those who responded so when asked in the American Religious Identification Survey 2001—*What is your religion, if any*? This was a nationally representative telephone survey of 50,000 households.[1] At first glance this unprompted question appears unproblematic for a population of believers such as Evangelical Christians but it works to exclude around one in five American Jews who appear in all manner of surveys and communal estimates but who responded "None," atheist, agnostic, humanist, etc. to this particular question. They will, however, respond positively if the category or prompt "Jewish" is explicitly used, for example: "Do you consider yourself Jewish?" or "Are you Catholic, Protestant, or Jewish?"

Of course, no question is unproblematic in social science and in fact the vast majority of those who are theologically identified as Evangelicals, by John Green and other experts, responded to ARIS with a variety of denominational responses such as Baptist, Lutheran, Nazarene or Assemblies of God. We are thus dealing with a group who identified themselves as Evangelical or Born Again to the exclusion of other denominational or congregational ties. This group definitely belongs in the Evangelical camp and can be envisaged as the core of this community. However, it would make no difference to the results on the belief and attitudinal items (see table 3.1) if they were substituted by denominational identifiers with a range of "Evangelical" groups such as Church of the Nazarene, Southern Baptists, or Assemblies of God.

Thus the data I shall present relate to two fractions of the two communities under investigation. In the Evangelical case, it is that small minority which ARIS estimated at just over one million adults whose primary response was "Evangelical" or "Born Again." In the Jewish case, it covers nearly three million adults—the majority of those normally termed the American Jewish community, i.e. those who answered "Jewish" to the exclusion of any other religious group or belief system. It thus excludes the most secularized elements in the

Table 3.1.   Indicators

	% Religious	% Somewhat Religious	% Somewhat Secular	% Secular
What is Your Outlook?				
U.S. Total Pop.	38	40	6	10
Evangelical	70	19	1	7
Jews	11	41	16	26

	% Agree Strongly	% Agree	% Disagree	% Disagree Strongly
God Exists				
U.S. Total Pop.	80	11	2	3
Evangelical	99	1	0	0
Jews	54	23	9	5

	% Agree Strongly	% Agree	% Disagree	% Disagree Strongly
God Helps Me				
U.S. Total Pop.	71	15	4	5
Evangelical	97	3	0	0
Jews	34	25	17	15

Household Membership in a Congregation	
U.S. Total Pop.	54%
Evangelicals	83%
Jews	53%

Source: The data is taken from the American Religious Identification Survey 2001. See Barry A. Kosmin and Ariela Keysar, *Religion in a Free Market* (Ithaca, NY: Paramount Market Publishing, 2006).

Jewish community, e.g. agnostics and Ethical Culturists along with those syncretist groups such as "JewBu's"—Jewish Buddhists. Nevertheless, I believe the data that follow do in fact provide important and valid insights into the overall nature of these two communities. They also throw considerable light on the nature of the contemporary differences in a number of social realms between the groups.

It is important to remember when viewing these statistics that they relate to adults, i.e. persons over the age of eighteen years. Table 3.1 deals with a range of religious and belief indicators.

HOW WIDE IS THE SOCIAL DISTANCE BETWEEN JEWS EVANGELICALS?

The first item on religious or secular outlook might be thought problematic but 97 percent of the ARIS respondents felt able to reply. The issue here should not be the question wording or terminology but the patterns of response. We can see that the two populations under scrutiny here deviate considerably from the national norm. If we take the first response item, we can see that Evangelicals "overachieve" by 32 percentage points and Jews "underachieve" by 27 points. So, in some ways, we can see at the outset that we are dealing with two fringe populations at either end of the national "outlook spectrum." Again we need to re-emphasize that these respondents are self-identified religious Jews—Jews by religion. In terms of denominational preference, our Jewish sample was 10 percent Orthodox. Most were Conservative and Reform, with the remainder "just Jewish." It is interesting to note that 42 percent of Jews by religion said they have a secular outlook of some kind. Either the term secular means something different to Christians than what it means to Jews, which may well be true, or Judaism operates very differently from other religions.

The findings related to the next two questions about the existence of the Divine and the efficacy of a personal relationship with the Divine strongly suggest that the thesis may well be true. The item on the existence of God shows that Jews deviate further from the national norm than do Evangelicals. In addition, Evangelicals are clearly a homogeneous group who believe in an efficacious personal God. Jews are much more skeptical in theological terms and much more diverse in their thinking about what God does for them personally.

With regard to current institutional ties to organized religion, Jews are average Americans while Evangelicals are much more congregationally involved.

The age structures of the two populations, as noted in table 3.2, are very different from both each other and the national norm. The demographic indicators, as a whole, show that Evangelicals are skewed toward the parenting generation in terms of age structure. So they are much more likely to be married than Jews or American adults in general. Jews are a much older population because many younger Jews—the offspring of these people—are to be found in the No Religion category. However, in terms of gender balance they are both normal populations.

As reflects their age structure, Jews have below average household size while in contrast Evangelicals live in larger household units. Jews are particularly noted for the high proportion of people who live alone—a rate three times as likely as for Evangelicals. In contrast, Evangelicals are more gregarious. One explanation for this is the number of children these populations produce. Half the Jewish households in the age range 18–60 years have no child present compared to only one in three homes among Evangelicals. In contrast,

Table 3.2.   Demographic Indicators

	% 18–29	% 30–64	% 65+	% Female	% Married
Adult Age Structure					
U.S. Total Pop.	23	61	16	52	59
Evangelical	19	72	9	49	74
Jews	14	58	28	51	60

	Average Household Size	% Single Person Households
U.S. Total Pop.	2.74 persons	24
Evangelicals	3.34 persons	11
Jews	2.24 persons	37

Number of Children in multi-person households with respondent aged 18–60			
	0	1–2	3+
U.S. Total Pop.	44%	44%	12%
Evangelicals	35%	39%	25%
Jews	52%	40%	8%

Evangelical households with three or more children are much more common. So in terms of familial orientation—at least at the nuclear family level—the Jewish family is small and rare while the Evangelical family is flourishing. The direction of the causality is open to question. Are family oriented adults especially attracted to Evangelicalism or is it Evangelical theology or ideology that successfully propels them to familialism?

Here I think we will begin to dispel some of the old myths about the social gap between these two communities. The past few decades have seen rapid rises in the national standards of living and education and so in the *embourgeoisement* of much of "white America." The data in table 3.3 show that this self-selected group of Evangelicals is by no means uneducated. In fact, educationally the Evangelicals are closer to the Jews than the U.S. norm in terms of college graduation rates.

On employment rates there is no differentiation at all across the groups, nor is there any in terms of the rate of home ownership. Jewish incomes are indeed above average and on a per capita basis the gap is wider still. Nevertheless, as the education and house owning data suggest, Evangelicals are neither poor nor ignorant people.

The technology data could be seen as providing an indication of discretionary spending patterns and overall openness to technical innovation. Interestingly, although in theory they have more discre-

Table 3.3.   Socioeconomic Indicators 2001

	College Graduates	18–64 Full-Time Employed	Home Owner	Median Household Income
Home Ownership 2001				
U.S. Total Pop.	33%	65%	71%	$42k
Evangelicals	49%	67%	75%	$54k
Jews	58%	66%	73%	$72k
	Large Screen TV	Video Games	PC Owner	Internet Access
Technology & Communications				
U.S. Total Pop.	13%	12%	20%	16%
Evangelicals	3%	6%	14%	12%
Jews	9%	5%	16%	15%

tionary income than average Americans, neither group are notable innovators or particularly prominent consumers of these communication devices. The only evidence of a cultural bias against the new media could be the low take-up of large TVs by Evangelicals and perhaps video games given their known bias toward young families. However, the statistics dispel negative myths about Jews—that they are the "great consumers" of ostentatious products such as large screen TVs.

The geographical data in table 3.4 show that the propinquity factor could explain much of the Jewish-Evangelical social distance. In terms of neighborhood, American Jews are much more suburban than Americans in general and very few are found in rural areas. The aphorism "Out of sight out of mind" comes to mind. Surprisingly, these

Table 3.4.   Geography

	Urban	Suburban	Rural	
Residence				
U.S. Total Pop.	30%	50%	20%	
Evangelicals	35%	47%	18%	
Jews	36%	60%	4%	
	Northeast	Midwest	South	West
Census Region				
U.S. Total Pop.	19%	23%	36%	21%
Evangelicals	18%	41%	17%	25%
Jews	43%	12%	25%	20%

Evangelicals are less rural than average Americans but are more likely to be found in the cities of the Midwest and Mountain states. Certainly few Jews and Evangelicals are likely to be neighbors even in the suburbs. We know that Jews are located mainly in the Northeast, Florida and California. On the other hand, this particular population of Evangelicals is overrepresented in the Midwest and the Mountain states. So, if regional cultures are still operating to differentiate Americans then this would suggest that these two populations are socially distant, too. Historically, the cultural home of Evangelicalism was the Midwest and it is interesting to note the continuation of this tradition in the popularity of this self-identification category in this region of the country.

The responses to three items of societal consequence are shown in table 3.5. Evangelicals are often seen as a "white population" like Jews. Certainly neither has many black identifiers. However, there is some evidence that there is a considerable and above average representation of the Hispanic minority in this particular population.

Another issue that affects religious belonging and behavior is the likelihood of living with somebody with a different religious outlook or loyalty. As America has become a more tolerant and socially integrated nation, social boundaries have fallen so marriages between people of different backgrounds have become more frequent. Interestingly, Evangelicals tend to live in slightly more religiously homogeneous homes than most Americans while Jews tend more than

Table 3.5. Social Indicators

	White	Black	Asian	Hispanic	Other
Race and Ethnic Composition					
U.S. Total Pop.	70%	10%	3%	12%	5%
Evangelicals	77%	3%	0%	20%	0%
Jews	92%	1%	1%	5%	1%

Percentage of Respondents with Spouse/Partner of a Different Religious Identity					
U.S. Total Pop.	22%
Evangelicals	18%
Jews	27%

	Republican	Democrat	Independent	Other/None
Party Political Preference 2001				
U.S. Total Pop.	31%	31%	30%	8%
Evangelicals	58%	12%	20%	10%
Jews	13%	56%	26%	5%

most Americans to reside in "religiously" mixed households. Again the myth of the "clannish Jews" and the intolerant Evangelical is dispelled by these statistics.

Finally, we turn to party politics. Here the data are not surprising to anybody with even a cursory knowledge of national politics. In statistical terms the results mirror the first table we examined on religious-secular outlook. Whereas Americans as a whole are balanced in their party preferences between the three main available options, Evangelicals are firmly Republican while Jews are heavily Democrat.

Thus, the overall conclusion pointed to by the hard evidence from the ARIS data is not unexpected. The two selected groups of respondents do, I believe, give us an indication of the areas and range of the gap in the overall social distance between these two communities. Clearly, Jews are figuratively and literally "blue state" Americans while Evangelicals are "red state" Americans. However, the source of the gap seems to lie in cultural and demographic areas rather than in the socioeconomic realm. This latter finding is important for communal relations because it explains why the economic antagonism against Jews, and market capitalism, which was common among Evangelicals in the early twentieth century, has largely disappeared as a political issue or point of conflict.

NOTE

1. See Barry A. Kosmin and Ariela Keysar, *Religion in a Free Market* (Ithaca, NY: Paramount Market Publishing, 2006).

4

The Organized Jewish Community and Evangelical America

A Brief History

Lawrence Grossman

The organized Jewish community's engagement with American Evangelicals, barely forty years old, has been fraught with ambivalence and contradiction. The Jewish stake in the relationship is clear. Not only are Evangelicals the fastest growing religious group in the United States both in numbers and political clout, but they also share with Jews a biblically-based Judeo-Christian heritage and the historical experience of living as a minority within a hostile majority religious environment. Of vital importance, Evangelicals—uniquely among Christian communities—share, on theological grounds, the Jewish commitment to the security of the State of Israel, perhaps the one issue on which all American Jews passionately agree.

But two other factors have hampered good relations. First, while other Christian groups have dropped from their agendas the drive to convert Jews, Evangelicals retain it as a priority, raising the specter, in Jewish circles, that Evangelical friendship is nothing but a proselytizing tactic. Furthermore, Evangelical political and social attitudes, always less liberal than those of most Jews, have turned increasingly rightward since the late 1970s, arousing Jewish suspicions of an intention to blur church-state boundaries and Christianize America. There are, then, contradictory forces simultaneously attracting Jews toward cooperation with Evangelicals and repelling them from it. Hence the constant ups and downs in the relationship.

The organized Jewish community discovered Evangelicals quite late. While formal contacts with Mainline Protestant institutions began in the late nineteenth century and with the Catholic Church in the 1920s, the world of Evangelicals remained terra incognita. For one thing, Jews and Evangelicals have tended to live geographically separate lives. American Jews have historically concentrated in the urban centers of the Northeast, the very places that show "the smallest conservative and Evangelical adherence rates among Protestants" in the country.[1]

Also, lack of familiarity led to mutual stereotyping. On the Jewish side, this meant painting Evangelicals as uneducated, bigoted, and single-mindedly out to convert Jews—hardly candidates for reasoned dialogue. In addition, Evangelicals, unlike Catholics and Mainline Protestants, were not well organized and lacked a public presence that might induce Jewish leaders to see them as potential interlocutors. Especially after World War I, Evangelicals tended to retreat from political involvement and the public arena, and so the Jewish community did not feel the need to take them into account in pursuing its agenda.[2] Even the phenomenon of "Christian Zionism," which saw some Evangelical ministers speaking out in favor of Jewish statehood in Palestine during the late nineteenth and early twentieth centuries, did not bring Jews and Evangelicals closer together. Its enthusiasts were isolated voices in their churches, often harbored clearly conversionary motives, and, in some cases, abandoned the cause once it left the realm of prophetic ideal and became, in 1948, the this-worldly and imperfect State of Israel.[3]

After World War II, when organized American Jewry concentrated its domestic efforts on civil rights, civil liberties, and strengthening the separation of church and state, it came to see Mainline Protestantism, and particularly its umbrella organization, the National Council of Churches, as an ally.[4] And, blinkered by a combination of cultural parochialism and wishful thinking, Jewish leaders acted as if the Mainline denominations were American Protestantism. The annual Joint Program Plan produced by the National Community Relations Advisory Council (NCRAC)—the closest thing to a policy platform of the Jewish community—referred repeatedly to relations with liberal Protestant groups but not to any others.[5] When Jews noticed them at all, Evangelicals were perceived as allies of the "radical right" and the John Birch Society.[6]

The Anti-Defamation League (ADL), the largest and best-known Jewish organization dedicated to fighting anti-Semitism, contributed to the negative stereotype of Evangelicals through its sponsorship of the research that produced the book *Christian Beliefs and Anti-Semitism* in 1966. The authors, Charles Y. Glock and Rodney Stark, found that among Christians, literal interpretation of New Testament teachings correlated with high levels of antagonism toward Jews, and therefore Baptists and other Evangelicals were far more likely than Mainline Protestants and Catholics to blame Jews for the crucifixion of Jesus and to insist that Jews could attain salvation only through conversion.[7]

Like so much else in American Jewish life, this simplistic attitude toward Evangelicals came into question in the wake of the Six-Day War of June 1967. Israel launched a preemptive strike against Egypt and Syria, which had threatened its destruction. Israeli forces captured the Sinai desert from the former and the Golan Heights from the latter, and when Jordan entered the war on the Arab side, Israel seized the West Bank of the Jordan River, including East Jerusalem. American Jews viewed the outcome as a quasi-miraculous deliverance of the Jewish state from the brink of annihilation, and were dismayed at the apparent indifference of the Christian bodies with which the organized Jewish community had been in dialogue. As the NCRAC Joint Program Plan noted that year, "Many Jews were appalled by the relative silence of the Christian world in the face of the threat of imminent destruction of the two and a half million Jews in Israel." It described "the prevailing 'official' Protestant response" as "a seeming desire to avoid taking sides."[8]

But Jews discovered that there were other Protestants, previously dismissed or ignored, who reveled in Israel's victory. Not quite sure of their theological taxonomy, the Joint Program Plan noted: "Among fundamentalists on the radical right, some saw in the Israeli victory a fulfillment of Biblical prophecy." Not until 1970 would the Plan get it right, announcing that "The Evangelical groups are staunchly pro-Israel."[9] The ADL, which had described Evangelicals as "inaccessible to dialogue" in December 1966, published the report of a long interview with the country's best known Evangelical, Rev. Billy Graham, one year later. Graham urged Israel not to relinquish land it had conquered if that might endanger the country's security. "The Jews are God's chosen people," said Graham. "We cannot place ourselves in opposition to Israel without detriment to ourselves." Evangelicals, concluded the interviewer, "are no longer inaccessible."[10]

The two major national Jewish community relations organizations, the ADL and the American Jewish Committee (AJC), moved to build relationships with Evangelicals. Both looked first to the Southern Baptists, who not only constituted the single largest Evangelical body, but also shared with Jews a common grievance—the suppression of their members' religious freedom in the Soviet Union—that added another bond, in addition to concern for the State of Israel, tying them to Jews.

The ADL led off with a symposium in Miami early in 1969 for its local chapter members and Baptist ministers and laymen. This became an annual event in the community and furnished a model for similar programs in other cities. An ADL-sponsored conference two years later at Baylor University, a Baptist institution, led to a series of other academically oriented Jewish-Evangelical meetings at campuses across the country.[11]

The AJC's first joint activity with the Southern Baptists was a three-day conference cosponsored with the Southern Baptist Convention Home Mission Board's Department of Work Related to Non-Evangelicals. Held at the Southern Baptist Theological Seminary in Louisville, Kentucky, it attracted some seventy scholars and members of the clergy. The conference program, noting that the two religious groups "share uniquely a common reverence for the Bible and its majestic teachings, as well as an historic experience of suffering to preserve freedom of conscience," declared the purpose of the get-together to be the removal of "stereotypes and mythologies" each had of the other. Significantly, Rabbi Marc Tanenbaum, interreligious affairs director of the AJC and initiator of the conference, delivered an address on "The Meaning of Israel: A Jewish View."

At the final session the participants agreed to work cooperatively "to defend the religious liberty of Baptists and Jews in the Soviet Union and other countries where both groups suffer discrimination." Another point of consensus that came out of the conference—surprising in retrospect, given the later rightward political tilt among Evangelicals—was a call to reverse national priorities by taking resources away from the "military-industrial complex" and investing them in the "war against poverty." The two organizations agreed to hold follow-up conferences "to advance understanding and cooperation," and specifically to address the most vexing area of potential conflict: the clash between the Baptist commitment to evangelism and Jewish insistence on the ongoing integrity and legitimacy of Judaism. Presciently, the conferees noted that attention to this knotty problem was a prerequisite for finding "a valid theological basis for religious coexistence."[12] A second AJC-Southern Baptist conference was held in Cincinnati in June 1971, concentrating on the need to cooperate on "such social issues as the Vietnam war, racism, pollution, and unemployment."[13]

These overtures bore fruit. In August 1972, the Baptist Convention in Israel, an affiliate of the Southern Baptist Convention, formally condemned anti-Semitism. It also acknowledged that Jewish persecution often "took place in so-called Christian countries" and was "rooted in

Christian anti-Semitism, deriving from the assumption that since the Jew rejected Christ, he was considered cursed of God and his sufferings deserved." The ADL's interreligious director, Rabbi Solomon Bernards, commented that the statement "encourages the active pursuit of meaningful Jewish-Christian encounter for the elimination of distrust and misunderstanding."[14]

The next step in Jewish-Evangelical relations came in December 1975, when the AJC ventured beyond the Southern Baptists and involved leaders of the broader Evangelical community. AJC, together with the Institute for Holy Land Studies—a Jerusalem-based Evangelical school—sponsored a three-day conference in New York City for scholars and religious leaders, "a first," noted *Christianity Today*, "in both Evangelical and Jewish circles." The sessions featured presentations, from Jewish and Evangelical perspectives, on the significance of the Messiah, the meaning of Israel, social concerns, the interpretation of Scripture, and religious pluralism. Once again, the most divisive issue was Evangelical insistence on converting everyone, including Jews, to Christianity. The Evangelical participants acknowledged the need to be more sensitive to Jewish feelings on this score.[15]

More dividends for the Jewish community were soon evident from its rapprochement with Evangelicals. The Israeli government, especially after the right-wing Menachem Begin became prime minister in 1977, found in the Evangelical community its strongest American Christian supporters. Newspapers carried ads signed by Evangelical leaders that backed Israeli control of the territories occupied in the 1967 war; many of the signatories had participated in joint Jewish-Evangelical conferences.[16]

The election of Jimmy Carter, a born-again Christian, to the presidency in 1976 symbolized the phenomenal growth of Evangelical Christianity, a trend that impressed Jewish organizations with the need to accelerate their outreach. Thus the American Jewish Committee invited Rev. Billy Graham to address its National Executive Committee meeting in 1977. Graham, who used the opportunity to affirm his support for Israel as a fulfillment of biblical prophecy, was given the organization's first National Interreligious Award.[17] By December 1980, when the AJC convened its second national conference with Evangelicals—this one held at Trinity Evangelical Divinity School in Deerfield, Illinois, in cooperation with the magazine *Christianity Today*—Prof. Marvin R. Wilson, an Evangelical biblical scholar, could cite an impressive record of dialogues, educational experiences, and social events that had drawn the two religious communities closer together.[18]

But working against the incipient alliance was the ongoing Evangelical insistence on evangelizing. Even as Evangelical and Jewish leaders congratulated themselves on erasing old stereotypes, one stereotype, that Evangelicals intended to convert the Jews, remained very real. In 1972, about 140 Christian groups announced a joint program, Key 73, to begin in early 1973, designed "to call the continent to Christ." While a number of Catholic dioceses and Mainline Protestant bodies signed on to the venture, many did not, and some that did gave only pro forma support. Key 73, then, had a decidedly Evangelical tinge. The activists saw themselves as following the Evangelical imperative of seeking to convert all people and did not specifically target Jews. They were, therefore, puzzled and hurt when Jewish leaders—adherents of a religion that did not seek converts—expressed resentment at the prospect of a missionary campaign that implicitly called into question the validity of Judaism.

The Union of American Hebrew Congregations and the United Synagogue of America—the congregational bodies of Reform and Conservative Judaism—took the lead in castigating Key 73 for its conversionary intentions. Both issued material to synagogues for distribution to young people refuting Christian theological claims. NJCRAC, which devoted a plenary session of its 1973 annual meeting to "Christian Evangelism and the Jews," warned its constituent organizations that Key 73 "threatens the principle of pluralism according equality to all religion in this country." In addition, "there is the possibility that friction between Evangelicals and Jews in the United States, arising out of the currently heightened level of proselytization in this country, may affect the attitudes of the Evangelical community toward Israel." NJCRAC urged rabbis and Jewish community leaders to convince their Evangelical friends and colleagues explicitly to exempt Jews from Key 73 efforts on the grounds that "Judaism is a living faith in its own terms."[19] A number of Evangelical leaders, most notably Billy Graham, did disavow any particular attempt to target Jews and pledged support for the principle of religious pluralism. In the end, Key 73 petered out with very little to show for itself, but it reinforced for Jews the fear that the ultimate aim of Evangelicals—no matter how forthcoming on other issues—was to convert them.

That Evangelicals—unlike most Catholics and Mainline Protestants—still delegitimized Judaism made the headlines again seven years later, during the 1980 presidential campaign, which pitted two Evangelicals against each other: Democrat Jimmy Carter, the liberal incumbent, and Ronald Reagan, the Republican challenger whose conservative politics would, in the end, prove more appealing to an increasingly rightward looking Evangelical community and to the electorate at large. (A third candidate, former congressman John Anderson, ran as an independent.) That August, at a pro-Reagan meeting in Dallas with the candidate present, Rev. Bailey Smith, president of the Southern Baptist Convention, declared that "God Almighty does not hear the prayer of a Jew." Reagan disavowed the remark, as did such leaders of the so-called Christian Right as Jerry Falwell and Pat Robertson.[20]

Jewish groups denounced Smith, who protested that he was "pro-Jew." Smith asked the ADL for a meeting, which took place in New York on December 18 with the press barred. After its conclusion Smith read a statement to the waiting reporters expressing "deep regret for any hurt to the Jewish community," affirming "an American pluralistic society," and opposing anti-Semitism. Had he known how his words would be "misinterpreted," said Smith, he would never have made the statement. Nathan Perlmutter, the ADL national director, declared himself satisfied. The ADL hosted Pat Robertson at its National Executive Committee meeting in October, where he spoke about his love for Israel. In November, after Reagan's victory, Israeli Prime Minister Menachem Begin conferred medals upon 100 Americans for "distinguished service to the State of Israel and the Jewish people." Among them was Jerry Falwell.[21]

From the standpoint of Israel's supporters, the Jewish-Evangelical bond proved its usefulness during the Reagan presidency as Falwell's organization, the Moral Majority, exerted strong influence within the Republican Party on Israel's behalf, with Prime Minister Begin's enthusiastic approval. The Reagan administration held regular briefings on the Middle East for American Jewish activists and Christian Right leaders such as Hal Lindsey, Jimmy Swaggart, Jim and Tammy Baker, Pat Robertson, and Tim LeHaye. After Israel bombed Iraq's nuclear facility in 1981, Begin called Falwell before calling President Reagan, and urged the Evangelical leader to "explain to the Christian public the reasons for the bombing." Falwell pledged to the Rabbinical Assembly, the organization of Conservative rabbis, at their meeting in Miami in 1985, to "mobilize 70 million conservative Christians for Israel and against anti-Semitism."[22]

But the election of 1980 and the Reagan ascendancy added another complicating ingredient to the Evangelical-Jewish encounter. No longer were conversionary intentions and delegitimation of Judaism the only reasons to fear the Evangelical embrace. The "new" Christian Right—if anything, even more pro-Israel than Evangelicals a decade earlier—was far more politically conservative, its views on many domestic issues diametrically opposed to the liberal stance of the American Jewish mainstream. These Jewish positions were, as the American Jewish Congress put it, "support for the separation of church and state and the protection of the public school classroom; support for the Equal Rights Amendment [barring discrimination against women] and the right of women to choose to have an abortion; support for human rights and opposition to all oppressive governments; support for the right to dissent and opposition to censorship; support for compassionate social welfare legislation and opposition to discrimination and poverty . . . the classic agenda of democracy."[23] The NJCRAC Joint Program Plan—as always, a faithful barometer of Jewish concerns—turned its attention to fighting administration initiatives to restore prayer and other religious practices to the public schools, enact tuition tax credits for private schools, and, more generally, break down the church-state divide, initiatives championed by the nascent, primarily Evangelical, Religious Right.[24]

A front-page article on the complicated relations between Evangelicals and Jews, based on interviews with leaders of both groups, appeared in *The New York Times* in early 1983. Evangelical enthusiasm for Israel was stronger than ever, manifested in "rallies and newspaper advertisements supporting Israel, participation of Evangelicals in synagogue services and the creation of pro-Israeli organizations among Christians." And yet some Jewish leaders were "uneasy," suspecting that these Evangelicals "want ultimately to convert the Jews and, on many political issues, often hold profoundly different, more conservative points of view." Those Jewish leaders who expressed skepticism, such as Rabbi Alexander Schindler, president of the Union of American Hebrew Congregations, felt that even Evangelical support for Israel was "intrinsically demeaning to Jews" since it was based on the idea that the ingathering of the Jews in their land was a necessary prelude to the Second Coming. More optimistic Jews, such as Rabbi Tanenbaum of the American Jewish Committee, believed that pro-Israel Evangelicals were gradually moving away from seeking the conversion of Jews and were also more politically diverse than commonly thought.[25]

Support for the optimists came from two surveys of Evangelical opinion released by the ADL, one in June 1985 and the other in January 1987. The first demonstrated that while it was true that most Evangelicals differed from the liberal positions held by most Jews on certain political and social issues (for instance, 90 percent of Evangelicals backed voluntary prayer in the public schools), on others they were split. Evangelicals favored Israel by a three-to-one margin—the degree of support for Israel correlating with frequency of church attendance—

and viewed Jews favorably by five to one. According to the second survey, negative religious stereotypes about Jews were not as common among Evangelicals as generally assumed. Fully 86 percent of Evangelicals disagreed with the assertion that God did not listen to the prayers of Jews and 90 percent disagreed with the notion that Christians were justified in holding negative attitudes toward Jews because "Jews killed Christ." ADL national director Perlmutter concluded from the 1987 data that Evangelical opposition to Jewish social policy positions "reflects different values," not bigotry or anti-Semitism.[26] This more relaxed view of the Evangelicals was reflected in the 1989 NJCRAC Joint Program Plan. It perceived "a growing division" among Evangelicals between "hard-core fundamentalists" and "moderates," and proposed that the Jewish community relate to Evangelicals as it did to other groups, "working in coalition on issues of mutual concern and parting company on those issues, both political and religious, where there are profound differences of view."[27]

But just as President Woodrow Wilson was reputed to have said in 1916 that any German U-boat captain had the power to falsify his campaign slogan, "He Kept Us Out of the War," so too, any small group of indiscreet or impolitic Evangelical leaders had the power to unsettle Evangelical-Jewish relations. That is what happened when fifteen Evangelical theologians from the United States and abroad, meeting in Bermuda in April 1989, issued a statement declaring not only that Christians were required to seek the conversion of Jews, but that "failure to preach the gospel to the Jewish people would be a form of anti-Semitism, depriving this particular community of its right to hear the gospel." The statement went on to describe Jews as "branches of God's olive tree" that had "broken off," and denied that Judaism "contains within itself true knowledge of God's salvation."[28]

While condemning anti-Semitism and declaring support for "the Jewish quest for a homeland with secure borders and a just peace," in the same breath these Evangelicals raised another inflammatory issue that would become increasingly divisive in the 1990s: whether a Jew might remain Jewish while accepting Christ. Their statement praised such Jews and encouraged them to seek the conversion of other Jews, albeit without "coercive or deceptive proselytizing." In a subsequent interview, one of the signers suggested that the statement was partially intended as a rebuke to the Mainline denominations, which had stopped seeking the conversion of the Jews. Jewish leaders reacted with dismay. Rabbi A. James Rudin, who had succeeded Tanenbaum as interreligious director of the American Jewish Committee, denounced the statement as "the worst kind of Christian religious imperialism and a theological assault upon the integrity of Jews and Judaism throughout the world."[29]

The Bermuda statement was a sign of things to come. With the collapse of the Moral Majority, the early 1990s saw the rise of a new organization claiming to represent the religious right, Pat Robertson's Christian Coalition. As accurately noted by the NJCRAC Joint Program Plan, this latest manifestation of primarily Evangelical political action focused on "the local level, such as candidates for school boards and other local elections articulating platforms of the 'religious right,' including attacking local school-board curricula and attempting censorship of schools libraries." The prominent role Robertson played at the 1992 Republican national convention, where he gave a prime-time address, worried Jewish organizations, raising "questions about the appropriate role of religion in public life." Exempted from taxes by registering as a nonpartisan group, the Coalition, charged NJCRAC, was seeking to elect enough "pro-family Christians" to gain control of Congress and the Republican Party, and then to legalize discrimination against homosexuals, return prayer to the public schools, enact government vouchers for attendance at private schools, lower taxes, and enact term limits—positions very much at odds with the Jewish communal consensus.[30]

The ADL published a book-length attack on the religious right in 1994. Most of the volume chronicled the rise and aims of Robertson, the Christian Coalition, and its legal arm, the American Center for Law and Justice, laying out the case that they intended to dismantle the separation between church and state. It included shorter descriptions of additional elements of the movement: Focus on the Family, Donald Wildmon's American Family Association, Paul Weyrich's Free Congress Foundation, and others. Appendixes to the book spelled out the differences between the terms Evangelical, fundamentalist, Pentecostal, and charismatic, and explained the Evangelical Christian approach to biblical prophecy.[31]

The book aroused considerable controversy, many conservative Christians and Jews calling it exaggerated and unfair.[32] On November 29, as a direct result of the furor, Jewish and Evangelical leaders met in Washington behind closed doors to try to restore mutual trust. According to some who were there, both sides agreed to use care in the language they used about the other, to support the right of everyone to participate in the political process, and to disagree on issues without maligning each other's motives.[33]

In early 1995, with the Christian Coalition battling allegations that Pat Robertson's writings contained anti-Semitic themes, the ADL invited Ralph Reed, executive director of the Coalition, to address its national leadership conference on April 3. Reed acknowledged that "religious conservatives have at times been insensitive and have lacked a full understanding of the horrors experienced by the Jewish people" and that some Christians bore "a measure of culpability" for the Holocaust. He pledged to uphold the separation of church and state, and declared it wrong to call the United States a Christian nation or to claim that God does not heed the prayer of a Jew. Evidence of his audience's skepticism was the fact that the only applause Reed received came after his insistence that Jerusalem must remain fully under Israeli control. Reed delivered essentially the same message— and evoked a similarly cool reaction—at the annual meeting of the American Jewish Committee the next month.[34]

As the Jewish community pondered the Christian Coalition's friendly new tone, the old issue of targeting Jews for conversion arose from a different quarter. A longstanding conflict between moderates and hardliners among the Southern Baptists—the largest single Evangelical group, with over 37,000 churches and 15 million members in the United States—was resolved in favor of the latter, and on June 13, 1996, the Southern Baptist Convention overwhelmingly passed a resolution to "direct our energies and resources toward the proclamation of the Gospel to the Jews." Money was appropriated to pay the salary of a full-time employee who would oversee the missionary effort. Far from being an anti-Jewish measure, explained one leader, it was in fact "the greatest act of respect, love, and honor a Christian can extend to a non-Christian."[35]

Jewish reaction was predictable. The ADL called the resolution "an insult to the Jewish people." B'nai B'rith, the large Jewish fraternal organization, launched a direct-mail campaign to 100,000 Jewish homes calling for postcards to be sent to Southern Baptist headquarters protesting the new policy; by November some 6,000 postcards had been mailed. The Jewish Council for Public Affairs (JCPA, successor to NJCRAC), reflecting the consensus of the organized Jewish community, noted the "outrage" of Jews and warned that the proselytizing efforts were likely to be directed toward support of Messianic Jewish groups that deceptively preached the compatibility of belief in Jesus with the maintenance of Jewish identity and practice.[36]

As numerous Christian leaders declared their opposition to the Southern Baptist position and asserted there was no need for a mission to the Jews,[37] the annual National Workshop on Christian-Jewish Relations, held on October 29, found the Southern Baptist representative, Philip Roberts, very much on the defensive. Roberts insisted that his denomination's resolution was motivated by "love" for Jews. But he angered the audience by insisting that a born Jew who was now a Southern Baptist and worked for the conversion of other Jews should be allowed to give a presentation. The request was turned down. Roberts accepted an invitation to speak at the ADL annual meeting in November, and used the opportunity to reiterate that love for Jews necessitated bringing them the word of Jesus. This prompted ADL national director Foxman to respond, "You cannot say to the Jewish people, we are opposed to anti-Semitism, but we want you to disappear as the people that you are."[38]

But the Southern Baptists were not to be deterred. In December, the Southern Baptist Convention sent a letter to all Reform rabbis explaining that its controversial resolution "does not suggest or imply that Jewish people should forsake their Jewish identity or their Jewish values." On the contrary, like the Apostle Paul, any Jew might accept "Jesus the Lord" and be saved. The letter expressed the hope that "our Jewish friends" would see the light "without coercion and no rejection, religious or social," and cited the example of the Messianic Jews. On January 29, 1997, the Convention sent a letter to the AJC and ADL proposing a meeting to mend relations. The two Jewish organizations indignantly rejected the invitation when it became clear that the Baptists intended to include "Jesus-believing Jews" in the discussions.[39] The Jewish-Southern Baptist dialogue had sputtered to an end. That October, Messianic Jews participated prominently in a Promise Keepers rally in Washington, in fact leading off the event by blowing the shofar, the ram's horn that Jews had blown the day before, Rosh Hashanah, in synagogues around the world.[40]

In September 1999, with the Jewish High Holy days coming up, the Southern Baptist Convention distributed a booklet, *Days of Awe: Prayer for Jews*, which directed Baptists to pray for the conversion of "Jewish people you know by name" during the holiday season, stressed that Jews could remain Jewish while "accepting Christ," claimed that most Jews today "are secularists or atheists" and thus ripe for conversion, and suggested that the acceptance of Christ would free Jews "of the strong influence of materialism." Chosen People Ministries, an organization of Messianic Jews, sponsored a conference entitled "To the Jew First in the New Millennium" on September 23–25 at Calvary Baptist Church in New York (the location chosen because it was "the heart of Jewish America"), which discussed strategies to win over more Jews. Many of the speakers expressed gratitude to the Southern Baptists for producing *Days of Awe*, and a decision was made to send thousands of missionaries into Jewish population centers.[41]

Expression of Jewish concern came quickly. The ADL was "offended and outraged," while the American Jewish Committee's interreligious affairs director called the conference "a spiritual salvo that's aimed at the Jewish people." The Jewish Community Relations Council of New York crafted a letter to the Southern Baptist Convention, signed by virtually all the city's Jewish organizations and the heads of the major rabbinical seminaries, stating "that conversion to Christianity removes one from participation in Jewish communal life and that the Christian belief in, and worship of, Jesus is incompatible with any authentic form of Jewish practice."[42]

The imminent arrival of the "millennium," two thousand years of the Christian era, in the year 2000, heightened tensions, both spurring on Evangelical enthusiasm to convert the world before the Second Coming and triggering Jewish fears of a possible anti-Semitic backlash in case Christ did not come again. Jewish fears, in fact, were overblown, as the only offensive public statement by a Christian leader was Jerry Falwell's assertion that the Antichrist was a living person and a Jew. He subsequently apologized and denied any anti-Jewish intent.[43]

Jewish dialogue with Evangelicals, begun in the aftermath of the Six-Day War with the aim of drawing the two communities closer, had evolved by century's end into a strange two-tier relationship. On the religious and domestic-policy planes the situation had clearly deteriorated. Jewish leaders vied with each other in denouncing Evangelical conversionary campaigns, especially those based on the idea that one could remain Jewish and believe in Christ. And yet many of the same Evangelical churches sponsoring such activities were also donating millions of dollars to Israel annually—not to mention the tourist dollars they brought with them on pilgrimages to the Holy Land—and exerting pressure on the U.S. government to back Israeli policies to the hilt.[44]

The election of President George W. Bush, a conservative Evangelical, in 2000 opened a new chapter in Evangelical-Jewish relations. Receiving just 19 percent of the Jewish vote in a close and disputed election, Bush was on record as a strong supporter of Israel. And, as in the Reagan era two decades earlier, organized American Jewry eagerly sought to get into the president's good graces, even if that meant setting aside, at least for the time being, its serious concerns about Evangelicals.

Both of the major mainstream Jewish communal organizations, the American Jewish Committee and the ADL, reached out to the administration and its Evangelical base. The AJC invited Bush to deliver the keynote address at its annual dinner in May 2001, his first public appearance as president before a Jewish audience. AJC executive director David A. Harris challenged the Jewish community with the question, "How can we expect Evangelical Christians to support our concerns if we support none of theirs?" Harris counted himself among those "who want to emphasize the convergence and commonality."[45]

Abraham Foxman, national director of the ADL, argued in 2002 for "Why Evangelical Support for Israel is a Good Thing," concluding that "American Jews should not be apologetic or defensive about cultivating Evangelical support for Israel," and that "fears that such support will undermine our impact on other concerns that American Jews have are overblown." And two years later, in the midst of the controversy over whether Mel Gibson's film *The Passion of the Christ* was anti-Semitic, Foxman, a vociferous critic of the film, reminded Jews that "Christian Evangelicals are our friends" on the issue of Israel's security, and that they had "influence with President Bush."[46]

As the Bush administration proceeded to demonstrate unprecedented support for Israeli policies, Evangelical enthusiasm for the Jewish state continued unabated with rallies, op-ed pieces, newspaper ads, and monetary contributions. Such Evangelical solidarity appeared in even bolder relief when contrasted to the behavior of some of the Mainline Protestant churches, which passed resolutions to consider or even implement divestment from Israel. Jewish organizations showed their appreciation: in 2002, the Chicago chapter of the Zionist Organization of America gave Pat Robertson its State of Israel Friendship Award; the following April the ADL invited Ralph Reed to speak at its national meeting on "Why Christians Support Israel."[47]

To be sure, at least one element of the Evangelical community, the Southern Baptists, still coupled a pro-Israel stance with vocal insistence on the need to convert Jews. In 2002 the Southern Baptist Convention's coordinator for Jewish ministries accused Catholics of anti-Semitism for granting Jews an "exemption" from proselytization and thereby "withholding the hope of Israel." The next year the president of a Southern Baptist seminary, calling for renewed attempts to convert Jews, compared Judaism to a "deadly tumor." And in 2005 the executive committee of the Southern Baptist Convention recommended that the Convention recognize the Southern Baptist Messianic Fellowship, a constituent group consisting of Jews who accepted Jesus, as "an evangelistic mission to the Jewish people." Each of these steps was sharply rebuked by the ADL, and in 2002 the Jewish Council for Public Affairs approved a statement condemning "the use of Jewish symbols and practices as deceptive and inappropriate in the marketing of Christian religious groups as legitimate forms of Judaism."[48]

But all through President Bush's first term the organized Jewish community preferred to emphasize the positive. In 2003 the JCPA passed an unprecedented resolution in praise of Evangelical-Jewish relations. Noting that Evangelicals "are often among the few significant non-Jewish communities routinely expressing support for an embattled Israel," the resolution acknowledged that one source of that support was an end-times theology that "many Jews view to be problematic;" nevertheless, according to "some Evangelical leaders," shared democratic values, opposition to terrorism, and "belief that Jewish sovereignty over Israel fulfills a biblical covenant" were more significant factors. The JCPA pointed to the "aggressive and misleading tactics" of some churches to convert Jews as "among the most significant topics" to be addressed in Jewish-Evangelical dialogue.

The resolution declared that the JCPA:

> Believes that increased dialogue between our communities could help each better understand the other and help build recognition of the range of issues on which Jews and Evangelical Christians are already working cooperatively: treatment of religious minorities in other lands, religious accommodation in the workplace, religious freedom restoration legislation, and social services. Where appropriate this dialogue might also address issues where differences may remain between some segments of the Jewish community and Evangelical Christians, e.g., church-state separation, the role of religion in public life, women's and reproductive health issues, and perceptions of Islam in the modern world. In short, dialogue will possibly diminish some of the objections to Jewish-Evangelical ties and the sometimes ill-informed negative stereotypes that characterize many in each community.

Community relations professionals were called upon to "pursue expanded interaction with Evangelical Christians, seeking to learn and to teach, to confront and to cooperate where appropriate."[49]

Contrary to the hopes of Jewish conservatives, the administration's pro-Israel stance did not win much additional Jewish backing for President Bush in his 2004 reelection campaign; estimates of his share of the Jewish vote ranged from 22 to 24 percent, as compared to 19 percent four years earlier.[50] Jewish voters remained overwhelmingly liberal and Democratic, but that did not seem to faze conservative American Evangelicals, who remained committed to Israeli security. On September 28, 2005, Richard Land, president of the Southern Baptist Convention's Ethics and Religious Liberty Commission, told a gathering of Christians and Jews that Evangelical support for Israel "has never been more widespread than it is today." He cited a recent poll showing that white Evangelicals constituted the most pro-Israel religious group in America, with 54 percent of them favoring Israel and only 7 percent favoring the Palestinians.[51]

Little could Land have imagined that barely five weeks later one of the best known Jewish leaders in the country would risk imperiling that support. On November 3, at the annual meeting of the national commission of the ADL, national director Abraham Foxman—the same man who had enthusiastically urged cooperation with Evangelicals not long before—issued a strong warning about "an effort to Christianize America," and identified it as "the key domestic challenge to the American Jewish community and to our democratic values." Foxman did not mention the word "Evangelicals," but he did not have to. He charged that such organizations as Focus on the Family, Alliance Defense Fund, the American Family Association, and others had "built infrastructures throughout the country" aimed at "restoration of a Christian nation." Foxman continued, "There is an open arrogance. The arrogance comes when you believe you have the exclusive truth. And it comes if you believe God has commissioned you to change this country." Acknowledging that "the Jewish community is not the prime target of this movement" and that it was not a matter of anti-Semitism, Foxman nevertheless claimed that "the imposing of one belief, one truth, above all others" threatened church-state separation and held potentially ominous implications for the security of Jews. And he released selected data from a recent ADL poll indicating that those Americans who attended church once a week were far more likely than others to support organized school prayer, the teaching of creationism, and display of the Ten Commandments in public buildings, and to believe that the courts had gone "too far" in separating church and state.[52]

Soon after, on November 19, another major mainstream Jewish leader, Rabbi Eric Yoffie, expressed similar sentiments at the 68th biennial general assembly of the Union for Reform Judaism (URJ), of which he was president. This organization, known until 2003 as the Union of American Hebrew Congregations, represents the synagogues of the Reform movement in Judaism, the largest branch of the religion in America. Though Yoffie's language was milder than Foxman's (perhaps because his presentation was in the form of a Shabbat sermon), his target was broader, encompassing not just matters of church and state but much of the Bush administration's policy agenda as well.

Like Foxman, Yoffie refrained from specifically mentioning the word "Evangelical." Castigating what he called "the Religious Right," Yoffie took offense at the notion that "unless you attend my church, accept my God and study my sacred text, you cannot be a moral person." He insisted that political liberalism could be, and was, in the case of Reform Judaism, an expression of sincere religious commitment, and that "family values" included health care for uninsured children, stem cell research to cure disease, the right "to prayerfully make decisions" about when to die, and legal protection for gay couples. And Yoffie urged conservative Christians to consult "our liberal Christian friends" as to how the teachings of Jesus might be used to promote a left-of-center social agenda. Noting his agreement with the Christian Right about the evil effects of the "coarsening of popular culture" and the need to battle religious persecution and sex trafficking around the world, Yoffie pledged to work together on these issues, but only on the understanding that "tolerance is an American value and a religious necessity" and that "religion is far too important to be entangled with government."[53]

Jewish leaders had, over the years, harshly criticized statements and policies they deemed offensive or dangerous emanating from Evangelical circles, but never before had they issued such broad, public denunciations. The precise motivations of Foxman and Yoffie are unknown, but several factors may have come into play.

The American Jewish community has been shrinking for some time, and organizations find themselves competing ever more aggressively for members and philanthropic dollars. Advised by advertising consultants to "brand" themselves so as to stand out from the crowd, Jewish groups are increasingly tempted to hunt headlines with belligerent rhetoric. In this particular case, a number of new issues had come up in the months just prior to the November speeches that set liberal Jewish teeth on edge: the Terry Schiavo case, in which the administration, at the behest of the Religious Right, sought to prevent the husband of a comatose woman from having her removed from life support; conflicts over the placement of the Ten Commandments on public property; the prospect that the appointment of new Supreme Court justices would lead to restrictions on abortion rights; the teaching of "intelligent design" in public schools as an alternative to evolution; and charges that Evangelical chaplains at the Air Force Academy were pressuring students to convert. By expressing outrage, Foxman and Yoffie were responding to the anxieties of countless Jews, both members of their organizations and others, and perhaps seeking to advertise their agencies to the community as prime defenders of the Jewish people.[54]

Before doing so, they must have given some consideration to the negative impact their words could have on Evangelical support for Israel. Yoffie and Foxman presumably decided that such support was unconditional and could not be endangered by criticism, a judgment that so far has been borne out. Whether Evangelicals will continue their pro-Israel activities over the long term if Jews continue to attack them remains uncertain.

There also might have been a political dimension to the November outbursts: they were, perhaps, the opening guns of the 2006 congressional campaign. Liberal Jews, never happy about having to bite their tongues over domestic policy in order to ingratiate themselves with the Bush administration for Israel's sake, already saw Bush in November 2005 as an unpopular lame duck. His policies—the Iraq war, the broader "war on terror," domestic spying, the response to Hurricane Katrina, and more—were costing Bush in the public opinion polls, although not yet with his Evangelical base. Perhaps hoping to stay ahead of the curve, the leaders of the ADL and the URJ sought to thrust themselves into the front lines of the political battle to elect a Democratic Congress and, in 2008, a Democratic president. By entering this fray, they were expressing the wishes of the great majority of American Jews.[55]

The political liberalism of American Jews, especially their aversion to the entry of religion or religious rhetoric into the public square, makes it unlikely that the organized Jewish community will ever feel entirely comfortable with the Evangelicals, who are their closest allies in defense of Israel.[56] Yet there are two demographic shifts taking place among American Jews—one geographic, the other religious—that might gradually narrow the distance between the two groups.

The Northeastern part of the United States is still the home of the lion's share of American Jewry, 43.6 percent, but that marks a decline from about 70 percent in 1900. Largely as a result of migration to the Sun Belt, the percentage of Jews living in the West has risen to 24.1 percent and in the South to 21.6 percent. If the trend continues, an increasing number of American Jews will be living in close proximity to Evangelicals. Many will find their stereotypes challenged, and the greater understanding of, and appreciation for Evangelicals could eventually percolate up to the decision makers of the national Jewish organizations, who, indeed, have already found that their Sun Belt constituents are not, as a rule, enthusiastic about picking fights with Evangelicals.[57]

Within American Judaism, the resurgence of religious orthodoxy has taken observers by surprise. While the Orthodox are still a minority, their relatively large families, minimal propensity to leave Judaism, and high levels of Jewish activity make it likely that the American Jewish community of tomorrow will have to reckon with them as never before.[58] Orthodox Jews never entirely bought into the political liberalism of the rest of the Jewish community, their traditional religious values actually placing them much closer to conservative Evangelicals on such issues as government aid to private schools, abortion, gay rights, and the negative effects of popular culture. Over the last several decades rising self-confidence has emboldened Orthodox organizations to diverge, sometimes vocally, from the Jewish communal consensus on these matters.[59] The signature of Rabbi Tzvi Hersh Weinreb, executive vice president of the Union of Orthodox Jewish Congregations, along with those of some fifty prominent Evangelical and Catholic leaders on "A Letter from America's Religious Leaders in Defense of Marriage," in support of a constitutional amendment defining marriage as "a union of male and female," may be more than just a straw in the wind.[60]

Stronger Orthodox influence on the broader Jewish community, like that of Jewish migrants to the Sun Belt, may mitigate strains between Jews and Evangelicals. But whether or not these forces bring a change in the posture of the Jewish community, the stake that both Evangelicals and Jews have in the direction of American public policy and in the survival of the State of Israel are sure to keep the two communities engaged with each other no matter what other forces work to pull them apart.

Evidence for optimism came on April 26, 2006, when Rabbi Eric Yoffie, the URJ president who spoke so harshly the previous November about the danger posed by the Religious Right, addressed some 9,000 students at Liberty University in Lynchburg, Virginia, upon the invitation of its founder, Rev. Jerry Falwell. Yoffie suggested that religious liberals like himself—and the great majority of Jews—should cooperate with conservative Evangelicals on support for Israel, a commitment to democracy, and concern about the cheapening of sexuality and the materialism of American culture, while at the same time disagreeing civilly on issues that divided them. Yoffie told his audience that he could "believe what I believe without calling you a homophobic bigot," and they "can do the same without calling me an uncaring baby-killer." Yoffie and Falwell spoke privately afterward, and Falwell, in subsequent remarks to reporters, declared, somewhat elliptically, "We can disagree about everything and still find common ground somewhere."[61]

NOTES

1. Lawrence Grossman, "Jews—Middle Atlantic and Beyond," in Randall Balmer and Mark Silk, eds., *Religion and Public Life in the Middle Atlantic*

Region: The Fount of Diversity (Lanham, MD: AltaMira Press, 2006), 95–98; James Hudnut-Beumler, "Protestant in the Middle Atlantic Region," ibid., 48.

2. Yaakov Ariel, "American Judaism and Interfaith Dialogue," in Dana Evan Kaplan, ed., *The Cambridge Companion to American Judaism* (New York: Cambridge University Press, 2005), 327–44. On conversion efforts see Ariel, *Evangelizing the Chosen People: Missions to the Jews in America, 1880–2000* (Chapel Hill, NC: University of North Carolina Press, 2000).

3. Yona Malachy, *American Fundamentalism and Israel: The Relation of Fundamentalist Churches to Zionism and the State of Israel* (Jerusalem: Hebrew University Institute of Contemporary Jewry, 1978).

4. Gregg Ivers, *To Build a Wall: American Jews and the Separation of Church and State* (Charlottesville: University Press of Virginia, 1995), 155, 161; Stuart Svonkin, *Jews Against Prejudice: American Jews and the Fight for Civil Liberties* (New York: Columbia University Press, 1997), 8, 17, 44, 63, 149.

5. *Joint Program Plan 1962–63*, 9–10; *Joint Program Plan 1963–64*, 15; *Joint Program Plan 1964–65*, 4–5; *Joint Program Plan 1965–66*, 21. Founded in 1944, NCRAC was renamed the National Jewish Community Advisory Council (NJCRAC) in 1969, and the Jewish Council for Public Affairs (JCPA) in 1999. It is an umbrella body encompassing the major national Jewish organizations and local Jewish community relations councils. Its *Program Plan* (renamed *Agenda* in 1999) reflects the consensus of these member agencies.

6. Jerome Bakst, "The Radical Right's $1,000,000 Preacher," *ADL Bulletin* (May 1962), 4–5 (on Rev. Billy James Hargis).

7. Charles Y. Glock and Rodney Stark, *Christian Beliefs and Anti-Semitism* (New York: Harper and Row, 1966).

8. *Joint Program Plan 1967–68*, 27, 7. For a summary of representative Christian statements at the time see Lucy S. Dawidowicz, "American Public Opinion," *American Jewish Year Book 1968* (New York: American Jewish Committee and Jewish Publication Society of America, 1968), 218–24.

9. *Joint Program Plan, 1967–68*, 6; *Joint Program Plan 1970–71*, 20.

10. Arthur Gilbert, ". . .Of the Jewish People We Ask Forgiveness," *ADL Bulletin* (Dec. 1966): 3; Gilbert, "Conversation with Billy Graham," *ADL Bulletin* (Dec. 1967), 1–2, 8.

11. *ADL Bulletin* (Feb. 1969), 7, (Feb. 1971), 6.

12. Program for "Jewish Baptist Scholars' Conference, August 18–20, 1969"; American Jewish Committee press releases, August 21, 24, 1969, all located in vertical file Christ-JRel, US/Baptists, Blaustein Library, American Jewish Committee.

13. American Jewish Committee press release, June 15, 1971.

14. ADL press release, Sept. 1, 1972.

15. "News: Jews and Evangelicals: Mutual Concerns," *Christianity Today* (Jan. 2, 1976). The proceedings were published as a book: Marc H. Tanenbaum, Marvin R. Wilson, and A. James Rudin, *Evangelicals and Jews in Conversation: On Scripture, Theology, and History* (Grand Rapids, MI: Baker Book House, 1978).

16. One ad, appearing in the *New York Times* and *Washington Post* on November 1, 1977, asserting that "most Evangelicals understand the Jewish

homeland generally to include the territory west of the Jordan River," drew the ire of James T. Wall, the liberal Protestant editor of the *Christian Century.* See Wall, "Israel and the Evangelicals," *Christian Century* (Nov. 23, 1977), 1083.

17. *American Jewish Year Book 1979* (New York: American Jewish Committee and Jewish Publication Society of America, 1979), 115. Graham, consistently pro-Israel and opposed to targeting Jews for conversion, was viewed by the Jewish community as a sincere friend, a reputation tarnished in February 2002 with the release of a 1972 tape on which he said derogatory things about Jews to President Nixon. The 83-year-old Graham apologized, declaring that he had no recollection of the Oval Office conversation. David Firestone, "Billy Graham Responds to Lingering Anger Over 1972 Remarks on Jews," *New York Times* (Mar. 17, 2002), sec. 1, 29.

18. Marvin R. Wilson, "Current Evangelical-Jewish Relations: An Evangelical View," in Marc H. Tanenbaum, Marvin R. Wilson, and A. James Rudin, *Evangelicals and Jews in an Age of Pluralism* (Grand Rapids, MI: Baker Book House, 1984), 14–16. This volume contains most of the presentations given at the Deerfield conference.

19. *American Jewish Year Book 1974–75* (New York: American Jewish Committee and Jewish Publication Society of America, 1974), 124–27; *Joint Program Plan 1973–74*, 42–44.

20. *American Jewish Year Book 1982* (New York: American Jewish Committee and Jewish Publication Society of America, 1982), 103.

21. "The Baptists and the Jews: Planning Ahead," *ADL Bulletin* (Feb. 1981), 3–4; Kenneth L. Woodward, "The Evangels and the Jews," *Newsweek*, Nov. 10, 1980, 76.

22. Donald Wagner, "Evangelicals and Israel: Theological Roots of a Political Alliance," *The Christian Century* (Nov. 4, 1998), 1020–1026, www .religion-online.org/showarticle.asp?title=216.

23. "Where We Stand: The Evangelical Right," *Congress Monthly* (Jan. 1982), 8.

24. *Joint Program Plan 1982–83*, pp. 50–54, *1983–84*, pp. 59–64, *1984–85*, pp. 31–35, *1985–86*, pp. 7–15, *1986–87*, pp. 38–40, *1987–88*, pp. 39–42.

25. Richard Bernstein, "Evangelicals Strengthening Bonds With Jews," *New York Times* (Feb. 6, 1983), A1.

26. "Evangelicals," *ADL Bulletin* (Sept. 1985): 9–10; "Religiously Conservative Christians: How Do They View Jews?" *ADL Bulletin* (Feb. 1987), 1, 13–14.

27. *Joint Program Plan 1988–89*, 54–55.

28. Peter Steinfels, "Evangelical Group Urges Conversion of Jews," *New York Times* (May 21, 1989), 37; Darrel Turner, "Evangelical Statement Stresses Importance of Witness to Jews," Religious News Service (May 9, 1989), 8–9.

29. Ibid.

30. *Joint Program Plan 1990–91*, 45; *1991–92*, 69; *1993–94*, 64; *1994–95*, 62–63.

31. *The Religious Right: The Assault on Tolerance and Pluralism in America* (New York: Anti-Defamation League, 1994). The book was compiled by David Cantor, an ADL researcher, with a foreword by ADL national director Abraham Foxman.

32. A sample of reactions is provided in "ADL Report Draws Both Praise and Blame," *ADL on the Frontline* (Sept. 1994), 6. See also the sharp critique by Midge Decter, a politically conservative Jewish writer, "The ADL vs. the Religious Right," *Commentary* (Sept. 1994), 45–47.

33. "The Beginning of the Beginning . . . Jewish, Christian Leaders Meet," *ADL on the Frontline* (Jan. 1995), 3, 7. The meeting was arranged by Rabbi Yehiel Eckstein, a former ADL staffer who had left the organization to found a new group, the International Fellowship of Christians and Jews, devoted to enhancing Jewish-Evangelical relations. See Zev Chafets, "The Rabbi Who Loved Evangelicals," *New York Times Magazine* (July 24, 2005), 22–27.

34. *ADL on the Front Line* (May/June 1995), 7; "Coalition Tries to Mend Jewish Relations," *Christian Century* (Apr. 26, 1995), findarticles.com/p/articles/mi_m1058/is_n14_v112/ai_16883520; "Focus on the Religious Right," *AJC Journal* (Aug. 1995), 5.

35. Gustav Niebuhr, "Baptists Move on Two Fronts in New Effort to Convert Jews," *New York Times* (June 14, 1996), A12; R. Albert Mohler, Jr., "Against the Stream: The Southern Baptist Resolutions," www.sbts.edu/fmohler.html.

36. "ADL: Southern Baptist Effort to Convert Jews Is an Insult to the Jewish People," press release (June 14, 1996), www.adl.org/PresRele/ChJew_31/2761_31.asp; Art Toalston, "Evangelism: Jews Oppose Baptist Outreach," *Christianity Today* (Nov. 11, 1996), www.ctlibrary.com/ct/1996/november11/6td03a.html; *JCPA Agenda 1997–98*, 37.

37. These included Catholics and Mainline Protestants, as well as the Alliance of Baptists, a small group of liberals that had broken away from the Southern Baptists some years earlier. Billy Graham commented that he had never targeted Jews for conversion. See Eric J. Greenberg, "Rev. Graham's Rebuttal," *Jewish Week* (New York: June 28, 1996), 14.

38. Debra Nussbaum Cohen JTA story, also NYJW; "'You Listen but You Don't Hear,' ADL Leader Tells Southern Baptists in Exchange on Resolution to Convert Jews," ADL press release (Nov. 21, 1996), www.adl.org/PresRele/ChJew_31/2856_31.asp.

39. "Rabbi Yoffie to Baptists, You Want It Both Ways," *National Jewish Post and Opinion* (Jan. 15, 1997), 3; "Baptists, Jews Fight Angry War of Words," *Forward* (Apr. 11, 1997), 11.

40. Elliott Abrams, "'Jews for Jesus' and the Evangelical Embrace," *Forward* (Oct. 24, 1997), 7.

41. Seth Mnookin, "Southern Baptists Pushing Proselytizing," *Forward* (Sept. 24, 1999), 15; Keith Hinson, "To the Jew First?" *Christianity Today* (Nov. 15, 1999), www.ctlibrary.com/ct/1999/november15/9td018.html.

42. "ADL Outraged by Southern Baptist Statements Rooting Jewish Conversion Appeals in Theology," ADL press release (Sept. 28, 1999), www.adl.org/presrel/ChJew_31/3472_31.asp; Gustav Niebuhr, "Baptists' Evangelism Concerns Jews," *New York Times* (Sept. 25, 1999), 9; Gustav Niebuhr, "Baptists' Ardor of Evangelism Angers Some Jews and Hindus," *New York Times*, (Dec. 4, 1999), 10. Rev. Billy Graham once again took the Jewish side, saying "I normally defend my denomination. I'm loyal to it. But I have never targeted

Muslims. I have never targeted Jews." Eric J. Greenberg, "Billy Graham Blasts Brethren," *Jewish Week* (New York: Jan. 7, 2000), 3.

43. *JCPA Agenda, 2000–01*, 60–61; "ADL: Rev. Falwell's Statement that the Antichrist is a Jew Borders on Anti-Semitism and is Rooted in Christian Theological Extremism," ADL press release (Jan. 19, 1999), www.adl.org. PresRele/asus_12/3311_12.asp.

44. See, for example, Debra Nussbaum Cohen, "Evangelical Christians Dig Deep, Raise Vast Sums for Jewish Causes," *Jewish Telegraphic Agency Daily News Bulletin* (Sept. 17, 1997), 1–2. To be sure, some American Jewish leaders were skeptical about Israeli policies, considering them too hard line. But the organized Jewish community overwhelmingly deferred to the lead of the Israeli government, and thus found themselves on the same side as the Evangelicals.

45. Tony Carnes, "Kosher Cooperation: Jewish Elites Broker New Relations with Evangelicals," *Christianity Today* (Oct. 2002), 19–20.

46. Abraham Foxman, "Why Evangelical Support for Israel is a Good Thing," *Jewish Telegraphic Agency Daily News Bulletin*, July 16, 2002; Foxman, "Though They Liked 'The Passion,' Christian Evangelicals are our friends," *Jewish Telegraphic Agency Daily News Bulletin*, Mar. 8, 2004.

47. Rod Dreher, "Evangelicals and Jews Together," *National Review Online*, Apr. 5, 2002, www.nationalreview.com/scrpt/printpage.p?ref=/dreher/dreher040502.asp; Craig Horowitz, "Israel's Christian Soldiers," *New York Magazine* (Sept. 29, 2003), newyorkmetro.com/nymetro/news/religion/features/n_9255; Rachel Pomerance, "Evangelicals Rally to Israel's Side as Protestants Consider Divestment," *Jewish Telegraphic Agency Daily News Bulletin* (June 29, 2005).

48. Ami Eden, "Baptist Calls Catholic Antisemitic; ADL Backs Bishops," *Forward* (Aug. 30, 2002), www.forward.com/issues/2002/02.08.30/news8.html; "ADL Condemns Southern Baptist Leader's Comparison of Judaism to a 'Deadly Tumor,'" ADL press release (June 19, 2003), adl.org/PresRele/ChJew_31/4272_31.htm; Bob Allen, "SBC Executive Committee Suggests Study of Mission to Jews," (Sept. 21, 2005), ethicsdaily.com/article_detail.cfm?AID=6322; JCPA Resolution on Misleading and Aggressive Proselytizing, adopted by JCPA Board (June 10, 2002).

49. JCPA Resolution on Evangelical-Jewish Relations adopted by the 2003 JCPA Plenum (Feb 24, 2003). Some of the discussion leading up to passage is available in "2003 JCPA Highlights," 12–14.

50. *American Jewish Year Book 2005*, 128.

51. Tom Strode, "Land: Evangelical Support for Israel Stronger Than Ever," www.bpnews.net/printerfriendly.asp?ID=21774.

52. "Religion in America's Public Square: Are We Crossing the Line," excerpts from an address by Abraham H. Foxman, Nov. 3, 2005, adl.org/Religious_Freedom/religion_public_square.asp. Foxman also called for a meeting of Jewish leaders to discuss strategy. Such a meeting was held at ADL headquarters, but, with the exception of Eric Yoffie, the representatives of other Jewish organizations who came evinced little enthusiasm for mounting a campaign against the Christian Right.

53. "Sermon by Rabbi Eric Yoffie at the Houston Biennial," Nov. 19, 2005, urj.org/yoffie/biennialsermon05. At Yoffie's behest, the gathering passed a resolution condemning the war in Iraq, which it subsequently sent to the president and members of Congress. Among other things, it blamed the war for "the growth of terrorism," called for a "clear exit strategy," and said that "we want our leaders to tell us the truth."

54. In late November, at the same time that the Foxman and Yoffie speeches were causing a stir, advance copies circulated of Rabbi James Rudin's *The Baptizing of America: The Religious Right's Plans for the Rest of Us* (New York: Avalon, 2006). Rudin, the retired former director of interreligious affairs for the American Jewish Committee, offered a book-length version of the same grim scenario: "It is the specter of our nation ruled by the extreme Christian Right, who would make the United States a 'Christian nation' where their version of God's law supersedes all human law—including the Constitution" (p. 1). Rudin noted that the views expressed in his book did not necessarily reflect those of the AJC.

55. One example of the wide political gap between Evangelicals and Jews: fully 70 percent of American Jews opposed the war in Iraq in November 2005, while 68 percent of white Evangelicals supported it. *2005 Annual Survey of American Jewish Opinion* (American Jewish Committee), www.ajc.org/site/apps/nl/content3.asp?c=ijITI2PHKoG&b=846741&ct=1740355; Charles Marsh, "Wayward Christian Soldiers," *New York Times* (Jan. 20, 2006), A17.

56. Significantly, Sen. Joseph Lieberman, the Orthodox Jew who ran for vice president on the Democratic ticket in 2000, was praised by Evangelicals for speaking openly about his religious commitment during the campaign; Abraham Foxman of the ADL, though, berated him for it.

57. Ira M. Sheskin and Arnold Dashefsky, "Jewish Population in the United States, 2006," *American Jewish Year Book 2006* (New York: American Jewish Committee and Jewish Publication Society of America, 2006), 160; Grossman, "Jews—Middle Atlantic and Beyond," 122.

58. Lawrence Grossman, "Jewish Religious Denominations," in Kaplan, ed., *Cambridge Companion to American Judaism*, 95–96.

59. Lawrence Grossman, "Mainstream Orthodox and the American Public Square," in Alan Mittleman, Jonathan Sarna, and Robert Licht, eds., *Jewish Polity and American Civil Society* (Lanham, MD: Rowman and Littlefield, 2002), 283–310. In the 2004 presidential election about three-quarters of American Jews voted against President Bush while almost the same percentage of Orthodox Jews voted for him.

60. David D. Kirkpatrick, "A Religious Push Against Gay Unions," *New York Times* (Apr. 24, 2006), A12; "A Letter from America's Religious Leaders in Defense of Marriage," www.religiouscoalitionformarriage.org. On the issue of stem-cell research, however, the Union, citing religious teachings, has lined up with the predominantly liberal Jewish organizations in favoring the research.

61. Jennifer Siegel, "Rabbi Enters Falwell's Bastion and Issues Plea for Tolerance," *Forward* (Apr. 28, 2006), 1, 5.

5

"Luckier Than Moses"

The Future of Jewish-Evangelical Alliance

George W. Mamo

Rabbi Yechiel Eckstein, founder and president of the International Fellowship of Christians and Jews, tells a story of one of his first trips to Israel that encapsulates the Evangelical fervor for Israel and the Jewish people. Some thirty years ago Rabbi Eckstein was asked to lead a Christian tour to the Holy Land. As a recent graduate from Yeshiva University, he told me that he really didn't know what to expect. But believing that any opportunity to go back to Israel is a good thing, he accepted the assignment. When he arrived in Jerusalem and he met his roommate, he started to question his initial enthusiasm. The Orthodox rabbi from New York, then in his twenties, had been paired with an eighty-five-year old black Baptist pastor from Virginia. During the first day of the tour, the pastor shared that coming to Israel—the "Land of the Bible"—had been a lifelong dream; he had been saving a little toward the trip each month for ten years and his sons had given him a gift so that he could make this trip. Rabbi Eckstein wondered, "Why Israel? Wouldn't a Christian want to go to Rome?"

Rabbi Eckstein found himself asking the same question many American Jews ask today when they encounter Evangelical Christians—"What could we possibly have in common?" The rabbi did not have to wait long for an answer. That first night in Israel, the pastor told the group he was going to bed early and headed for his room; some time later Rabbi Eckstein went upstairs. He entered the room quietly, expecting to find his roommate asleep; he was instead kneeling beside the bed with his arms lifted toward Heaven praying. And this was his tearful prayer:

"Thank You Lord, I'm luckier than Moses! You only let Moses see the Promised Land.[1] You've let me walk in it. Thank You Lord." In that overheard prayer, Rabbi Eckstein found the answer to his question. "What could an Orthodox rabbi and a black Baptist pastor have in common?" Israel—their common love for Israel. For the New Testament tells us that Christians have been grafted into the olive tree that is Israel and that we are nourished and supported by the root of that vine, the Jewish root of Christianity.[2]

Today, many American Jews are coming to realize, just as Rabbi Eckstein came to appreciate, that some of Israel's best friends are Christians.

I have been involved in Jewish-Christian relations and Christian-Israeli relations vocationally for only six years. But in that time I have had the opportunity to speak with thousands of Jews and Evangelicals about the deep well of Evangelical support for Israel and the Jewish people. Despite my lack of academic credentials or decades of experience in this field, I hope that some of what I have learned will add to this dialogue.

For a Christian, recognizing this shared "root" means recognizing that without the Jewish people, we wouldn't have most of our Bible, and there would never have been a rabbi named Jesus. Increasingly, we also recognize that Jesus was born, lived and died a Jew. Accepting and wanting to better understand the Jewish roots of our own faith and the Jewishness of our Savior is part of what motivates Christians, and particularly Evangelical Christians, to be the largest component of Israel's tourism economy. Each year, nearly half a million[3] Christians step away from their families and day-to-day responsibilities to make a pilgrimage[4] to Israel to walk where our God, the God of Abraham, Isaac and Jacob, revealed Himself to all humankind. But the pilgrims I have led did not just go as tourists; they also went to serve their elder brothers and sisters in the faith. Groups that I have taken to Israel also see and work in projects and programs that Evangelicals have supported. We visited projects like Migdahl Ohr, the orphanage founded by Orthodox Rabbi Yacob Grossman; we served lunch to the poor of Jerusalem in Chabad-run soup kitchens, and visited secular day care centers in Beit She'an.

As an aside, Evangelical supporters of Israel are demographically different from the "typical" Federation donor. For example, the group that I led to Israel in December 2005 was more typical of our supporters than any of the three other groups I've led. There was not a single major or "mega" donor in the group. These were people who give sacrificially; folks who give out of their need, rather than their surplus.

These are people who support Israel because they—like me—believe God has told Christians to support Israel and the Jewish people. This is a group that will cite not only the familiar Genesis 12 promise to Abraham[5] that we will be blessed as we bless Abraham's children, but are just as likely to quote the words of the Apostle Paul who tells us in Romans 15:27 that we (believers in Jesus) "owe it to the Jews to share with them their material blessings."[6]

Evangelicalism is a recent phenomenon. Most people trace modern Evangelicalism to just after World War I when it was seen as a backlash to fundamentalism. Evangelicalism grew in prominence with the advent of Billy Graham and his citywide revivals and the establishment of such publications as *Christianity Today*. But it was only when Jerry Falwell founded the Moral Majority and Pat Robertson and Ralph Reed launched the Christian Coalition that "Evangelical" began to register with the media. Even with the flexing of newfound political muscle, for much of the twentieth century, most people—including most American Christians—equated the term "Evangelical" with faith healers, holy rollers, and counterfeit preachers. "Born-again" Christianity was seen as a thing of high emotion, white suits, big hair, and too much makeup.

Then in the 1970s, prominent figures by the scores—in politics, sports and entertainment—freely spoke about "being born again"[7] and their faith in Jesus. And in the United States' bicentennial year we elected our first "born-again" Christian as the Republic's thirty-seventh president. Since Jimmy Carter, we have elected two more Evangelicals to the presidency. The first, Bill Clinton, was a liberal democrat like Carter; but the next one, our current president—George W. Bush—few would call liberal.

These three presidents show rather vividly that Evangelicals—who, according to the results of one survey represented 26.3 percent of voters in the 2004 elections[8]—take no single approach to American politics (or American problems). Make no mistake; the majority of Evangelicals are Republican[9] and it is largely this political "clout" that explains why Washington's policies toward Israel and the Middle East are so different from those of European countries.

In the words of the cochair of the Fellowship's Stand for Israel program, Gary Bauer, Evangelical voters tend to:

> see our foreign policy in moral terms, and they see Israel as the good guy, a democracy, a nation much like ours. And they see Israel's opponents as a collection of thugs, dictators and self-appointed kings.[10]

So who are the Evangelicals? Just as there is no definition that can encompass Chabad, Orthodox, Conservative, Reform, and Reconstructionist Judaism, there is no easy way to define and talk about "Evangelicals." And just as there is no single leader or spokesman for Judaism, there is no Pope or single voice that speaks for the tens of millions of Americans who call themselves "Evangelicals." Insofar as there is no inclusive definition that accompanies all Evangelicals, Evangelicals resemble Jews.

Within Evangelicalism there are a number of distinct subgroups including fundamentalists and Pentecostals, who have experienced the "baptism of the Holy Spirit"[11] and practice such divine "gifts" as speaking in tongues and miraculous healing by prayer. The rest are mainly conventional Protestants who hold to the authority of the Bible and to orthodox Christian doctrines.

All Evangelicals—regardless of what else they may disagree on—believe that one must make a conscious commitment to Christ. It is this spiritual encounter, whether gradual or instantaneous, that is known as being "born-again."

Most estimates say that roughly one in four Americans identify themselves as "born-again." If these estimates are correct, then 70 million Americans are "born-again" (Evangelical) Christians. Just for comparison—according to sociologists, there are about 5.5 million Jews in America, nearly half of whom select "other" when asked for their religious preference.[12]

Craig Horowitz, writing in the *New York Magazine*, called Christian support for Israel a "bizarre mixed marriage."[13] If we can stick with this metaphor for a while, then the Evangelical-Jewish (mixed) marriage was formalized (dare we say consummated?) in 1980 when Prime Minister Menachem Begin presented the "Jabotinsky Centennial Medal" to Jerry Falwell for his work on behalf of Israel.

In the quarter century that followed, the relationship between American Jews and Evangelicals was, at best, lukewarm. Evangelical overtures to the Jewish community were generally met with skepticism. Many Jews believed—and many still believe (especially given the recent comments of two of organized Jewry's most influential spokesmen)—that Christian support for Israel is part of a bigger scheme to convert Jews to Christianity or to persuade them to move to Israel as part of some devious plan to hasten the end of the world as laid out in the Christian Bible. But, a few—and at first it was very few—saw there was a big difference in believing that something should or would happen and believing there was anything you could do to make it happen.

One of the first to recognize this important distinction and to appreciate the Evangelical thirst to understand the Jewish roots of Christianity was Rabbi Yechiel Eckstein. Today he is being joined by organizations as diverse as AIPAC[14] and the JCPA. I had the privilege of presenting the Evangelical point of view during the JCPA's historic 2003 meeting when the delegates approved a resolution urging local JCRCs (Jewish Community Relations Councils) to seek out Evangelical support and cooperation. AIPAC and the JCRCs are joining the longstanding outreach efforts of the Embassy of Israel and individuals like Rabbi Eugene Korn. Despite all of this, there is still a lot of suspicion about Evangelical Christians in the Jewish community. Some of the suspicion, unfortunately, is well founded.

Christians are compelled to share our faith.[15] But, we are also taught and know that we cannot cause a change of heart or conversion; that work is entirely in God's hands. Our responsibility is simply to share our faith. This has not always been so. The pages of Church history are filled with the record of inquisitions, pogroms, Holy Week attacks and forced and coerced "conversions." These pages, which are unknown to many Christians, are often the only pages of church history that Jews do know. For this I apologize. But, some of the suspicion (maybe most of it) is also rooted in ignorance—ignorance about Christianity in general and ignorance about Evangelical Christianity in particular.

Just as many of our donors tell us they have "never met a Jew," many American Jews have only "met" Evangelicals through TV or movies—where the portrayal is none too flattering. Despite Hollywood's caricature:

We're not all Elmer Gantry holy rollers.
We're not all Southerners.
We don't all drive pickup trucks.
We're not all poorly educated rednecks.
And most of us have never owned a white suit.

Yet these are the pictures that form in most people's minds when they're asked to describe a "typical Evangelical." Now, while Hollywood has done us no favors, we're responsible for some of the caricaturing ourselves—"Christian" TV has not exactly presented our "best and brightest."

I can remember a time when my son, Chip, was about five. We had gone out somewhere and left the TV on. When we came home, he like most kids ran immediately to the "tube." And he just froze. After a while, he turned to me and asked "Daddy, what's wrong with that man?" I had a hard time explaining "tongues" (glossolalia) to my five-year-old son.

For the last several years when I have addressed the question of "why do Evangelical Christians support Israel," I have routinely pointed to the sea change in Jewish acceptance of that support. Where I used to talk about how appreciative Israelis were to receive Christian support; in recent years, I've routinely pointed to Abe Foxman's changed attitude as exemplary of American Jews' changed attitude toward Christians. However, the recent comments by Abe Foxman and Rabbi Eric Yoffie berating the "religious right" have the potential to set back relations between our communities by decades.

By way of background, let me tell you how far we *had* come. In November 2000 when the UJC (United Jewish Communities) held its General Assembly (GA) in Chicago, they presented an award to Rabbi Eckstein for his groundbreaking work in building non-Jewish support for Israel through the International Fellowship of Christians and Jews. For years afterwards, it seemed every time Mr. Foxman was interviewed he made a point of saying how he had walked out of the GA and how he could not believe the UJC was honoring a man who was *schnorring* from non-Jews to help Jews by asking Christians to help meet the basic survival needs of Jews in the former Soviet Union and Israel. Foxman also told the *Forward* that regardless of how much money it raised [from Christians], he found Eckstein's portrayal of Israeli poverty "distasteful."[16]

But this all changed a few years ago when Mr. Foxman said, in an article published by the Jewish Telegraphic Agency:

> American Jews [should be] highly appreciative of the incredible support that the State of Israel gets from a significant group of Americans—the Evangelical Christian Right. In many ways, the Christian Right stands out as the most consistently supportive group of Israel in America.[17]

After using Mr. Foxman as exemplar of the change in the attitude of the organized American Jewish community, I would mention *Hadassah Magazine*'s lead story—"Jews and Christians: Some of our best friends . . ."[18] or Craig Horowitz' "Israel's Christian Soldiers" for *New York Magazine*[19] as proof that Evangelicals were finally being seen as real, rather than convenient, allies in the fight for a strong and secure Israel.

But in the last weeks of 2005, it all swung the other way. In a speech delivered at an ADL meeting, Foxman identified the Christian Right as the principal threat to Jewish life in America, claiming it is attempting to "Christianize America" by discarding "the constitutional balance that protects our public square."[20] Later the same month, Rabbi Yoffie likened Evangelical opposition to gay marriage to Nazi oppression.[21]

Criticism has also come from *Vanity Fair*, which published "American Rapture—Evangelical Christians and the Big Business of Being Born Again."[22] *Salon*[23] has declared that "Evangelicals support Israel for their own eschatological reasons," that "there have been threats, implicit and explicit, that such support might weaken if Jews oppose their domestic agenda too aggressively," and that "sensitivity has vanished from today's religious right." *Mother Jones* has weighed in, describing Evangelical activists as "out-of-reach zealots . . ."[24]

Shmuel Rosen, Chief U.S. Correspondent for *Ha'aretz*, has voiced the re-emerging suspicion well:

> Supporters of Israel face a complex problem: Do they continue to uphold their wonderful friendship with their devoted supporters, or should they first assess the long-term significance of this support whether it does indeed pose a threat to the stability and security of America's Jewish community—and work this assessment into the overall picture that determines the depth of these ties?[25]

In the waning months of 2005, the motives of Evangelicals are not only again being questioned, Evangelicals are being attacked. Why? I think it is because we are falling back into old stereotypes, and well-painted stereotypes can play on latent fears and (importantly) raise lots of money. Let's look at the players in this.

American Jews are mainly urban, educated, liberal Democrats, nearly half of whom identify as secular.[26] Jews in America tend to be uncomfortable with "God talk"—even when it is other Jews doing the talking. Christians who support Israel tend to be politically conservative, and unabashed in expressing their love for Jesus and their devotion to the Gospel. On nearly every key domestic issue—whether it is abortion, gay rights, school prayer or school vouchers—pro-Israel Christians and most Jews hold opposite positions. Only the Orthodox, as Rabbi Dr. Shlomo Riskin of Ohr Torah Stone told me when I addressed his students on Memorial Day, vote similarly to Evangelical Christians. Politically, most Jews and most Evangelicals disagree about nearly everything. Yet on Israel, some Christians and Jews have nearly 100 percent agreement. But pro-Israel Christians are not the Mainline Christians that organized Judaism has traditionally partnered with on social issues. Generally speaking, pro-Israel Christians are not Catholics, they are not Episcopalians, they are not Lutherans, they are not the United Church of Christ, and they are not Presbyterians. The

Christian supporters of Israel tend to belong to Baptist, Pentecostal or Charismatic churches. And this is a large part of the dilemma that organized Jewry is faced with today—their traditional allies have largely abandoned or openly attacked Israel, while the Evangelical community has embraced the Jewish State as never before.

Hillel Halkin writing in the November 10, 2005 issue of the *Jerusalem Post* put it this way:

> The Christian Right is today Israel's main bastion of political support in the United States at a time when the liberal Left has turned increasingly against it. One can certainly understand that this is a source of embarrassment and bewilderment for American Jews, who find themselves deserted by old friends and embraced by perceived aliens.[27]

If the organized Jewish community is really interested in the group that supports Israel, it has to shift its focus from the Mainline Churches that have long been allied with Jews on social and political issues, to the much larger Evangelical community.

But it seems that now, Abe Foxman and others are ready to lead a grand retreat from the alliance that was just putting down roots. Foxman and others are once again telling the Jewish community and the non-Jewish liberal political community that the only group Jews *can't* work with is the very group that most vocally supports Israel.

And while the ADL cites their survey results, no one is looking at the facts—because facts sell neither newspapers nor memberships. Whether you examine the results of the 2004 Pew Poll on Religion and Politics[28] or the Fellowship's 2002 Tarrance Group[29] survey, Evangelicals overwhelmingly support Israel for the "right" (no pun intended) reasons.

We're told that the "religious right" supports Israel to hasten the return of Jesus and the onset of Armageddon—yet the Tarrance survey data show that only one in three Evangelicals supports Israel "because it is the place prophesized for the second coming of Jesus." What is the most often cited reason Christians support Israel? Forty-three percent said they support Israel because of Israel's democratic values and its role as our strong and reliable ally in the war against terrorism. In other words, four in ten self-identified Evangelicals support Israel because of our shared democratic values and the common enemy that is targeting America and Western values along with Israel.

When we pressed respondents for the "theological" reasons they supported Israel, 59 percent cited the promises of God to Abraham—including Genesis 12:3 ("I will bless those that bless you and I will curse those that curse you") and God's covenant promise to the Jewish people that the land would be theirs forever.[30] By the way, roughly two in three Jews also pointed to God's covenant with the Jewish people as their main theological reason for supporting Israel. The reasons Evangelicals support Israel are rooted in shared democratic ideals and in the beginning of the Bible in the Hebrew Scriptures—not in the "end times" of the book of Revelation.

Evangelicals are committed to Israel. And through programs like Stand for Israel,[31] The Fellowship's advocacy initiative, or John Hagee's CUFI (Christians United for Israel) we're going to make sure that the pro-Israel voice at the White House, on Capitol Hill, in fifty state capitals and in neighborhoods and newspapers across this nation is not always a Jewish voice.

But the reality is we are most effective when we partner with our friends—our brothers and sisters in the Jewish community—as we did in September when Jews and Evangelicals packed the JW Marriott ballroom for Stand for Israel's second Washington Briefing.

We need to forge a true partnership—a partnership based on what we agree on. A partnership is never an agreement to agree on everything. More often it is an agreement to set aside differences in order to accomplish a common goal—partnership is first an agreement to disagree. For this alliance of Evangelicals and Jews to be successful, we have to agree to disagree on a lot of things. We have to focus on the one point of indisputable agreement—we are all committed to the preservation of the Jewish people and the Jewish homeland within secure, defensible borders. For this to happen, the organized Jewish community has to follow the lead of the JCPA; it has to be willing to treat Evangelicals as it has treated other partners.

The Jewish community was able to work with the Democratic Party—because they could separate the Democratic Party from George Wallace. The Jewish community has worked with Black America, because they know that neither Jesse Jackson nor Louis Farrakhan speaks for all of the American Black community. Why should an Evangelical alliance be held to a different (and higher) standard?

And while Israel has accepted—indeed welcomed—Christian political and economic support, the organized American Jewish community by and large still doesn't "get it" (although Israel clearly does). In late 2005, former Prime Minister Binyamin (Bibi) Netanyahu said:

> The greatest support Israel has today is in the United States. And the greatest support Israel has in the U.S., besides the Jewish community, is that of Evangelical Christians.
>
> These people . . . support us not because of a shared ethnic identity, but because of a broader partnership based on values.[32]

But it seems that Abe Foxman and Rabbi Yoffie believe *our values* are so tainted that we just can't be trusted. Still, I believe Christian support will be undiminished. Because—and even Abe Foxman has said this—"There's never been a quid pro quo for our support of Israel."

NOTES

1. Dt 34:4–5, "Then the LORD said to him, "This is the land I promised on oath to Abraham, Isaac and Jacob when I said, 'I will give it to your descendants.' I have let you see it with your eyes, but you will not cross over into it. And Moses the servant of the LORD died there in Moab, as the LORD had said." *Holy Bible, New International Version*, (International Bible Society, 1984—hereafter, NIV).

2. Rom 11:17b–19 (NIV), ". . . you, though a wild olive shoot, have been grafted in among the others and now share in the nourishing sap from the olive root, do not boast over those branches. If you do, consider this: you do not support the root, but the root supports you."

3. 2004 statistics, State of Israel Ministry of Tourism.

4. Most Christian supporters of Israel cite God's promise to Abraham that He "would bless those who bless you" as one of their biblical reasons for supporting Israel. But Christians who make pilgrimage will often cite Ps 84:5 (NIV), "Blessed are those whose strength is in you, who have set their hearts on pilgrimage."

5. Gn 12:3 (NIV), "I will bless those who bless you, and whoever curses you I will curse; and all peoples on earth will be blessed through you."

6. Rom 15:27 (NIV), "They were pleased to do it, and indeed they owe it to them. *For if the Gentiles have shared in the Jews' spiritual blessings, they owe it to the Jews to share with them their material blessings.*" (Emphasis added).

7. The term "born-again" is often used interchangeably with "evangelical." It has its origin in Jesus' dialogue with Nicodemus, a Pharisee and "ruler of the Jews" in the third chapter of the Gospel of John: "3 In reply Jesus declared, 'I tell you the truth, no one can see the kingdom of God unless he is born again.' 4 'How can a man be born when he is old?' Nicodemus asked. 'Surely he cannot enter a second time into his mother's womb to be born!' 5 Jesus answered, 'I tell you the truth, no one can enter the kingdom of God unless he is born of water and the Spirit. 6 Flesh gives birth to flesh, but the Spirit gives birth to spirit. 7 You should not be surprised at my saying, "You must be born again.""'" (NIV).

8. Pew Forum on Religion and Public Life, Fourth Survey of Religion and politics, 2004, pewforum.org/publications/surveys/green-full.pdf.

9. Ibid.

10. Craig Horowitz, "Israel's Christian Soldiers," *New York Magazine* (Sept. 29, 2003), 51–52.

11. The "charismatic" and "Pentecostal" branches of Evangelicalism believe that the "gift of tongues" is a key manifestation of salvation (Acts 2:4 (NIV), "4 All of them were filled with the Holy Spirit and began to speak in other tongues as the Spirit enabled them") where other Evangelical denominations (most notably Southern Baptists) believe the "sign gifts" ceased (1 Cor 13:8b (NIV), ". . . where there are prophecies, they will cease; where there are tongues, they will be stilled") with the canonization of scripture.

12. City University of New York Graduate Study, Oct. 2001. www.gc.cuny .edu/press_information/current_releases/october_2001_aris.htm.

13. Horowitz, "Israel's Christian Soldiers."

14. AIPAC—the American Israel Public Affairs Committee has recently hired full-time staff to court "religiously motivated pro-Israel Americans."

15. Evangelical Christians are told to share their faith with everyone in numerous passages including Acts 1:8 (NIV), "But you will receive power when the Holy Spirit comes on you; and you will be my witnesses in Jerusalem, and in all Judea and Samaria, and to the ends of the earth" and Mt 28:19–20 (NIV) (the so-called Great Commission), "Therefore go and make disciples of all nations, baptizing them in the name of the Father and of the Son and of the Holy Spirit."

16. Ami Eden, "Pariah Rabbi Converts Foes of Evangelical Outreach," *Forward* (July 12, 2002).

17. Abraham Foxman, July 16, 2002, JTA.org.

18. "Jews and Christians: Some of our Best Friends. . ." *Hadassah Magazine* (June/July 2003).

19. Horowitz, "Israel's Christian Soldiers."

20. Address by Abraham Foxman to ADL National Commission Meeting, Nov. 3, 2005, www.adl.org/Religious_Freedom/religion_public_square.asp.

21. Sermon by Rabbi Eric Yoffie, Union for Reform Judaism 68th General Assembly, Nov. 19, 2000, urj.org/yoffie/biennialsermon05/index.cfm?.

22. Craig Unger, "American Rapture—Evangelical Christians and the Big Business of Being Born Again," *Vanity Fair* (Dec. 2005).

23. Nov. 29, 2005, www.salon.com.

24. Adam Piore, "A Higher Frequency," *Mother Jones* (Dec. 2005).

25. Shmuel Rosen, "Where Does the Wonderful Friendship End?" *Ha'aretz* (Oct. 11, 2005).

26. *2001 American Jewish Identity Survey*, Graduate Center, City University of New York, www.gc.cuny.edu/faculty/research_studies/ajis.pdf.

27. Hillel Halkin, "Foxman's Hypocrisy," *Jerusalem Post* (Nov. 10, 2005). To fully appreciate the degree of desertion, consider the divestment and anti-security fence resolutions passed by the Jewish Community's traditional partners such as the Presbyterian Church (USA) and the United Church of Christ. [The Presbyterian Church (USA) reversed its divestment decisions in June 2006]

28. pewforum.org/publications/surveys/green-full.pdf.

29. The survey, commissioned by the International Fellowship of Christians and Jews, found that 62 percent of conservative Christians say they support Israel and its policies and actions toward Palestinian terrorism.

30. Gn 13:14–15, 17 (NIV), "14 The Lord said to Abram after Lot had parted from him, 'Lift up your eyes from where you are and look north and south, east and west. 15 All the land that you see I will give to you and your offspring forever . . . 17 Go, walk through the length and breadth of the land, for I am giving it to you.'"

31. See www.StandForIsrael.org for examples of pro-Israel political advocacy.

32. Edgar Lefkowitz, "Bibi: Evangelicals are Israel's Best Gentile Friends," *Jerusalem Post* (Nov. 8, 2005).

6

On the Road

The Jewish Community Relations Encounter with Evangelical Christians

Ethan Felson

LOCAL EXPERIENCE: FROM SAN ANTONIO
TO HOUSTON AND BEYOND

Two hundred miles along Interstate 10 connect the Texas cities of San Antonio and Houston. Tall buildings give way to suburbia, then exurbia, then rural countryside, then the markings of another city on the horizon. This four-hour journey also traverses the relationship between Jews and Evangelical Christians in America.

The downtowns of both San Antonio and Houston are dotted with venerable Mainline Protestant churches. Over the past generation, as Evangelical churches flourished in the South, their influence grew with their numbers. Among them is the ministry of Reverend John Hagee, one of America's most prominent Christian Zionist leaders. Hagee's career started in the 1960s in downtown San Antonio. In 1975, with one hundred parishioners, he started his own nondenominational church in a northern suburb of San Antonio. Twelve years later, along the highway that marks the outer band of San Antonio, he opened the 5,000 seat Cornerstone Church which today boasts 17,000 members.

In 1978, Hagee traveled to Israel and returned, in his words, "a Zionist."[1] The modern state of Israel is, to Hagee, a fulfillment of a biblical promise of land to the Jews—and a necessary precursor for his particular strand of Christian Zionism, one that is rooted in premillennial dispensationalism and is linked to an apocalyptic battle between good and evil that will occur in the Holy Land as a part of the end of days.

Hagee spoke boldly about an end of days that was upon us—and the belief that it is biblically mandated to support the modern State of Israel, which is itself a biblically predicted precursor to the end of days.

Hagee made support for Israel a pillar of his ministry and reached out to the local Jewish community, offering not just fellowship but funds. He was and is a consummate fundraiser. His donor base, committed Christians, reached deep into their pockets to support the State of Israel. In the early 1980s, he began hosting an annual "Night to Honor Israel." However, since Hagee's theology flowed from the farther reaches of Christian theology, he represented a challenge to much of the Jewish community at the time. He has also been aligned with politically conservative positions that are often diametrically opposed to the traditional stances of the American Jewish community on a gamut of issues from separation of religion and state, to women's rights.

In the San Antonio Jewish community, since the inception of the event, there has been a diversity of opinions as to the role they should assume in that event. A local Orthodox rabbi who is a close friend of Hagee has provided a consistent Jewish presence at the event and has pressed for the local Jewish community to follow his lead. San Antonio's Jewish community, however, has been where most of the American Jewish community has been in terms of solidifying a relationship with Evangelical Christians—both curious and skeptical.

The Jewish Federation of San Antonio, for many years, declined to be a sponsor of the program. Their concerns have reflected a standard litany—proselytizing, theological motivation, politics, and personality. Should they reject a partnership with a conservative, premillennialist, Evangelical Christian? Should the community eschew Hagee's support and his dollars because of his theology or the effect a partnership might have on liberal Protestants for whom Hagee's brand of Christianity is pure anathema? Others feared alienating the Muslims, about whom Hagee can be sharply critical—casting them essentially in the language of the Antichrist. Still others have been skeptical of the man himself.

Hagee did not have to travel far to find a Jewish community that would embrace him. In Houston, Jewish Federation director Lee Wunsch placed a different prism on the encounter between Jews and Evangelical Christians. To Wunsch, the boundary would be drawn at proselytization and the misappropriation of Jewish customs and practices—à la Hebrew Christians who combine Jewish practices with their Christian messianic beliefs. But for that, Hagee's support and his dollars were welcome. From that acceptance, a friendship grew that, in Wunsch's words, allowed him to press the pastor on a range of concerns including proselytization and even political topics such as Israel ceding land to Palestinians.[2]

Wunsch developed a close relationship with Hagee. Satisfied that Hagee's missionary yearnings did not cross his bright line, he "picked up the check" that others had left on the table. At Hagee's 2004 "Night to Honor Israel," the San Antonio church hosted a reception for the Jewish Federation of Greater Houston where they presented Wunsch with a check for $1 million to support his Exodus campaign to resettle in Israel Jews from the former Soviet Union. Wunsch praised not only Hagee's pro-Israel philanthropy but "his annual six-figure commitment to the Jewish Federation of Houston's Annual Campaign—a campaign that supports our Hillels, our day schools, and our major social service Agencies." Wunsch added, in a November 23, 2004 letter to his community, "we should embrace Pastor Hagee as a friend, a supporter and a strong advocate of Israel. He distances himself from those who would convert us and from those messianic groups who would have you believe that you can be Christian and Jewish at the same time. And, if there are other issues on which we disagree, then we can agree to disagree—that, after all, is what our great American democracy is all about."[3]

Just two years later, Wunsch would be on hand as Hagee donated $7 million to five different pro-Israel causes at the twenty-fifth annual "Night to Honor Israel." Representatives of the San Antonio federation did sit alongside Wunsch at the event, but the federation continued to withhold its cosponsorship, citing divergent community viewpoints. Also seated next to Hagee would be his wife, wearing a "Lion of Judah" pin to signify her major gift to the Jewish Federation women's division . . . in Houston.

Across the Bible Belt and the rest of America, many local Jewish communities have made the philosophical journey from San Antonio to Houston. For some it has been an easy ride. For others, not.

The Memphis Jewish community came to know another Evangelical Christian powerhouse. The late Rev. Ed McAteer was a founder of the Moral Majority in the 1970s and a passionate supporter of Israel. Also a premillennial dispensationalist, McAteer organized massive prayer breakfasts, often with major Israeli political figures as keynote speakers. In 1998, toward the end of his life, McAteer formed Christian Friends of Israel. That group held rallies, engaged in pro-Israel advocacy, and raised funds that were channeled through the local Jewish federation to purchase an ambulance for Israel. The Jewish Federation, in that effort, refused support from a local Hebrew Christian congregation. Although the Evangelical group respected this boundary, they later challenged the Jewish Federation on a policy matter when they opposed Israeli disengagement from Gaza. Their position put strain on the relationship due to the federation's stance in support of decisions made by Israel's democratically elected government. Still, the perception of a close Evangelical-Jewish relationship was present enough to cause concern when anti-Israel divestment campaigns were waged in the Mainline Churches, so much so that the federation and its community relations council needed to articulate that they were not aligned exclusively with Evangelicals.

Of course, the terms Evangelical, Mainline Protestant, and Christian Zionist are not mutually exclusive. In reality, they can be seen more as overlapping circles in a Venn diagram. In many communities, Jewish organizations and leaders have forged close ties with pro-Israel Christians, both inside and outside the Mainline Churches, some of whom are Christian Zionist and/or Evangelical. The benefits of these relationships would play a critical role in an important drama of 2006.

Birmingham Jewish federation director Richard Friedman has, for many years, advocated closer relationships across the spectrum of the Protestant community. Jewish Community Relations Council director Joyce Spielberger has presented several forums and speakers to the JCRC on the topic of Evangelical-Jewish relations. A 2004 JCRC forum, featuring a Christian Zionist elected official, sparked a lengthy conversation about the nature of this relationship. In the main, the community favored reaching out—certainly not a surprising development given the demographic realities of the South and the barriers that are broken down by familiarity. The relationships the Birmingham Jewish community developed would prove invaluable when the national Presbyterian Church held its 2006 General Assembly in Birmingham—the convention at which the church would reconsider several controversial resolutions adopted two years earlier. In the catbird seat was the strongly pro-Israel pastor of Birmingham's South Highland Presbyterian Church, Rev. Ed Hurley, a longstanding friend of the Jewish community, and Birmingham Rabbi Jonathan Miller. Hurley sponsored a resolution to rescind the church's divestment stance—and served as a broker between numerous factions of the church.

Warm and cooperative relations with Evangelicals have not been the sole province of the Belt. In Southern New Jersey, a five-year-old relationship between the JCRC and a locally based national Christian Zionist group, Friends of Israel, has produced a significant amount of advocacy in defense of Israel including several press conferences, solidarity rallies, and missions to Israel. In all those activities, according to council director Alan Respler, the local council reports that FOI rejects participation by those who would use the interaction to proselytize.

This experience, however, is far from universal. In San Diego, the Evangelical megachurch Mission Valley Christian Fellowship (MCFV) places support for Israel at the center of many of its activities. They organize annual missions and, at one event alone, raised more than $500,000 for the New Jerusalem Foundation, a nonprofit created by Ehud Olmert when he was Mayor of Jerusalem. The local Jewish federation has not joined hands with MVCF, however, because of the church's refusal to step back from its proselytizing efforts—activities which have caused additional anxiety due to the church's active presence in Israel with Russian immigrants and exchange programs with Ariel, an Israeli settlement whose population is almost half immigrants from the former Soviet Union. The decision not to partner with MVCF was not without its critics, though, including the local Israeli consulate. The federation, in deciding not to sponsor, did enjoy the support of the city's rabbinical association.

THE NATIONAL EXPERIENCE:
CAUTION, CONFRONTATION, AND COOPERATION

The experience of local Jewish communities mirrors the national community relations encounter with this issue. Rabbi James Rudin, American Jewish Committee's director of the Interreligious Affairs Department, coauthored a series of publications on Evangelical-Jewish relations and Christian Zionism throughout the 1980s, educating Jews about the Evangelical community, calling for increased cooperation and dialogue. However, prior to the 1990s, most policy statements by American Jewish organizations regarding Evangelical Christians were cautionary at best.

In 1980 the JCPA, then the National Jewish Community Relations Advisory Council Joint Program Plan (JPP), recognized that the relationship with Evangelicals "has been a mix of cordiality and cooperation (as to Israel) and misunderstanding and hostility (as to conversionary activity)."[4] The statement advanced the prevailing perception of the day that Evangelical support for Israel was grounded in premillennialism. The policy recommendations were to study the Evangelical community and identify potential areas of cooperation. The policy's only action item was to sensitize Evangelicals to the Jewish community's deep concern about conversionary activity. In 1982, the JPP continued to seek partnership with moderate Evangelicals with policy positions on social issues that "closely correspond to those of the Jewish community." Such partnerships, it was hoped, would "ameliorate the tensions triggered by the strong current of pro-Arab, anti-Israel sentiment among some members of the Governing Board of the National Council of Churches."[5]

That same year, a policy on political activism stated that those religious leaders who urge their members to "vote Christian," evidence an intent "glaringly incompatible with the constitutional prohibition of religious tests for public office." A concern that grew in the 1984 election in which more overt organizing by the Religious Right was manifested in situations such as the congressional race against a Jewish member of Congress that included a call to "put a Christian in Congress."[6]

In the late eighties, policy statements supported an approach to Evangelical-Jewish relations that would be similar to relations with other religious and ethnic groups. In 1987, the JCPA favored "working in coalition on issues of mutual concern and parting company on those issues, both political and religious, where there are profound differences of views."[7]

JCPA policies in the late 1980s declared the Religious Right to be in retreat due to a series of scandals involving televangelists. However, local communities reported that there were increased efforts by school board and other local candidates to "articulate platforms of the 'religious right,' including attacking local school-board curricula and attempting censorship of school libraries."[8]

The Religious Right, however, was deemed to be resurgent by 1992—and concerns about "stealth candidates" for office gave way to a recognition that Evangelical Christians had fully exited the revival tent and taken seats of power across the nation. Policies called for monitoring of Religious Right political activity, noting Christian Coalition founder Rev. Pat Robertson's pledge to gain "effective control" of the Republican Party by 1996.[9]

A national alarm was sounded, and a highly charged conversation followed, when Anti-Defamation League director Abe Foxman published *The Religious Right: The Assault on Tolerance and Pluralism in America* in 1994. In that tome, Foxman said that "an exclusionist religious movement in this country has attempted to restore what it perceives as the ruins of a Christian nation by more closely seeking to unite its version of Christianity with state power."[10] Later that year, the political power of Evangelicals was demonstrated through the Republican sweep of Congress in the 1994 midterm election. Although the Contract with America touted by the new House Speaker Newt

Gingrich avoided contentious social issues such as abortion and school prayer, the die was cast. A political agenda popular with Evangelical Christians was now a part of the national political agenda. Foxman held a series of rapprochement meetings with Evangelical leaders.

THE PERFECT STORM: DURBAN, CAMP DAVID, *INTIFADA*, AND 9/11

Any expectation that American Jews and Evangelical Christians might be headed on opposite trajectories was seriously challenged by a "perfect storm" of events starting in 2000. In Israel, the hope that peace might finally be achieved was dashed in the summer of 2000. Palestinian Authority Chairman Arafat walked out of the Camp David Accords with Israeli Prime Minister Barak and American President Clinton. Arafat returned to Gaza and unleashed a spate of riots and suicide bombings, allegedly in response to Ariel Sharon's visit to the Temple Mount.

A few months later, the historically close American election brought a clean sweep to Washington. For the first time, the United States House of Representatives, Senate, and now the White House would be led not just by Republicans but by religious conservatives, more closely aligned with Evangelical Christianity than any other religious community.

In 2001, a siege mentality had taken hold as Jewish organizational leaders, already responding to an anti-Israel onslaught regarding the new *intifada*, prepared for the United Nations World Conference Against Racism to open the last week in August in Durban, South Africa. Preconference language suggested that a significant battle was mounting over whether anti-Semitism would be considered a form of racism.

The news from Durban, however, was worse than most expected. The WCAR unfolded as an Israel-bashing festival. Palestinian activists wore "Zionism is Racism" t-shirts, donned "Israeli Apartheid" buttons, distributed copies of *The Protocols of the Elders of Zion*, and carried signs with cartoons that depicted Israelis savoring the blood of Palestinians. Language condemning anti-Semitism, Holocaust denial, and Israel-delegitimization was stricken from the written declarations. Colin Powell, the African American U.S. Secretary of State had looked forward to the WCAR, but worries about anti-Jewish developments led the administration to take a wait-and-see approach. In a move warmly welcomed by Jewish groups, Bush declined to send Powell. After four days, the American delegation exited, followed soon by Israel and the Jewish caucus to the concurrent NGO conference.

The final WCAR NGO resolution deemed Israel "a racist apartheid state," guilty of war crimes and genocide. Jewish participants praised the few civil rights groups that condemned the process and its product. But they stood in shock at the silence of the interfaith partners they would have to return to America and face. A conservative administration supported the Jewish communal position while representatives of the Mainline Protestant churches abandoned the Jewish community and Israel during a very dark hour.

Returning to America, the Jewish NGO representatives who attended Durban were bewildered at the lack of support from the Mainline Churches. Years later, participants would say that had another news story not stolen the headlines, we might still be talking about what happened at Durban. Three days after the conference officially closed, though, two planes felled the World Trade Center buildings in New York, and another two careened into the Pentagon and a field in Pennsylvania. A war against terrorism was upon America.

Two weeks after the September 11th attacks, a group of prominent civil rights groups in Washington issued a statement expressing concern about how the nascent war on terrorism would impact civil liberties. The list of signatory organizations for such statements, until that point, would generally have included several national Jewish organizations. No Jewish organization opted to join this statement, in part because of the stress of the moment, but also because no consensus remained to stay the prior course. One prominent Jewish lobbyist commented to this author, "I don't think we'll be saying anything to criticize this President." Another said, "this is no longer business as usual." Although a political realignment that had been predicted by some did not materialize, the perfect storm had shuffled the decks in terms of Jewish alliances—and American Jews circled their wagons.

As the Palestinian *intifada* continued, American Jews looked with some bewilderment as criticism of Israeli policies mounted. To friends of Israel who had followed closely both the peace talks and subsequent violence, the Palestinian position seemed unsupportable absent a true animus to Israel. The ADL, in 2002, paid for a pro-Israel full-page *New York Times* ad, written and signed by then Christian Coalition director Ralph Reed. Foxman said, "American Jews should not be apologetic or defensive about cultivating Evangelical support for Israel. The need for support by an Israel under siege is great. Fortunately, Evangelical support is overwhelming, consistent, and unconditional. And the fears that such support will undermine our impact on other concerns that

American Jews have are overblown, since we will continue to articulate in forceful ways our significant disagreements on social issues."[11]

Perhaps the most public manifestation of the embrace of Evangelical Christians took place on the Mall in Washington in April 2002. Having witnessed more than a year of attacks on Israel for its defensive measures in the Palestinian *intifada*, several major national Jewish agencies, including the United Jewish Communities and the Jewish Council for Public Affairs, cosponsored a massive Israel solidarity rally in Washington, DC. In addition to Israeli and American political and Jewish community leaders, the rally featured leaders from traditional allies such as the Urban League and AFL-CIO. Representing the Christian community, however were Sister Rose Theiring, the President of the National Christian Leadership Conference for Israel—a coalition of theologically liberal, moderate, and conservative Christian supporters of Israel and, strikingly, Janet Parshall, the conservative Evangelical radio talk show host and head of the powerful Religious Broadcasters of America. At one point in her remarks, Parshall shouted "We will never give up the Golan!" to the cheers of some and the stunned silence of others. She had broken a taboo by embracing a "pro-Israel" policy position that reached well beyond that of most of the Jewish organizations represented at the rally. There was, however, no follow-up or clarification to Parshall's policy declaration.

Parshall, of course, was not the first to make such a bold assertion rejecting land for peace—nor was the Jewish community's ignoring her statement unique. In 1996, Hagee himself had written that the assassination of Yitzhak Rabin was biblically predictable, reflecting a divide in Israel between those who believe that Jews have a 'holy deed' to the land and those who "put more faith in man than in God" and thus return land.[12] These events seemed to add a second boundary, a political one, alongside the conversionary boundary, for Evangelical-Jewish ties. And as a testament to his commitment to work *with* the Jewish community, several years later Rev. Hagee would "take a walk" on Israel's disengagement from Gaza.

In the aftermath of the 2002 Washington rally, the JCPA undertook a study of Evangelical-Jewish relations. One forum in Baltimore, standing room only, was seminal. George Mamo,[13] the founding director of Stand for Israel, a program of the International Fellowship of Christians and Jews (IFCJ) was among the speakers. The IFCJ is a group whose leader, Rabbi Yechiel Eckstein, has pushed the envelope and the buttons of the organized Jewish community, raising millions of dollars from Christian Zionists. Some participants at the Baltimore forum came looking for fireworks. They were disappointed. Mamo framed a rationale for mainstream Jewish support for a deepened relationship with Evangelicals. He startled his audience when he described polling commissioned by his agency that challenged much of the prevailing wisdom of American Jews regarding Evangelicals. Shared values, an abhorrence of terrorism, and a strong relationship with the United States were among the most common reasons for supporting Israel. When pressed, three in five Christian Zionists pointed to the biblical promise to bless Israel and the Jewish people as their theological motivation for support of Israel. By contrast, less than three in ten cited biblical prophecy related to the end of times.[14]

In February 2003, the JCPA debated a resolution on relations with Evangelical Christians. Although mostly a restatement of long-held principles, the debate around the resolution was very contentious. In Chicago, an affiliate of a national Jewish organization exercised its veto right, scuttling that community's sponsorship of the resolution. Chicago JCRC Director Jay Tcath later noted that the issue of Evangelical-Jewish relations had become the "third rail" of American Jewish community relations. Tcath noted that the Jewish community placed Evangelicals in a unique place, allowing controversies to stand in the way of relationships—noting absolutist objections to Jewish-Evangelical ties often flowed from ill-informed negative stereotypes.

The JCPA resolution identified Evangelical support for Israel as a force that had motivated many Jews to "revisit the question of relationships with Evangelical Christians" on both domestic and international issues.[15] In addition to supporting coalitional work on shared interests, the resolution broke some new ground. It rejected the notion of a quid pro quo for partnering with Evangelical Christians. For years, some Jewish leaders had suggested that an aggressive domestic agenda including issues such as gay rights and abortion might alienate much needed Evangelical support on Israel. The resolution rejected that, placing the Jewish community on record opposing those who asserted that the Jewish community should temper its actions on contentious issues. Interestingly, one such threat would come later that year—from no less than the director of the National Association of Evangelicals, Ted Haggard, who suggested that Jewish opposition to Mel Gibson's film *The Passion of the Christ* risked alienating Evangelical support for Israel. He was roundly criticized for that remark and quickly reframed it in less strident terms.

The resolution also dealt with proselytizing with added nuance. Rather than expressing discomfort or opposition regarding conversionary activities, the line would be drawn at "aggressive and misleading" proselytization. This development reflected a recognition that "spreading the gospel" is an intrinsic and cardinal tenet of the Christian faith and that the misappropriation of Jewish customs and practices along with some of the more tenacious activities such as those by street evangelists pose the real problem in the relationship.

Welcoming the resolution, Evangelical-Jewish relations expert Professor Gerald McDermott,[16] of Roanoke College said, "Jews should fear proselytizing that is coercive, but they should not fear friendly persuasion that they are free to reject."[17] Lastly, the resolution noted that those approaching relationships with Evangelical Christians should do so taking into account "local and other dynamics," recognizing that the relationship with Evangelical Christians is significantly influenced by their prevalence on the local landscape.

The resolution was broadly welcomed in the Evangelical community. In an interview with the *Baltimore Sun*, Southern Baptist Convention leader Rev. Richard Land welcomed the sentiments expressed in the resolution. "It could be the beginning of a new era of understanding and common cause at a whole new level between Evangelicals and Jews."[18] He also clearly framed Evangelical support for Israel in a context that did not relate to the end of days. "We don't believe any human being or human event can manipulate the second coming," said Land. "The second coming will come when God has foreordained it will come."[19]

NEW HORIZONS

Subsequently, in 2004, the Jewish community was blindsided by the passage of four resolutions by the Presbyterian Church (USA) at its biennial General Assembly in Richmond, Virginia. The Mainline Church narrowly rejected a motion to cease financial support for a Hebrew Christian church in Philadelphia with funds earmarked to expand the denomination's waning membership.[20] A resolution rejecting Christian Zionism was adopted by a wide margin[21] as was a resolution calling on Israel to remove in its entirety the security barrier that was being constructed to separate Israelis and Palestinians.[22] The resolution which gained the most attention, however, was one favoring the so-called Geneva Accord, modeled after the Camp David agreement rejected by the Palestinians four years earlier. That resolution included language mandating a process of "phased, selective divestment" of church assets in companies operating in Israel. A firestorm ensued.[23]

Observers of the debate around divestment noted that it was, in many ways, a proxy for the centuries-old battle between the liberal and conservative strands in American Protestantism. The Mainline Churches have experienced a sharp decrease in membership and political influence, largely due to the burgeoning Evangelical movement. One vestige of power maintained by the Mainline Churches, however, is their sizable endowments and pension funds. The divestment resolutions symbolized a striking back of sorts. The PCUSA, with $7 billion in such assets, placed them down as markers against the political influence of the pro-Israel community, both Christian and Jewish.

The national Jewish community relations agencies rejected suggestions to confront the church directly at the national level—or to create a Presbyterian-Jewish alliance against the church. Despite the priority given to challenging the Presbyterian action, no editorials, op-eds, or full page ads were placed in the national media. Instead, communities were encouraged to approach their Presbyterian counterparts on the local level.

The encounter was instructive. More than 100 communities held meetings with their Presbyterian counterparts. In addition to learning that the vast majority of Presbyterians were unaware that divestment would be considered, the Jewish community learned of the strong pockets of support for Israel—and opposition to church policies—that permeated all segments and regions of the church. It was one thread of this support that opened a new paradigm in interfaith relations and pro-Israel advocacy.

In community after community, dialogue sessions revealed a sizable community of Presbyterians who were deeply disaffected by their own denomination's actions with regard to the Israeli-Palestinian conflict. Although these individuals were leaders within their Mainline denominations, they more closely resembled the passionate pro-Israel voices that had emanated almost exclusively from the Evangelical Churches.

In a twist of irony, the person who did the most successful organizing of these Christian Zionists within the Mainline Churches, Shari Dollinger, is the niece of the San Antonio Reform rabbi who has been a leading spokesperson against an alliance with Pastor Hagee. Dollinger, a former employee of the American Israel Public Affairs Committee and the Israeli Embassy, serves as an organizer of pro-Israel activities for a consortium of donors spearheaded by Newt Becker of California. These donors have funded a spectrum of more hawkish or conservative programs—and in some ways their engagement on divestment was intended to be no different.

Dollinger cobbled together an alliance of groups known to embrace a confrontational Israel advocacy approach, including the David Project, Stand with Us, and the American Jewish Congress. A consummate community organizer, Dollinger also brought together a broad and impressive array of Christian Zionists from within the Presbyterian Church—some of whom were already well connected. Among these leaders were individuals associated with "Renewal" groups—a nemesis of the Mainline denominations due to their persistent challenges of church dogma on matters such as abortion, ordination of gay clergy, and, quite prominently, Middle East policy. Also aligned were theologically liberal Presbyterians, led by Presbyterians Concerned for Jewish and Christian Relations, a group with whom the organized Jewish community already had close relations.

What looked like it may have been a strategy in direct conflict with the one adopted by the national community relations groups such as ADL, AJC, and JCPA, materialized quite differently. Dollinger's coalition, known more for bombast and protest, worked in close cooperation with the mainstream groups. An alliance of Presbyterians from left and right, together with a broad array of Jews, worked in concert to encourage commissioners to the 2006 Presbyterian General Assembly to change course. The net effect was surprising to all. Commissioners were given well-coordinated packets of materials on divestment, and were given the opportunity to hear speakers, participate in Sabbath services, and to find a common ground that would move the church back toward a more moderate stance on the Israeli-Palestinian conflict. A highway billboard commissioned by the Presbyterians, that was initially to have had the word "Divestment" with a line through it, morphed over several drafts, into one that sported a dove and the moniker "Presbyterians for Peace."

In the end, after an unprecedented grassroots dialogue effort by Jewish community relations agencies, the alliance of pro-Israel Presbyterians carried the baton over the finish line. The General Assembly overwhelmingly adopted a reconciling resolution, turning back several efforts to weaken or scuttle the language. The church replaced the language it had adopted in 2004 mandating an Israel-focused divestment process, with one that instead suggested that the church's longstanding social investment principles be applied—and be applied across the region, not just to Israel.[24] The church apologized for the hurt caused by its prior actions and called for a new season of interfaith cooperation. In a separate resolution, the church even revised its prior call for Israel to remove its entire security barrier, regardless of its location.

Instead the church stated that it should track the 'green line.'[25] Interestingly, these pro-Israel Presbyterian leaders did not, at that General Assembly, make strong efforts to stem another tide, namely the attacks from the church against Christian Zionism itself. Resolutions were submitted, but failed to gain traction in light of the attention paid to the issue of divestment. The 2004 resolution adopted by the PCUSA was nothing short of a shot across the bow of Evangelical Christians and Christian Zionists within the denomination. It indeed called Christian Zionism "anti-evangelical" because it "undermines the presence and witness of the indigenous Middle East Christians" . . . and creates "a false image of Christianity, one that is militant, western, and Zionist." All Christian Zionists are reduced to being divisive factors in the church who distort sacred texts "into apocalyptic scenarios for the end times in a predictive and reductionist form of prophecy." Most tellingly, the overture deems Christian Zionism off-limits theologically, stating that it is "contrary to the Reformed principles of interpreting Scripture."[26] A subsequent PCUSA fact sheet on Christian Zionism went beyond classifying all Christian Zionists as premillennialist, to painting them as indifferent to the suffering of Palestinians and called on Presbyterians to "speak out against the corrosive spiritual and political aspects of Christian Zionism."[27]

In an ironic twist, the 2004 resolution on Christian Zionism concluded by stating that "premillennialist interpretations that underlie Christian Zionism ultimately exclude any validity of the continuity or efficacy of God's covenant with the Jewish people themselves, and ultimately are anti-Semitic."

This irony has captured the imagination of the Rabbinic Scholar on staff at the Jewish United Fund in Chicago. Rabbi Yehiel Poupko[28] has been on a mission for more than two years to educate Mainline Protestants that their blanket rejections of Christian Zionism are inherently a rejection of any Jewish claim to our homeland and an endorsement that any such claim is nullified in the coming of Christ. It is a brand of supercessionism. He is also engaging Evangelical Christians to articulate better the theological underpinnings of their support for Israel that do not flow from prophecies about Armageddon. The Jewish people, according to Poupko, are caught between two extreme theologies, one that says we have no connection and the other which says we have a connection only because Jesus is coming:

> The Mainline Protestants and the Evangelicals now meet to do theological battle on the playing field that is the Jewish people and the State of Israel. We have become their soccer ball. In effect, the Main-

line says, "How can Christians support Israel out of a theology that is based on biblical literalism, inerrancy of prophecy, and the assertion that one can look at contemporary events and know God's will?" Indeed, the Mainline is thus holding the Jewish people and Israel accountable for Evangelical support, and is saying, "How justified can Zionism and Israel be if their strongest support in the Christian community is coming from Evangelical quarters?" And in effect, the Evangelical turns to the Jewish community and says, "For decades, many of you have made common cause with the Mainline Protestants, with the liberals, with the Democratic party on a whole series of social, political, and economic issues. And now, when it comes to Israel, which we Evangelicals know matters most to you, they are not your friends, and we are."[29]

Indeed, the "battle" that Rabbi Poupko identifies is nothing less than the bumpy road from San Antonio to Houston. Almost every element of the organized Jewish community is programmed to align with liberal Protestants on a vast array of issues and to turn a blind eye to their anti-Zionism. Similarly, the community had seemed programmed to reject those from the Evangelical community who embrace Zionism, as an odd "other" with a hidden agenda.

More than a decade of experience, setting boundaries around political matters and proselytization, have moved the American Jewish community, reluctantly at times, to a position of increased comfort in working with Evangelical Christians. The very actions of the Mainline Protestants, in attacking both Israel and any theological position that could support a Jewish homeland there, have been catalysts in this transition. Along the journey the Jewish community has found an increased comfort zone that has enabled the long-sought partnerships on domestic issues such as religious accommodation legislation, environmental protections, and the rights of religious minorities in other lands.

It is often the case in communities without a large Evangelical presence that the Jewish community will seek some nonofficial representation at events like Rev. Hagee's "Night to Honor Israel"—which has itself become a bit of a Christian Zionism roadshow. But with each experience where Jews recognize that their support most often comes from a genuine place of shared interest, the barriers fall and the relationship grows. The Jewish community must be vigilant, however, to embrace this alliance in a manner that does not alienate their nemeses in the Mainline Churches who, perhaps unknowingly, continue to set the stage for a supremely uncomfortable and unwinnable Christian-on-Christian battle about the Jewish homeland.

NOTES

1. Ron Kampeas, "A Gift Horse or A Trojan Horse," *Jewish Telegraphic Agency*, July 6, 2006.

2. Author's conversation with Lee Wunsch.

3. Letter from Lee Wunsch to Jewish Community, Nov. 23, 2004.

4. *Joint Program Plan for Jewish Community Relations of 1980–1981*, National Jewish Community Relations Advisory Council, 43.

5. *Joint Program Plan for Jewish Community Relations of 1982-1983*, National Jewish Community Relations Advisory Council, 52–53.

6. Ibid.

7. *Joint Program Plan for Jewish Community Relations of 1987–1988*, National Jewish Community Relations Advisory Council, 45.

8. *Joint Program Plan for Jewish Community Relations of 1985–1986*, National Jewish Community Relations Advisory Council, 43.

9. *Joint Program Plan for Jewish Community Relations of 1993–1994*, National Jewish Community Relations Advisory Council, 64.

10. Abraham Foxman, *The Religious Right: The Assault on Tolerance and Pluralism in America* (New York: Anti-Defamation League, 1994).

11. Abraham Foxman, "Why Evangelical Support for Israel is a Good Thing," *Jewish Telegraphic Agency*, Op-Ed, July 16, 2002.

12. *The End of Days: Fundamentalism and the Struggle for the Temple Mount*, Oxford University Press, New York, 2001, 165, citing John Hagee, "The Beginning of the End," as chapter 5 in this volume

13. An essay by Mamo appears elsewhere in the volume.

14. Ed Goeas and William Stewart, *Study: American Christians and Support for Israel*, The Tarrance Group, October 3–6, 2002.

15. *Resolution on Evangelical Jewish Relations*, adopted by 2003 JCPA Plenum.

16. An essay by McDermott appears as chapter 8 in this volume.

17. February 26, 2003, Metro Desk John Rivera, *Baltimore Sun*.

18. Ibid.

19. Ibid. Metro Desk John Rivera, *Baltimore Sun*.

20. *Overture On the Relationship Between Christians and Jews and PCUSA Evangelism*, adopted by 2004 Presbyterian Church (USA) General Assembly in Richmond, VA.

21. *Overture on Christian Zionism*, adopted by 2004 Presbyterian Church (USA) General Assembly in Richmond, VA.

22. *Overture On Calling for an End to the Construction of a Wall by the State of Israel*, adopted by 2004 Presbyterian Church (USA) General Assembly in Richmond, VA.

23. *Overture On Supporting the Geneva Accord*, adopted by 2004 Presbyterian Church (USA) General Assembly in Richmond, VA.

24. *Overture On Rescinding and Modifying Certain Actions of the 216th General Assembly (2004) Regarding the Israeli-Palestinian Conflict*, adopted by 2006 Presbyterian Church (USA) General Assembly in Birmingham, AL.

25. Ibid.

26. *Overture on Christian Zionism*, adopted by 2004 Presbyterian Church (USA) General Assembly in Richmond, VA.

27. *Christian Zionism* fact sheet by the Presbyterian Church USA.

28. Poupko has contributed chapter 9 to this volume.

29. Yehiel Poupko, "Evangelicals: A Brief Description and Some Jewish Considerations," March 27, 2006.

7

Evangelical Ironies

Theology, Politics, and Israel

Gary Dorrien

This chapter presents a liberal Protestant perspective on the making of American Evangelicalism and the politics of the Christian Right, beginning with a few generalizations. Most American Evangelicals are politically conservative, which has enabled Christian Right leaders to build a powerful Evangelical network within the Republican Party. A vital minority stream of the Evangelical movement, however, is politically liberal or progressive, and American Evangelicals in general are not as politicized as the organized Christian Right.

Most American Jews, on the other hand, are politically liberal or moderate, and not principally identified (in the manner of Evangelicals) with a particular theology. But many American Jews and Evangelicals have formed an unusual alliance over the politics of supporting and defending Israel. This alliance, on the Jewish side, is much wider than its neoconservative wing, and neoconservatism is not an exclusively Jewish persuasion. However, neoconservatism is an important force in American politics; Jewish intellectuals and activists have played a leading role in the neoconservative movement; and the alliance between American neoconservatism and the Christian Right is politically potent. This essay will unpack these generalizations, focusing on the making and identity of American Evangelicalism.

WHAT IS EVANGELICALISM?

Modern American Evangelicalism is an offshoot of the fundamentalist revolt against the modernization of the Mainline American Protestant churches in the late nineteenth and early twentieth centuries. Historically, Protestant Evangelicalism has featured three broadly distinct forms of theology and ecclesial practice. The first type, classical Evangelicalism, derives from the confessional and dissenting movements of the sixteenth-century Reformation. It is grounded in the doctrinal heritage of the continental Reformation traditions, which includes the Reformationist and scholastic phases of orthodox Protestantism, as well as the confessional and Anabaptist forms of these traditions. The second historic type of Evangelicalism, Pietism, broke away from the classical emphasis on absolute divine sovereignty, forensic justification, and scholastic inerrancy, emphasizing experiences of conversion, sanctification, spiritual regeneration and healing. Nineteenth-century American Evangelicalism was dominated by groups in this category, especially Baptist and independent church communities, Methodists, Wesleyan holiness groups, Oberlin Perfectionists, Campbellite Restorationists, and New School Presbyterians. In recent years an extraordinary sociological phenomenon, the nondenominational megachurch movement, has morphed out of the Pietist tradition. It chucks the hymnals, sings praise music off the wall, often preaches a consumer-oriented gospel of health and wealth, and packs huge auditoriums with born-again believers.

The third historic type of Evangelicalism, fundamentalist evangelism, is a product of the antimodernist reaction of the late nineteenth and early twentieth centuries. Fundamentalism turned the scholastic doctrine of perfect biblical inerrancy—which Luther and Calvin did not espouse—into the basis of all other doctrines, insisting on the necessity of literal beliefs impugned by modern criticism. It also propounded an apocalyptic millennialism that often divided the Bible along dispensational lines.

The term "Evangelical" derives from the Greek *euangelion*, which means "gospel" or "message of good news." In the root sense of the term, an "Evangelical" is anyone who accepts the gospel message that Jesus is savior and lord. For this reason there is an element of presumption in the attempt by any group to claim the term exclusively for itself. All Christian theology is rooted in the gospel proclamation of the incarnation, saving death and resurrection of Jesus Christ. By definition all Christian theology is Evangelical. The modern tendency to identify Evangelicalism with theologically conservative forms of

Protestantism slights the presence of gospel faith in other forms of Christianity. Historically and theologically, conservative Protestants have no more right to an exclusive claim over the term "Evangelical" than to the word "Christian."

Yet the conservative Protestant claim to "Evangelicalism" does signify something worth naming. Luther and Calvin judged that the gospel message of salvation by faith through grace was obscured, if not fatally subverted by the paganizing tendencies of the Catholic Church. These included the development of an ecclesiastical system in which extrabiblical functions were recognized as sacraments, the sacrament of Holy Communion was construed as a priestly sacrifice, and the Pauline doctrine of salvation by faith was blended with a doctrine of works righteousness. By accommodating the gospel message to paganizing theological and ecclesiastical motifs, the Reformers argued, Roman Catholicism distorted the distinctive "Evangelical" message and character of biblical faith. To be *Evangelisch* in this continental sixteenth-century context was to be a protester. The Reformation summarized the Evangelical message in great Latin slogans: *sola gratia* (salvation only through divine grace), *sola fide* (justification by faith alone), and *sola Scriptura* (Scripture as the single rule of faith and practice). Evangelical Christianity, the Reformers insisted, is defined by its faithfulness to these scriptural motifs.

Classical Protestant Evangelicalism stressed that salvation is an unmerited gift of grace bestowed by an absolutely sovereign God through faith in Christ. In its scholastic phase Protestant orthodoxy defended its forensic understanding of salvation from any creeping Catholic influence. Lutheran and Reformed confessional statements emphasized double predestination, absolute divine sovereignty, and salvation by grace through faith. Right doctrine sharply limited all claims about the sanctifying work of the Holy Spirit. The Pietist movements in Germany and England were reactions against the spiritual coldness and troubling moral implications of Protestant orthodoxy. The early Pietists (Philipp Jakob Spener, August Hermann Francke, Gerhard Tersteegen) and their famous successors, John Wesley and George Whitfield, did not challenge the classic Protestant preoccupation with individual salvation, but emphasized the themes of holiness, good news, spiritual freedom, and new life in the Spirit. They urged that believers are not merely justified from without, but given a new life of Spirit-filled holiness through their faith in Christ. Eventually the Pietist movement challenged the classic emphasis on predestination and absolute divine sovereignty. If God predestines most people to eternal torment, Wesley declared, God is not loving and merciful. For Wesley that was a nonstarter: "So ill do election and reprobation agree with the truth and sincerity of God! But do they not agree least of all with the scriptural account of his love and goodness: that attribute which God peculiarly claims wherein he glories above all the rest."[1]

The Wesleyans and German Pietists, believing that they recovered the full spiritual heritage of the gospel, regarded themselves as true Evangelicals. But the classic Evangelicals never surrendered or shared the term. In Germany the Pietists were never called *Evangelisch*, but *Pietismus*, followers of "the awakening movement" *(Erweckungsbewegung)*. Only Lutherans were real Evangelicals. In the modern period a third Protestant movement reclaimed the mantle of Evangelical faith, this time in protest against the liberalization of the Protestant churches. The fundamentalist doctrine of "perfect errorlessness" was prefigured in seventeenth-century Protestant orthodoxy, but in its modern context, fundamentalism is a byproduct of modern historical consciousness. Nineteenth-century conservatives confronted the rise of biblical criticism and Darwinian theory. How was the authority of the Bible to be defined and secured against these challenges? The conservatives who came to be called "fundamentalists" replied that biblical authority could not be secured apart from biblical inerrancy. If the Bible contains any errors, it cannot be God's Word; and if it is not God's verbally inspired Word, it cannot be a secure source of religious authority.

That was the foundation on which the doctrines of Christ's incarnation, virgin birth, substitutionary atonement, miracle-working power, and resurrection were said to depend. In 1875 conservative Evangelicals launched the Niagara Bible Conference, an annual summer resort meeting that became the prototype for hundreds of Bible conferences at which Evangelicals defended the fundamentals. By 1878 the Niagara Conference had identified fourteen fundamentals, one of which, dispensational eschatology, was of very recent vintage. Major Evangelical leaders such as Presbyterians Nathaniel West, James Brooks, William J. Erdman, and Henry Parsons and Baptist A. J. Gordon urged that millennialist apocalypticism was as fundamental to Christian orthodoxy as the incarnation of Christ. The Niagara Conference of 1878 made it official, enshrining a sectarian novelty with the authority of orthodoxy, one that plays a significant role in contemporary Evangelicalism.

In the eschatological trade, a millennialist is anyone who fastens on the idea of a utopian kingdom of God on earth, usually lasting one thousand years. The dominant Christian eschatology has been amillennialist. Augustine taught that the kingdom of God is spiritual, not social or political, which convinced Pope Gregory I, most of the papal tradition, Thomas Aquinas, Martin Luther, and John Calvin. Augustine developed his view against the premillennialism of the early church, especially its Greek-speaking Eastern theologians. Premillennialism is the view that Christ will return to earth to establish an earthly kingdom. The Radical Reformation went back to this chiliast view of the kingdom, as did most of the Puritans who settled New England, though neither tradition prescribed a detailed scheme. A third eschatology with some historic standing is postmillennialism, which interprets the kingdom of God as a historical utopia in which the world will be Christianized through evangelism and social transformation. In the postmillennial interpretation the reign of God is realized before Christ returns; thus the return of Christ is postmillennial. Much of the Calvinist tradition has been postmillennialist, notably Jonathan Edwards and Lorraine Boettner, as were John and Charles Wesley, much of the Methodist tradition, and most of the Social Gospel tradition.

The nineteenth-century reactionary movement that, in 1920, acquired the name "fundamentalist" had a powerful conviction of the world's hopelessness. Thus it took the apocalyptic option in eschatology, in novel forms deriving from recent sectarian movements, even though most of the early "fundamentalist" leaders were members of established Protestant denominations. Many groups in the nineteenth century proclaimed that the world was in its last days. History was doomed to destruction. People may be saved in history, but history has no future and is not worth saving. This powerful sense of the futility and darkness of the world fueled the preaching of the Shakers, the Millerites (who believed the world would end in 1844), and John Nelson Darby, who fashioned a detailed apocalyptic scheme that served as the prototype for many successors. Darby taught that at the end of the present age Christians will be raptured out of the world; Jews and all others will endure a seven-year period of Great Tribulation, during which some Jews will be converted to Christ; and Christ will return after the Great Tribulation to rule on earth for one thousand years. Despite Darby's world-weariness, his theology made a spectacular success.

J. N. Darby (1800–1882) was a traveled Irish sectarian and former Anglican priest who preached throughout the U.S. Midwest and Northeast, converting the Plymouth Brethren movement to his spiritual vision. He shared Calvin's belief that God predetermined everything in history; on the other hand, whereas Calvin and Luther experienced the book of Revelation as something alien to the gospel faith, Darby believed that Revelation and Daniel contained the key to history. Darby's intolerant temperament and supreme confidence in God's personal guidance caused him to spurn relations with like-minded Christian groups. These qualities made him a formidable sectarian leader. He taught that God has two plans of salvation—one for Israel and the other for the gentile church—and that the secret "rapture" of the church (a term from the Latin Vulgate Bible's translation of 1 Thessalonians 4:17) would occur in an "any-moment coming." These ideas were expounded in his system of dispensations, which explained the necessity of a Jewish return to Palestine, the hope of raptured deliverance for the faithful remnant that followed Jesus, and the promise of a millennial kingdom based in Jerusalem.[2]

Though Darby insisted on his absolute originality in gleaning the true meaning of scriptural prophecy, his version of premillennialism was a variant of competing schemes. It was distinctive in its doctrine of the "any-moment" secret rapture and its insistence that God has two different plans operating in history. According to the Bible, Darby argued, God has one plan for an earthly people (Israel) and a separate plan for a heavenly people (the church). To read the Bible rightly is to "rightly divide" it between these two programs, interpreting every passage literally in terms of its dispensational context.

Darby's successors debated the precise timing of the rapture and the placement of dispensational lines. After dispensationalism became a defining feature of American fundamentalism, some dispensationalists denied their connection to Darby. All of them, however, stressed what Darby and C. I. Scofield called "rightly dividing the Word of Truth." This scheme rested on Revelation 20 (the only text in Scripture that explicitly mentions a future millennium) and a handful of other texts, especially Daniel 2:1–49, Daniel 9:24–27, and 1 Thessalonians 4:16–17. According to dispensational theology, God tests humanity through a distinct plan of salvation described in the Bible. Each era ends with a catastrophic divine judgment for humanity's failure to meet the ascribed test. The first dispensation ended with the human Fall from sin and expulsion from Eden, the second ended with the Flood, the third with the Tower of Babel, the fourth with the end of the Hebrew exodus from Egypt, the fifth comprised the period of the Law from Exodus 12 to Acts 1 (Pentecost), and the sixth is the age of the church. The seventh dispensation will be the millennial reign of Jesus in Jerusalem.[3]

Dispensationalism turned the Bible into a kind of secret code containing divine messages about the future of the world. It decentered the incarnation, death, and resurrection of Christ by consigning these events to the period of the Law. And it nullified centuries of biblical interpretation. To read the Bible truly was to crack its code, perceiving that a seemingly obscure passage in Daniel 9 actually contains a precise prediction of the end of the fifth dispensation, the inauguration and entire history of the church, and the arrival of the future messianic age. Daniel 9:24–27 refers to a period of seventy weeks that must be completed "to put an end to sin and to atone for iniquity" before the inauguration of the kingdom. Dispensational theology calculates that "seventy weeks" actually means seventy weeks of years (that is, 490 years, or seventy "sevens"). With a bit of strenuous figuring, it holds that the first 483 years of this period (seventy weeks and sixty-two weeks) were taken up by the latter stage of the fifth dispensation, specifically, the period that fell between the rebuilding of Jerusalem described in Ezra and Nehemiah and the death and resurrection of Jesus.

Of course, Jesus did not return seven years after his death to establish his kingdom. Dispensationalism deals with this difficulty by appealing to a "postponement theory" that stops the clock between the sixty-ninth and seventieth "week." A historical interval between the sixty-ninth and seventieth "weeks" not clearly foreseen by the Hebrew prophets begins after the completion of the last 483 years of the fifth dispensation. This interval is the sixth dispensation, which is the entire age of Christianity. The Christian church has no prophecies of its own, but exists in a kind of time warp or "great parenthesis" that interrupts the fulfillment of God's promise to Daniel.

In its strange and novel way, dispensational theology broke from the supersessionism of Catholic and Protestant orthodoxy. It explicitly denied that the Christian covenant displaced or replaced God's covenant with Israel. Evangelicals debated this aspect of Darby's scheme from the beginning of the fundamentalist movement. Even the dispensationalist mainstream of American fundamentalism, however, never really absorbed its challenge to the logic of supersessionism. Dispensational theology may have been mostly about Israel, not Christianity, but the kingdom of Christ still swallowed everything else. God was concerned primarily with the Jews, but for the Jews to be saved, they had to convert to Jesus. Because God worked with only one people at a time, the church had to be removed from the scene before God could resume his dealings with Israel. In dispensationalist teaching, the Great Tribulation was foretold in Daniel 9:24–27, and the proof text for the rapture was Paul's odd remark in 1 Thessalonians 4:16 that living believers in Christ will be caught up in the clouds together with the dead in Christ after Jesus descends from heaven. The church will escape the Great Tribulation by being whisked from the earth, Darby taught, and since it exists in nonhistorical time, the (pretribulational) rapture could occur at any moment. Before the tribulation Christ will come to rescue his saints; after the tribulation he will return with his saints to defeat the Antichrist and establish his millennial kingdom. The beginning of the tribulation marks the resumption of Daniel's seventieth week. Biblical history will resume after certain prophecies from Daniel and Revelation are fulfilled: the appearance of the "anti-Christ," the rise of the nation-uniting Beast foretold in Daniel 2:1–49, the return of the Jews in unbelief to Palestine, the conversion of some Jews, the terrible persecution of converted Jews during the first three and one-half years of the great tribulation, and the triumphant return of Christ to earth foretold in Revelation 19:11–21.[4]

CHRISTIAN RIGHT POLITICS AND THEOLOGY

Tens of millions of American Evangelicals believe that this is what history is about and where it is going. To them, Armageddon is not something to resist, but God's very will and deliverance. Israel matters to God because God works on only one plan of salvation at a time; Israel matters to Christians as the vehicle of their own deliverance from the world. I am not suggesting that dispensationalist teaching is the sole or controlling basis of the Christian Right's hawkish support of Israel. Many Evangelicals are not dispensationalists or even premillennialists. The biblical teaching that God has granted Israel a divine right to rule over historic Palestine is a more unitive and fundamental principle for Evangelicals than any particular eschatology. Many Evangelicals, no differently from liberals like me, have been motivated to support Israel by their perception that Israel and the United States share crucial values and a common spiritual heritage, and, more importantly, that supporting Israel is the least that Christians and all morally decent people can do in response to ongoing centuries of anti-Jewish prejudice, persecution, and oppression. Many Evangelicals also make the geopolitical calculation that supporting Israel is the best way to advance the cause of democratic progress in the Middle East.

But the latter factors taken together do not account for the Christian Right's distinct fixation with Israel and identification with its political right wing. In the liberal Protestant churches we usually try to hold together moral concern for the rights of Israelis and Palestinians, advocating a two-state solution with secure borders hewing not far from the Green Line. In the Christian Right there is very little holding together. Evangelical organizations and publications that rarely speak about other foreign policy issues take a hard line on Israeli/Palestinian matters, routinely echoing the right wing of the Likud Party. Certainly, some of the key Evangelical players in this field do not subscribe to premillennial theology, much less its dispensational version. But some Christian Right leaders are fervently millennialist, and more importantly, a huge popular base within American Evangelicalism takes millennial theology and politics for granted. In much of the Evangelical world, millennial theology is the story behind the other stories about Christianity, America, democracy, and the world's future. It is the key to the Bible and the meaning of all things.

In the late nineteenth century, under the leadership of R. H. Torrey, C. H. Mackintosh, W. E. Blackstone, James H. Brookes, Arno Gaebelein, and especially Dwight Moody, dispensationalist teaching was grafted onto Evangelical orthodoxy. Dispensationalists sharply debated whether the church would be raptured before or after the Great Tribulation, a dispute that led to the demise of the Niagara Conference in 1901. But the pretribulationist view prevailed among fundamentalists, owing partly to the enormous success of the Scofield Reference Bible, first published in 1909, which featured an extensive system of annotations and cross references. To generations of Scofield Bible readers, dispensationalism was literally *in* the Bible. Its orthodoxy was inscribed in the text. Today millennialism has a more powerful following than ever before, as reflected in the incredible *Left Behind* series, which has now sold over 60 million copies.[5]

The sheer size and influence of this phenomenon makes it perilous for Evangelical leaders to say a critical word about it, not to mention politicians courting Evangelical support. In the 1890s Princeton theologian and fundamentalist leader Benjamin B. Warfield tried to stop the millennialist tide. Warfield and his Princeton disciple, J. Gresham Machen, pleaded against fundamentalist otherworldliness, perfectionism, and literalism, urging that the reference to Christ's thousand-year reign in Revelation 20 is a symbol for the peace of eternal life. They also accepted Darwinian evolution. Despite its Bible-thumping, they protested, the fundamentalist movement contributed greatly to the decline of biblical literacy in American churches. Instead of reading scripture inductively in its widest historical and canonical contexts, dispensationalists fixed on a few apocalyptic texts ripped out of context and applied literally to the future. In the name of recovering fundamental full-gospel Christianity, they promoted bad exegesis and displaced the biblical doctrine of salvation with a bizarre schematism only remotely derived from scripture.[6]

A century ago the most respected Evangelical theologians said these things plainly and loudly. Today the most respected and accomplished Evangelical theologians still reject Darby-style exegesis, but you have to be a close observer to know it. From the beginning of the "new Evangelicalism" in the 1940s, when Harold Ockenga, Carl Henry, E. J. Carnell, and Billy Graham vowed to overcome the reactionary reputation and spirit of their tradition, American Evangelical leaders have struggled with their movement's apocalyptic impulse.

Henry and Carnell perceived that "fundamentalist" had become an unredeemable term. They set out to rehabilitate the intellectual foundations of fundamentalist Evangelicalism and make it worthy of respect. On occasion they admonished each other that their movement needed prestige desperately. Theologically they harkened back to a classical Protestant orthodoxy that rejected millennialism and separatist ecclesiology. As Baptists, they looked especially to their Reformed Puritan heritage, but always in a way that interpreted this heritage through the lens of the ongoing fundamentalist battle against modernism. With Ockenga and other founders of Fuller Theological Seminary and the National Association of Evangelicals, they embraced the term "neoevangelicalism"—later shortened to "Evangelicalism"—to mark their claim that something new was happening in conservative American Protestantism. The fundamentalists of the 1930s had retreated to sectarianism after losing the struggle for the historic denominations and seminaries. The new Evangelicals called off the fundamentalist retreat from the world, and built the foundation of a religious empire. There was such a thing as an intellectual version of Evangelical orthodoxy, they insisted. The writings of Henry, Carnell, and Bernard Ramm made a vigorous case for this claim, laying the groundwork for a renewed Protestant conservatism. In 1942 the National Association of Evangelicals (NAE) was founded as an alternative to the Federal Council of Churches. For many years the NAE was comprised mostly of groups far outside the mainstream of American religion. As late as the early 1960s more than two-thirds of its members came from the Assemblies of God, the Church of God (Cleveland), the International Church of the Foursquare Gospel, the Pentecostal Church of God, and the Pentecostal Holiness Church.

Remarkably, this remnant of a defeated theology went on to become America's strongest religious tradition. It capitalized on the revival fame of Billy Graham, the movement building of the NAE, the success of *Christianity Today* magazine, the ability of Evangelicalism to expand beyond its ethnic families of origin, the Evangelistic prowess of Campus Crusade for Christ and InterVarsity Fellowship, the great skill with which Evangelicals developed their own media and music, the seriousness with which Evangelicalism reached out to young people, the development of the megachurch movement, and the decline of the liberal Protestant churches. When Jimmy Carter, in 1976, described himself as "born again," much of the country, especially the media, was incredulous. Carter's staff spoke of the issue ruefully as "the weirdo factor." But later that year *Newsweek* magazine declared that 1976 was "the year of the Evangelical," and sociologically speaking, one might say that every year since has been the "year of the Evangelical." By the mid-1980s the Evangelical subculture had become the Mainline. Today the term "Evangelical" is so widely treasured that it lacks a common point of reference. There is no golden thread that unites the unwieldy profusion of Calvinists, Wesleyans, Pentecostals, fundamentalists, neo-Barthians, nondenominationalists, Emergent Church followers, and others who claim the name. Classical Evangelicalism is different from the Evangelicalism of the Wesleyan Holiness movements; both are considerably different from the antimodernist fundamentalism that still claims a large share of the Evangelical world; and the nondenominational megachurch movement is changing the face of the Evangelical streams that feed into it.

Historically, one of the chief features of fundamentalism was its separatist impulse. The tendency to associate fundamentalism with a sectarian politics and ecclesiology always raised difficult problems for historians who sought to account for the many fundamentalists who never left the historic Mainline denominations. It raised equally perplexing problems for those who tried to explain the existence of fundamentalist currents within conservative denominations such as the Christian Reformed Church, the Wisconsin and Missouri Synod Churches, and the Southern Baptist Convention. Because these churches never drove their fundamentalists into exile, they did not reproduce the exile-and-separation pattern of other fundamentalist groups.

By the mid-1970s, however, even old-style fundamentalists like Jerry Falwell and Cal Thomas had resolved to take back the dominant culture. The ascension of a liberal Evangelical to the White House spurred right-wing Evangelicals to create organizations that opposed Carter, liberalism, and the erosion of Christian America. The prototypes were the National Christian Action Council (1977), Focus on the Family (1977), American Family Association (1977), Christian Voice (1979), Concerned Women for America (1979), Religious Roundtable (1980), and most importantly, the Moral Majority (1979), which propelled thousands of Evangelicals into electoral politics.[7]

The second wave of Christian Right organizing was launched in 1991, with Pat Robertson's founding of the Christian Coalition of America. Robertson had run for president in 1988; in the 1990s his organization, directed by Ralph Reed, became a political juggernaut that played a significant role in winning Republican control of Congress. In 1994 alone the Christian Coalition mailed 30 million postcards opposing President Clinton's health care plan and made more than 20,000 phone calls urging support for the balanced budget amendment. With ample justification the Christian Coalition regularly boasted that it was the most powerful religious organization in American politics and the most powerful grassroots political organization in the nation, period. The group has lost some of its political clout in recent years, following the resignations of Reed and Robertson from leadership positions. Nonetheless, during the 2004 presidential election it distributed 70 million voter guides throughout all fifty states; it boasts over 2 million supporters; and it still claims to be "the largest and most active conservative grassroots political organization in America." The Christian Coalition lobbies Congress and the White House, holds grassroots training schools around the country, distributes legislative scorecards on favored and unfavored politicians, and plays a careful hand with its IRS status. Its legislative agenda is heavy on bills dealing with gay marriage, abortion, the Pledge of Allegiance, and displays of the Ten Commandments, yet its top legislative priority in 2005 was to pass President Bush's Social Security reform with personal accounts; number two was to make permanent Bush's 2001 federal tax cuts. Repeatedly the coalition boasts of its own political might and that of the Christian Right more generally, as on November 3, 2004: "In the election outcome yesterday, Christian Evangelicals made the major difference once again."[8]

After 30 years of politicking the Christian Right is long on household names and political gains and short on policy achievements. Its leading figures include Pat Robertson, Jerry Falwell, Paul Weyrich, Tim LaHaye, Richard Land, James Dobson, Gary Bauer, Charles Stanley, Paige Patterson, Alan Keyes, James Kennedy, and Franklin Graham. Its rather modest list of policy achievements has given rise to in-house debates about its strategy and a host of new organizations including the American Center for Law and Justice (1995, a litigation-oriented spin-off of the Christian Coalition), Focus on the Family Action (2004, Dobson's political and lobbying arm), and the Moral Majority Coalition (2005, Falwell's revival of the Moral Majority). It is remarkable enough that a religious tradition so emphatically concerned with heaven, hell, otherworldly salvation, and the apocalypse should become so deeply politicized. That its political activity should extend into the foreign policy arena is more remarkable still, which confirms the importance of the movement's millennialist background. We used to think that millennialism, at least of the fundamentalist variety, naturally went with sectarianism. Now we have stunning examples of apocalyptic worldliness—premillennialist movements that are deeply involved in electoral politics and foreign policy.

The Christian Right is routinely nationalistic and interventionist in foreign affairs. It supports higher military spending, the invasion of Iraq, and an aggressive view of the U.S. role in the world. Christian Right leaders, like political theorists and pundits of the old right, are often bitterly critical of America's degenerate culture, but unlike the old right they give little sign of worrying about the projection of American culture and capitalism throughout the world. On the politics of Israel the Christian Right opposes the road map process and the goal of a two-state solution. After Bush came out for a Palestinian state in 2001, Christian Right leaders repeated their opposition to it. Christian Coalition president Roberta Combs declared: "You can have a Palestinian state or you can have a Jewish state; you cannot have both." Later she complained: "There's been too much talk of a Palestinian state. This only encourages the terrorists to keep murdering innocent civilians in hopes of forcing Israel to reach a settlement which would imperil its survival."[9]

In his writings and television appearances Robertson contends that the Bible's geography of the Promised Land is normative for Christian theology and U.S. policy in the region. He teaches that the gathering of Jews in modern Israel is a prelude to Christ's second coming at which Jews will be converted to Christianity or condemned to hell. To take a right-Likud line on the settlements and the Palestinians is simply to obey God's Word, taking God's side. Though Robertson has also promulgated lurid conspiracies about the role of unbelieving Jews in forging an evil New World Order, his leadership on Israeli settlements and defense issues has won him a special pass in neocon circles. Norman Podhoretz, while allowing that Robertson holds paranoid, even "demented" views about Jewish bankers, the Trilateral Commission, and the Council on Foreign Relations, indulges his attacks on the evil destructiveness of liberalized Jews. Podhoretz explains that despite the anti-Semitic pedigree of Robertson's conspiracy theorizing, he is an invaluable advocate of a militant Israel. Neither does it matter why Robertson ardently takes this position; what matters is that he does so.[10]

Most Evangelicals are not as deeply politicized as the leadership of the Christian Right, and even Christian Right activists tend to be more militant about abortion politics and the Supreme Court than about foreign policy. Among the many Evangelicals that I met while writing my book on Evangelical theology, very few were passionately invested in the politics of the Middle East. Two-thirds of Israelis support a two-state solution with secure borders and a clear national identity. In my experience of American Evangelicals, most of them do not presume that they know better than Israelis what is good for Israel or what God's position is on the matter. But the leading Christian Right organizations take a hard line on both aspects of the matter, causing them to swing back and forth over President Bush's policy toward Israel.

When Bush shunned Yasir Arafat, demanded new Palestinian leaders, gave mere lip service to the road map, and supported Sharon's invasion of the West Bank, the Christian Right cheered him on. When Bush came out for a Palestinian state, got behind the road map, criticized the wayward boundary of the Wall, and famously told Sharon, seven days after he invaded the West Bank, that "enough is enough," the Christian Right fumed in disappointment, like the neocons. Christian Right leaders have campaigned against the road map and a Palestinian state, supported moving the Israeli capital to Jerusalem, called for expanded settlements, and opposed Sharon's judgment that it was not viable for 8,000 Jews to continue living in one-third of the Gaza Strip, surrounded by 1.3 million Palestinians.

Because most American Evangelicals are not as dogmatic about Israeli politics as their leaders, Bush has not lost Evangelical support for his endorsement of a two-state settlement. More broadly, Evangelicals rightly perceive that Bush's piety, though skillfully politicized, is also sincere on a personal level. For this reason the Evangelical community is deeply bonded to Bush, who convincingly speaks its language. Until his conversion to a Pietist form of Evangelicalism Bush was hurtling straight toward alcoholism, divorce, further business failure, and a wasted life. He owes his personal and political success to his religious conversion, and he knows it. He also knows how to court the Evangelical vote—a skill he acquired during his father's presidency—and he realizes that the Evangelical community is broader and more forgiving than its activist organizations.

The Harriet Miers fiasco demonstrated the political power of the Christian Right and Bush's dependence on it. The Evangelical vote is not necessarily Republican; Clinton, it is hard to remember, won the Evangelical vote twice. But the Christian Right got its second wind by opposing Clinton, and Bush's political viability rests on his good relations with it.

PROGRESSIVE EVANGELICALISM

Having stressed that Evangelicalism is a broader phenomenon than the Christian Right, I want to close by stressing that it has a significant left wing. There is a current Evangelical community that claims its kinship with the antislavery, feminist, temperance, and social gospel Evangelicalisms of the nineteenth century and that incorporates contemporary progressive concerns. Jim Wallis and *Sojourners* magazine, Tony Campolo, and Eugene Rivers speak for this brand of Evangelicalism in the public square. Leading theologians and ethicists in the progressive camp include Ronald Sider, Glen Stassen, Nicholas Wolterstorff, Donald Dayton, Charles Kraft, William Dyrness, and the late Stanley Grenz. President Bush got a taste of progressive Evangelicalism last spring when he spoke at Calvin College's commencement in Grand Rapids, Michigan, only to learn that half the faculty was vocally opposed to his politics and theology, especially his foreign policy. Ethically and politically, the progressive Evangelicals protest that the radical, prophetic, egalitarian spirit of the gospel message, and of early American Evangelicalism, was obliterated by the first generation of fundamentalists. A great American tradition of emancipatory social Christianity was betrayed by its reactionary successors.[11]

The first glimmerings of Evangelical protest against this arrangement arose in the early 1970s, with the coming of age of the 1960s generation. To young Evangelicals like Jim Wallis, Donald Dayton, and John Alexander, who supported the civil rights movement and opposed America's war in Vietnam, the monolithic political conservatism of the Evangelical establishment was deeply disturbing. They argued that Evangelical theology should lead to forms of political engagement that oppose war and promote equality. Wallis' magazine the *Post-American* (later *Sojourners*) pressed hard on this theme and found a like-minded audience. Antipoverty activist Ron Sider became a leading Evangelical voice for economic justice and antimilitarism; Virginia Ramey Mollencott and Nancy Hardesty tried to build a feminist constituency. In its early years, the *Post-American* featured very conservative theological articles next to articles that stridently condemned American militarism and social injustice. For several years the magazine made the case for Christian anarcho-pacifism in nearly every issue while carefully avoiding in-house debates over biblical inerrancy.[12]

The success of *Sojourners*, in particular, gave the progressive stream a footing and voice in the Evangelical world. Thousands of Evangelicals found the magazine's political radicalism more compatible with the gospel ethic than the stodgy conservatism of the Evangelical establishment. Many of them were galled by the treatment that *Christianity Today* gave to the civil rights movement. Under Carl Henry's leadership, the magazine defended "voluntary segregation," claimed that civil rights integrationism was communist, and condemned Martin Luther King, Jr.'s campaigns of civil disobedience. *Christianity Today* denounced the 1963 March on Washington as a "mob spectacle." It condemned interracial marriage, and when James Meredith sought to enter the University of Mississippi as a student, *Christianity Today* applauded the state of Mississippi for refusing to admit him. The magazine also plugged hard for the Vietnam War, rebuking war protestors and calling for harsh sanctions against draft resisters.[13]

The Evangelical establishment's defense of segregation and military intervention drove Dayton, Evangelical historian David Moberg, and others to figure out what had gone wrong. The greatest nineteenth-century revivalist, Charles Finney, was a fervent abolitionist and anti-militarist; the holiness movements were the first to ordain women to the preaching ministry; William Jennings Bryan made his early fame as a fiery populist. Why was modern Evangelicalism so repressive by comparison?

How did it happen that Evangelical leaders could be counted on to defend some of the worst aspects of American society? Why was it impossible to criticize the Vietnam War at any Evangelical college or seminary without being condemned as a communist? Moberg judged that Evangelicals became politically conservative as soon as they had privileges to defend. Dayton stressed the Evangelical swing from post-millennialism to dispensationalism, and the difficulty of sustaining radical movements of any kind.[14]

Finney-style revivalism thrived on spiritual intensity and moral fervor, but even the Wesleyan movements cooled over time. Some of them formed new sects and others were absorbed by the Mainline denominations, but in both cases, the children of the revivalists were less inclined than their parents to prize their alienation from the dominant culture. They did not regard strangeness or countercultural purity as signs of their salvation, but wanted to belong to America. The sheer horror of the Civil War dispelled the optimism and hope that had fueled much of Oberlin-style revivalism. Once slavery was abolished, the moral issues that got politicized were more personal. Evangelicals devoted themselves to temperance and Godly living. Moreover, the movement's theological choices had social consequences. Dispensationalism was the antithesis of the social gospel. Armed with Darby's theology, fundamentalists denied that the church had a mission to promote social justice. This contention strengthened the alliance be-

tween popular fundamentalism and the guardians of Princeton orthodoxy, who had opposed abolition, racial integration, and feminism in
the first place. Three-quarters of a century later, the new progressives
started over by going back to an egalitarian politics.

But Evangelicalism is a deeply theological tradition, and eventually the new progressives began to produce not merely a different kind
of politics, but also a different style of Evangelical theology, one that
struggled with the problems of hermeneutics and cultural pluralism.
Under the influence of cultural and hermeneutical theory, social criticism, postmodernism, post liberal theology, and the experiences of
missionaries, Evangelicals developed interactionist models that construed biblical meaning as a circular process of narrative-framed understanding. Traditional Evangelicalism spurned hermeneutics on the
ground that criticism impugns the authority of the text, replacing the
Bible's authority with that of the Bible scholar. It taught that the best
interpretations take nothing from the interpreter's situation into the
interpretive process. Progressive Evangelicals such as Charles Kraft,
Stanley Grenz, and William Dyrness replied that this position disas-
trously sets theology against the social sciences, ignoring the social
character of understanding.

We always come to the text from where we are. We cannot participate in a discussion or even a process of indoctrination that excludes
our embodiment and situation. Scriptural meaning must be discerned
by beginning with one's embodied communal life in the world, not
with a doctrine of Scripture. The progressives urged that a priori bibli-
cism begs the questions of interpretation and context. Communicat-
ing the Word is never a mere process of translation, but rather a two-
way conversation that draws upon and encodes distinctive cultural
practices and meanings. It is harmful to all parties, including Christianity, to impose a version of North American religious culture on the
rest of the world in the name of a cross-cultural revelation. If one does
not interrogate the cultural assumptions, favorite themes, and unac-
knowledged worldviews that one brings to the text, one will surely
read them into it.[15]

For progressive Evangelicals, the scriptural text becomes authoritative only when its creative and redemptive power is manifest
through the lives of faithful communities. The point is to recover the
biblical sense of truth as revelatory narrative. The truth of gospel
faith is primarily story truth. To take it seriously is to give up the
traditional exaltation of the single interpretive voice. Stories are dynamic, participatory and multivalent; they invite interpretation
from many angles. A theology that takes the story form of scriptural

truth seriously must call upon a choir of interpreters to capture the interplay of symbolic riches in Scripture. It is not new to Christianity to say that a religious tradition is true primarily as true story; neither is it new to conceive religious truth as polyphonic and multivalent. But these are new themes for Evangelicalism. At bottom the progressives are challenging their tradition to stop being threatened by the inexhaustible interplay of meaning that religious traditions contain. The Word is rich and complex because the story at its center bears these attributes inexhaustibly.

To the extent that the progressives have made inroads within Evangelicalism, the confrontational spirit of Evangelical fundamentalism is giving way to the discourse of a generous orthodoxy, one that lives more peaceably and graciously within a religiously plural world. It speaks to the sensibility of young Evangelicals who yearn for gospel-centered teaching that does not violate their own experience of living in a pluralistic, multicultural, postmodern society. Contemporary Evangelicals have reason to say, "it started with Billy Graham." Billy Graham conducted racially integrated crusades throughout the South in the 1950s, he sought to broaden the ecumenical common ground within Evangelicalism, and he had respectful relationships with Catholics and Jews, all of which made him an object of loathing to fundamentalist leaders like John R. Rice. At his 1957 crusade in New York, Graham introduced Martin Luther King, Jr. as the leader of a great and necessary social revolution. Graham was a close friend of Rabbi Marc Tanenbaum, and in 1977 he won the American Jewish Committee's National Interreligious Award for his efforts to strengthen mutual respect between Evangelicals and Jews. In later life he surprised interviewers by remarking that he had long regarded himself as a theological conservative and social liberal.[16]

But Graham's movement had less of a social conscience than he; his own was repeatedly compromised by his intimate access to power; and today much of the Evangelical movement is stridently dogmatic, mean-spirited, and virtually fundamentalist. Former Southern Baptist Convention president Bailey Smith saw nothing wrong with proclaiming that God does not hear the prayers of a Jew. How could it be otherwise if Jews are cut off from God's saving grace? Billy Graham's son, Franklin Graham, has done important work in the field of emergency relief, directing a charitable enterprise named Samaritan's Purse that works in desperately impoverished areas, and he has a more conversational preaching style than his father. But the content of his preaching is fundamentalist hellfire evangelism: Jesus is the only way to salvation; every knee shall bow; most knees will bow in

Hell, where it will be too late. Franklin Graham gives short shrift to the suggestion that God may embrace Jews or anyone else on any other terms, and he is colorfully direct in correcting President Bush about Islam. Islamic terrorism is not a perversion of Islam, he insists; it is the essence of Islam.[17]

It is a curious fact that the Christian Right, holding such views and commanding extraordinary power in the Republican Party, has been content thus far to be represented by neoconservatives in the foreign policy field. Despite its immense political power, the Christian Right is not a major player in the making of Republican foreign policy. For the most part it supports neoconservative positions and defers to neocon policymakers in this area. Christian Right leaders endorse the aggressive American nationalism and neo-imperialism that are trademarks of the neoconservative movement; they take essentially the same policy line toward Israel as the neocons; and each group trades on the other's strength. The Christian Right has a large popular base, but lacks a foreign policy brain trust. Neoconservatism has no popular base, but its brain trust is famously productive and influential.

I believe that this strategic alliance in the foreign policy area is likely to erode. The Christian Right as a whole has been much stronger on lobbying, grassroots electoral politics, and movement politics than on policy scholarship, and the latter shortcoming is especially acute in the foreign policy area. Sooner or later it is bound to develop its own foreign policy experts, journals, and think tanks, seeking to wield its political power directly. At its 2004 convention, the NAE featured a large banner proclaiming: "What can Evangelicals get if they mobilize? Anything they want." That spirit is likely to prevail in the foreign policy field, and more broadly, the field of policy scholarship.

But American Evangelicalism is a more diverse and contested ground than that of its politicized, Christian Right sector. To the extent that the Christian Right seeks to capitalize on its wider base, it must reckon with Evangelical viewpoints at the center and moderate left of American politics, where majorities of American Jews, Catholics, and Mainline Protestants already live.

A bit of evidence for this view can be found in the only movement reader yet published by Evangelicals on public policy, *Toward an Evangelical Public Policy: Political Strategies for the Health of the Nation* (2005), which grew out of discussions in the NAE. Edited by Ronald Sider (president of Evangelicals for Social Action) and the late Diane Knippers (president of the neoconservative Institute for Religion and Democracy), the book contains a foreword by NAE president Ted Haggard, who laments the defeat of the Federal Marriage Amendment in

Congress and warns of the "holistic extrication of the Judeo-Christian value system from American public policy." The editors acknowledge at the outset, however, that Evangelicals have not made an impressive case for their approach to politics. Despite the recent success of the Evangelical movement in gaining political power, they observe, it has produced nothing that compares to Catholic or liberal Protestant scholarship on social policy. Evangelicals routinely make pronouncements about policy issues without bothering to develop a theoretical or empirical base. Their writing and activism often amount to "ready, fire, aim," lacking any basis in a coherent political philosophy or structure of evidence.[18]

Toward an Evangelical Public Policy does not present a coherent vision, either; it is an essay collection that carefully balances, and sometimes integrates, the conservative and progressive streams of Evangelicalism. David P. Gushee and Dennis P. Hollinger, writing on ethical method, describe five types of Evangelical ethics: Mainstream (Carl Henry), Reformed (Richard Mouw), Anabaptist (John Howard Yoder), Wesleyan (Stephen Mott), and Anglican (Oliver O'Donovan). The authors observe that these perspectives are Evangelical because they root ethical reflection and practice in a personal relationship with Christ, treat the entire canonical Bible as the eternal Word of God, and accept the divine authority of the Bible's specific moral commands. Tom Minnery and Glenn T. Stanton, writing on family integrity, uphold the norm of exclusive heterosexual marriage while disclaiming any interest in being traditional or progressive. The book's chapter on war and peacemaking, authored by Glen Stassen, urges Christians to focus on a different question than the one addressed by pacifist and just-war theorists. Instead of focusing on whether it is right or wrong to make war, Stassen's "just peacemaking" approach develops effective ways to prevent terrorism and war. It urges pacifists to concentrate on actually *making* peace and just warriors to further develop the principles of last resort and just intention. Just peacemaking supports nonviolent direct action, takes independent initiatives to reduce threats, acknowledges personal and collective responsibility for violence and injustice, promotes democracy, human rights, and religious liberty, fosters just and sustainable economic development, builds cooperative forces in the international system, strengthens the United Nations and other multilateral institutions, advocates reductions in offensive weapons, and encourages grassroots peacemaking efforts. This approach is not superior to pacifist and just-war theory, Stassen acknowledges, and it is not a substitute for addressing the question of the morality of war. It is simply that which all Christians should pursue whether they support pacifism or just war.[19]

Stassen appropriately emphasizes the mainstream status of just peacemaking theory, which is advocated by Christian ethicists across the spectrum of theologies, especially liberal Protestants and Catholics active in the Society of Christian Ethics. There is something a bit strange, however, about presenting this perspective as a representative Evangelical position. Stassen's emphasis on multilateralism, international cooperation, disarmament, social justice, and resistance to war is very far removed from the policy platforms advocated by the Christian Right within and outside the Republican Party. It contradicts the positions persistently taken by Christian Right leaders and preached from many Evangelical pulpits. Yet it is also undeniably rooted in an Evangelical understanding of the gospel message and formulated by an ethicist from a major Evangelical seminary (Fuller Theological Seminary). The very willingness of an NAE group to be associated with Stassen's perspective, and the failure of its opponents to prevent him from representing Evangelicalism in this showcase forum, show the internal difficulties that Evangelicals are likely to face when they seriously enter the foreign policy institute business. Christian Rightism is an ideology, like neoconservatism; but the National Association of Evangelicals cannot be true to its name without representing social and political possibilities more diverse than the Christian Right.

Having devoted this much effort to understanding and analyzing a theological tradition not my own, I want to end with a personal word that is characteristic of my religious perspective, but not exclusive to it. We need new forms of community that arise out of but transcend religious affiliation, culture, and nation. All of our religious traditions have propensities for dogmatism and prejudice that must be uprooted. If we fail to interrogate the violence that is in all our religious traditions, religion will remain part of the problem. If those of us who are Caucasian fail to interrogate whiteness and its privileges, we will resist any recognition of our own racism. If those of us who are male fail to interrogate our complicity in sexism, we will perpetuate it. If those of us who are Christian fail to repudiate anti-Semitism and Christian supercessionism, we will perpetuate the evils that come with them. If those of us who are heterosexual fail to stand up for the rights of gays and lesbians, we will be oppressors. If those of us who are middle class guard our class privileges, we will perpetuate injustice. If we swear our highest loyalty to our nation, we will share in the guilt of our nation's international bullying. That we need a wider community of the divine good is certain.

NOTES

1. Phillip Jacob Spener, *Pia Desideria, or Heartfelt Desire for a God-Pleasing Reform of the True Evangelical Church, Together with Several Simple Christian Proposals Looking Toward this End* (1675), trans. Theodore G. Tappert (Philadelphia: Fortress Press, 1964); *Pietists: Selected Writings*, ed. Peter C. Erb (New York: Paulist Press, 1983); John Wesley, "Predestination Calmly Considered," *John Wesley*, ed. Albert C. Outler (New York: Oxford University Press, 1964), quote 445. This chapter adapts material from Gary Dorrien, The Remaking of Evangelical Theology (Louisville: Westminster John Knox Press, 1998).

2. J. N. Darby, *The Collected Writings of J. N. Darby*, ed. William Kelly, Doctrinal No. 1, vol. 3 (Sunbury, PA: Believers Bookshelf, Reprint 1971), 1–43; Ernest R. Sandeen, *The Roots of Fundamentalism: British and American Millenarianism 1800–1930* (Chicago: University of Chicago Press, 1970); George M. Marsden, "Fundamentalism as an American Phenomenon," *Reckoning with the Past: Historical Essays on American Evangelicalism from the Institute for the Study of American Evangelicals*, ed. D. G. Hart (Grand Rapids, MI: Baker Book House, 1995), 303–21; Nathan O. Hatch, "Millennialism and Popular Religion in the Early Republic," in Leonard I. Sweet, ed., *The Evangelical Tradition in America* (Macon, GA: Mercer University Press, 1984), 112–14; C. Norman Kraus, *Dispensationalism in America: Its Rise and Development* (Richmond, VA: John Knox Press, 1958). On the Millerites, from whom the Seventh Day Adventist movement later evolved, see Ruth A. Doan, *The Miller Heresy, Millennialism, and American Culture* (Philadelphia: Temple University Press, 1987); and Jonathan Butler, "The Making of a New Order: Millerism and the Origins of Seventh-Day Adventism," in Ronald Numbers and Jonathan Butler, eds., *The Disappointed: Millerism and Millenarianism in the Nineteenth Century* (Bloomington, IN: Indiana University Press, 1987), 189–208.

3. C. I. Scofield, *Rightly Dividing the Word of Truth* (Westwood, NJ: Revell, 1896), 3; for Darby's discussion of the pretribulation rapture, see Darby, *The Collected Writings of J. N. Darby*, Prophetic No. 4, Vol. 11 (Winschoten, Netherlands: H. L. Heijkoop), 110–67. For a classic exposition of this eschatology, see Nathaniel West, *The Thousand Year Reign of Christ* (Grand Rapids, MI: Kregel Publications, 1993, 1st ed. 1899).

4. Darby, *The Collected Writings of J. N. Darby*, Prophetic No. 1, Vol. 2 (Winschoten, Netherlands: H. L. Heijkoop), 278–383. For discussions of the counting of the seventy weeks, see Timothy P. Weber, *Living in the Shadows of the Second Coming: American Premillenialism*, 18–19, 247–48; and Weber, "Premillenialism and the Branches of Evangelicalism," in Donald W. Dayton and Robert K. Johnston, eds., *The Variety of American Evangelicalism* (Downers Grove, IL: InterVarsity Press, 1991), 9–11. For the most popular early formulation of dis-

pensational theology, see William E. Blackstone, *Jesus Is Coming* (New York: Revell, 1908). See also James H. Brookes, *Israel and the Church* (St. Louis: Gospel Book and Tract Depository, n.d.); Samuel H. Kellogg, "Is the Advent Pre-Millennial?," *Presbyterian Review* 3 (1882), 475–502; Kellogg, "Premillennialism: Its Relation to Doctrine and Practice," *Bibliotheca Sacra* 45 (1888), 234–74. On the postponement theory, see C. H. Mackintosh, *Papers on the Lord's Coming* (Chicago: Bible Institute Colportage Association, n.d.), 101–102.

5. For later elaborations of dispensational theology, see Lewis Sperry Chafer, *Dispensationalism* (Dallas: Dallas Theological Seminary Press, 1936); Henry C. Thiessen, *Introductory Lectures in Systematic Theology* (Grand Rapids, MI: Wm. B. Eerdmans Publishing Company, 1949); John Walvoord, *The Rapture Question* (Grand Rapids, MI: Zondervan Publishing House, 1979); Charles F. Baker, *A Dispensational Theology* (Grand Rapids, MI: Grace Bible College Publications, 1971). One of the bestselling books of all time is a dispensationalist primer, Hal Lindsey's *The Late Great Planet Earth* (New York: Bantam Books, 1973).

6. The number one thousand represents absolute perfection and completeness in biblical symbolism, Warfield observed: "When the saints are said to live and reign with Christ a thousand years the idea intended is that of inconceivable exaltation, security and blessedness—a completeness of exaltation, security and blessedness beyond expression by ordinary language." Benjamin B. Warfield, *Biblical Doctrines* (Edinburgh: Banner of Truth Trust, 1988), 643–64, quote 655.

7. See Allen D. Hertzke, *Representing God in Washington* (Knoxville: University of Tennessee Press, 1988); Matthew C. Moen, *The Christian Right and Congress* (Tuscaloosa: University of Alabama Press, 1989); William Martin, *With God on Our Side: The Rise of the Religious Right in America* (New York: Broadway Books, 1996); John C. Green, Mark J. Rozell, and Clyde Wilcox, *The Christian Right in America* (Washington, DC: Georgetown University Press, 2003).

8. Website Homepage, Christian Coalition of America, "America's Leading Grassroots Organization Defending Our Godly Heritage: About Us," www.cc.org/about.cfm, accessed Sept. 27, 2005; Christian Coalition of America, "Our Legislative Agenda," www.cc.org/issues.cfm, accessed Sept. 27, 2005; Christian Coalition of America, "Christian Coalition Says 'Christian Evangelicals Made the Major Difference in the 2004 Presidential Election,'" Press release Nov. 3, 2004, www.cc.org/content.cfm, accessed Sept. 27, 2005.

9. Christian Coalition of America, "Christian Coalition of America Opposes Creation of a Palestinian State," press release June 18, 2002, www.cc.org/content.cfm, accessed Sept. 27, 2005; Christian Coalition of America, "Christian Coalition Commends Rumsfeld for Defense of Israel," press release Aug. 7, 2002, www.cc.org/content.cfm, accessed Sept. 27, 2005.

10. Pat Robertson, *The New World Order* (Dallas: Word, 1991); Norman Podhoretz, "In the Matter of Pat Robertson," *Commentary* 100 (August 1995), 27–32; Podhoretz, "The Christian Right and Its Demonizers," *National Review* 52 (Apr. 3, 2000), 30–32.

11. Jim Wallis, *God's Politics: Why the Right Gets It Wrong and the Left Doesn't Get It* (New York: HarperCollins Publishers, 2005).

12. Ronald J. Sider, *Rich Christians in an Age of Hunger* (Downers Grove, IL: InterVarsity Press, 1977, rev. ed. 1984); Sider, "An Evangelical Theology of Liberation," in Richard John Neuhaus and Michael Cromartie, eds., *Piety and Politics: Evangelicals and Fundamentalists Confront the World* (Washington, DC: Ethics and Public Policy Center, 1987), 145–60; Virginia Ramey Mollenkott, *Women, Men and the Bible* (Nashville: Abingdon Press, 1977); Mollenkott, "Evangelicalism: A Feminist Perspective," *Union Seminary Quarterly Review* Vol. 32 (Winter 1977), 95–103; Nancy Hardesty, *Women Called to Witness: Evangelical Feminism in the Nineteenth Century* (Nashville: Abingdon Press, 1984); Letha Scanzoni and Nancy Hardesty, *All We're Meant to Be* (Waco, TX: Word Books, 1974).

13. John Oliver, "A Failure of Evangelical Conscience," *The Post-American* (May 1975), 26–30; Donald W. Dayton, *Discovering an Evangelical Heritage* (New York: Harper & Row, 1976), 2–3.

14. John Oliver, "A Failure of Evangelical Conscience," *The Post-American* (May 1975), 26–30; Donald W. Dayton, *Discovering an Evangelical Heritage* (New York: Harper & Row, 1976), 2–3.

15. Charles Kraft, *Christianity in Culture: A Study in Dynamic Biblical Theologizing in Cross-Cultural Perspective* (Maryknoll, NY: Orbis Books, 1979); Stanley Grenz, *Revisioning Evangelical Theology: A Fresh Agenda for the 21st Century* (Downers Grove, IL: InterVarsity Press, 1993); William A. Dyrness, "How Does the Bible Function in the Christian Life?" in *The Use of the Bible in Theology: Evangelical Options*, ed. Robert K. Johnston (Atlanta: John Knox Press, 1985), 159–74.

16. See David Rausch, "Chosen People: Christian Views of Judaism Are Changing," *Christianity Today* (Oct. 7, 1988); CT News, *Christianity Today* (Nov. 18, 1977), 57; Peter J. Boyer, "The Big Tent: Billy Graham, Franklin Graham, and the Transformation of American Evangelicalism," *New Yorker* (Aug. 22, 2005), 42–55.

17. Boyer, "The Big Tent: Billy Graham, Franklin Graham, and the Transformation of American Evangelicalism," 42–55.

18. *Toward an Evangelical Public Policy: Political Strategies for the Health of the Nation*, eds. Ronald J. Sider and Diane Knippers (Grand Rapids, MI: Baker Books, 2005), Haggard quote, 6; editors' quote, 9.

19. David P. Gushee and Dennis P. Hollinger, "Toward an Evangelical Ethical Methodology," *Toward an Evangelical Public Policy: Political Strategies for the Health of the Nation*, 117–39; Tom Minnery and Glenn T. Stanton, "Family Integrity," ibid., 245–64; Glen T. Stassen, "The Ethics of War and Peacemaking," ibid., 284–306.

8

Evangelicals and Israel

Gerald R. McDermott

INTRODUCTION

For understandable reasons, Jews have been wary of Evangelicals for a long time. Recently the world's most famous Evangelical, Billy Graham, was revealed to have told Richard Nixon in 1972 that Jews had a "stranglehold" on the American media and that unless that were broken, "this country's going down the drain."[1] This only seemed to confirm the worst fears of many Jews: that even the pro-Zionist sentiments of Evangelicals masked inner hostility. Jews also remember the recent Southern Baptist Evangelistic campaign targeting Jews, which suggested to some Jews that they would not be fully accepted unless they converted to Evangelical Christianity. As Yaakov Ariel, another contributor to this volume, has put it, while Evangelical and fundamentalist missionaries to Jews have shown much goodwill and appreciation for Jews and their cultural heritage, they have not believed that the Jewish religion could "provide its adherents with spiritual comfort, moral guidelines, and, most important of all, salvation."[2]

Most Jews, then, are not surprised to learn that Evangelicals think Judaism is only a stepping stone to something else. But they may be surprised to discover the role Evangelicals have played in the history of modern Israel. Consider the following vignettes:

Evangelical William Hechler was Theodor Herzl's "first . . . most constant and most indefatigable . . . follower."[3] It was Hechler who helped open doors for Herzl to Europe's palaces and corporate boardrooms, and Hechler who helped Herzl formulate his vision for a Jewish state. In the decade before his 1931 death Hechler repeatedly warned his Jewish friends of an impending massacre of Jews in Europe that would make the Crusades and Spanish Inquisition look like "child's play."[4] Hechler's warnings were dismissed by all who heard them.

President Harry Truman, an active Baptist who had a conservative approach to the Bible and its prophecy about Israel, defied the State Department and nearly all his advisors both when he supported the American-led United Nations resolution to establish the State of Israel in 1948, and when he declared American recognition of the fledgling state. When he was introduced at the Jewish Theological Seminary as "the man who helped create the State of Israel," Truman protested, "What do you mean 'helped to create'?! I am Cyrus! I am Cyrus!"[5]

Jimmy Carter, who campaigned for the American presidency as a self-declared Evangelical, was the architect of the 1978 Camp David peace agreement between Egypt and Israel.

When Benjamin Netanyahu came to Washington in January 1998 to discuss Israel's stalled withdrawal from parts of the West Bank under the Oslo Accords, he was feted at a rally organized by Voices United for Israel, an organization of conservative Evangelical and fundamentalist Christians and Jews. His advisor Bar-Illan told journalist Gershom Gorenberg that "the applause Netanyahu received at the Washington rally, and when he spoke to the [Evangelical] Christian Embassy's Tabernacles gatherings, exceeded any reception he got from his own Likud Party."[6]

On April 15, 2002, a major pro-Israel rally in Washington, DC featured Janet Parshall, a prominent Evangelical talk-show host. That same month Evangelical leader Gary Bauer defended Israel against Palestinian spokesmen in several TV debates. Two Republican lawmakers linked to conservative Christians, Kentucky Senator Mitch McConnell and Texas Rep. Dick Armey, collaborated with Jewish Democratic colleagues on several congressional resolutions supporting Israel and castigating Yasir Arafat. In May 2002 seven prominent conservative Christians, among them leaders of the Southern Baptist Convention and the National Association of Evangelicals, implored President Bush to "vigorously" condemn anti-Semitism. They said this was "keeping faith with our own virtues."[7]

This chapter is divided into four sections. First, I will define what I mean by "Evangelical," and distinguish that movement from "fundamentalism." Second, I will explore the history of Evangelicals' relationship to Zionism and the modern State of Israel. Then I examine how Evangelicals have approached the question of land theologically. In the conclusion, I reflect briefly on what all this suggests for Evangelicals and Jews as they think about the modern Jewish state.

WHAT IS AN EVANGELICAL?

The word "Evangelical" is derived from the Greek noun *Euangelion*, which means "glad tidings," "good news," or "gospel," the last of which goes back to an Old English word for "God talk."[8] Three times the New Testament says that someone who proclaims the gospel of Christ dying for our sins is an *Euangelistes* (Evangelist).[9] There are signs of what could be called an Evangelical spirit[10] throughout church history, from the early church and its fathers, through Augustine, Ambrose, Bernard of Clairvaux, Thomas Aquinas, and Pascal, to the Reformation precursors Wycliffe, Hus, and Savonarola. But the word was first used of Catholic writers who, early in the sixteenth century, tried to revert to more biblical beliefs and practices than were current in the late medieval church. Then at the Reformation the name was given to Lutherans who focused on the doctrine of justification by grace through faith and sought to renew the church based on what they found in Scripture.[11]

The more recent roots of today's movement lie in the trans-Atlantic revivals of the 1730s and 1740s, led by Jonathan Edwards, John Wesley, and George Whitefield, who highlighted the authority of Scripture, the work of Christ in salvation, and the New Birth. This movement was shaped by the Puritan legacy of preaching and conversion, but stressed more emphatically the sense of assurance of salvation. It was also molded in part by Pietism, which emphasized warmth of feeling, sometimes at the expense of doctrine, and by Enlightenment modes of thinking, which appealed to the authority of John Locke and used his method of testing opinions by experience.

These Enlightenment influences were strengthened during the high tide of common sense philosophy in the nineteenth century, which promised the unerring value of intuition. While Edwards had insisted that fallen reason can never know the majesty of God, Charles Hodge suggested that to know the words of Scripture was to know the realities to which the words pointed.[12] In this century Carl Henry put more emphasis on intellectual principles one can derive from Scripture than on the biblical narratives, a pattern which Hans Frei has identified as characteristic of the Enlightenment mentality.[13]

Today's Evangelicalism emerged as a self-conscious reaction against fundamentalism, which began shortly after 1910 as a series of pamphlets making reasoned arguments against Protestant liberalism but then degenerated into a reactionary "oppositionalism" which lost its link with the historic creeds of the church and tended to ignore the social demands of the gospel. As one scholar has described it, it was "too otherworldly, anti-intellectual," legalistic, moralistic, and anti-ecumenical.[14]

The deliberate use of the term "Evangelical" in this century dates to the formation of the National Association of Evangelicals in 1942, which was a careful attempt to distinguish Evangelicalism from fundamentalism. In contrast to the fundamentalist separation from modern culture, the "new Evangelicals" (led by E. J. Carnell, Harold Ockenga, Carl Henry, and Billy Graham) were committed to engaging with culture in an attempt to transform it through the gospel.[15]

In the half century since, Evangelicals have become prominent players on the American landscape.[16] They have gained political clout and numerical strength. Recent studies suggest that "Evangelicals now constitute the largest and most active component of religious life in America." A 1992 survey identified 25.7 percent of the population as "white Evangelicals" and another 7.8 percent as "black Protestants," most of whom could be classified as Evangelicals. More recent estimates put the number of Evangelicals somewhere between 40 and 75 million Americans.[17] Evangelical theology has matured at the same time that many Evangelicals have concentrated on peripheral matters (such as the "rapture" and other questionable eschatological details) and equated the logical conclusions of dogma with dogma itself (particular formulations of biblical inerrancy, double predestination, the second blessing, the millennium).

Although Karl Barth is not an Evangelical in the American or British sense of the word, his definition of the word aptly summarizes what I consider to be the best work in Evangelical theology today: "*Evangelical* means informed by the gospel of Jesus Christ, as heard afresh in the sixteenth-century Reformation by a direct return to Holy Scripture."[18] Many scholars have attempted to delineate in more detail what Evangelical theology is about, but Alister McGrath's six "fundamental convictions" seem to capture the most important distinctives:

1. The majesty of Jesus Christ, both as incarnate God and Lord and as Savior of sinful humanity;
2. The lordship of the Holy Spirit, Who is necessary for the application of the presence and work of Christ;
3. The supreme authority of Scripture, recognizing that the language of Scripture is culturally conditioned but that through it God has nevertheless conveyed the eternal, unconditioned Word. Scripture is to be interpreted with the help of reason and the best tools of scholarship, with attention to differing genres;
4. The need for personal conversion. This is not necessarily an emotional experience but at least involves personal repentance

and trust in the person and work of Christ, not simply intellectual adherence to doctrine;

5. Commitment to evangelism and missions;
6. The importance of religious community for spiritual nourish-
   ment, fellowship, and growth.[19]

Every one of the above six distinctives is shared by most other
Christians. What makes this list Evangelical, however, is the degree of
emphasis which Evangelicals place on the six marks, and the forms
which they take. For example, all Christians say evangelism is important at one level or another, but not all define the Evangelistic message
in the Christocentric terms that Evangelicals do. Some regard social
service as evangelism, and others do not consider conversion to faith
in Christ to be necessary. Nor do all regard evangelism with the same
urgency. When Billy Graham conducted his first crusade in New York
City, some Protestant Mainline leaders ridiculed his efforts—not only
because he did not emphasize structural social reform, but also because they regarded personal evangelism as theologically wrong-
headed.[20] Now some of those same churches speak of personal evangelism as essential to the growth of the church in the world, but they
send out fewer missionaries and do less to train their members for the
task of evangelism than their Evangelical counterparts typically do.
And while all Christians speak of the need to turn from the world to
Christ, Evangelicals have placed more emphasis on conversion because of the Puritan and Pietist legacies from which Edwards, Whitefield, and Wesley learned.

Evangelicalism is most often confused with fundamentalism, so I
will also identify points at which these two approaches diverge. I
should say at the outset that, as for all generalizations, there will be
plenty of exceptions to the "rules" that follow, and that these are no
more than tendencies or directions in which members of these two
constituencies move. They should be regarded as ideal types that are
valuable not so much for their historical value (there may be no one
individual who perfectly fits either type) as for their heuristic import.
The sum total for each type roughly approximates a distinctive pattern
of thinking.[21]

1. Interpretation of Scripture. Fundamentalists tend to read Scripture more literally, while Evangelicals tend to look more carefully at genre and literary and historical context.[22] Another way
   of saying this is that fundamentalists tend to assume that the
   meaning of Scripture is obvious from a single reading, while

Evangelicals want to talk about layers of meaning. For example, more fundamentalists will understand the first three chapters of Genesis to contain, among other things, scientific statements about beginnings, while Evangelicals will focus more on the theological character of those stories—that the author/editor was more interested in showing that the earth has a Creator, for example, than precisely how the earth was created.

2. Culture. Fundamentalists question the value of human culture that is not created by Christians or related to the Bible, whereas Evangelicals see God's "common grace" working in and through all human culture. For them, Mozart may not have been an orthodox Christian and quite possibly was a moral failure as a human being, but his music is a priceless gift of God. Culture is tainted by sin, as are all other human productions, but it nevertheless can reflect God's glory.

3. Social action. There was a time when fundamentalists considered efforts to help the poor to be a sign of liberal theology, because proponents of the social gospel during the modernist controversy of the 1920s were theological liberals.[23] Until recently many fundamentalists limited their view of Christian social action to struggles for religious freedom and against abortion. Evangelicals have been more vocal in their declarations that the gospel also calls us to fight racism, sexism, and poverty.[24]

4. Separatism. For many decades in this century fundamentalists preached that Christians should separate themselves from liberal Christians (which sometimes meant Evangelicals) and even from conservatives who fellowshipped with liberals. This is why some fundamentalists refuse to support Billy Graham—Graham asks for help from Mainline Protestant and Catholic churches, and sends his converts back to these churches for further nurture. Evangelical theology puts more emphasis on engagement with culture with the aim of transforming it, and working with other Christians toward common religious and social goals.

5. Dialogue with liberals. Fundamentalists have tended in the past to believe that "liberal" Christians (those who denied Jesus' resurrection, the sinful nature of humanity, the efficacy of the atonement, or fundamentalist views of biblical inerrancy) were Christian in name only, that there was nothing to learn from them, and there was no use trying to talk to them once they refused to accept the fundamentalist version of the gospel.

The Evangelical approach is to talk with those of more liberal persuasions in an effort to persuade and perhaps even learn.[25]

6. The nature of Christian faith. Although most fundamentalists preach salvation by grace, they also tend to focus so much on rules and restrictions (do's and don'ts) that their church members could get the impression that the heart of Christianity is a set of laws governing outward behavior. There is a similar danger in Evangelical churches, but Evangelical theology focuses more on the person and work of Christ as the heart of the Christian faith.

7. Fissiparousness. Many Evangelical groups have fractured and then broken again over what seem to later generations to have been minor issues. But the tendency seems worse among fundamentalists, for whom differences of doctrine, often on rather minor issues, are considered important enough to warrant starting a new congregation or even denomination. Because Evangelical theology makes more of the distinction between essentials and nonessentials, Evangelicals are more willing to remain, for example, in Mainline Protestant churches.

Here I will argue that these two groups diverge on Israel as well. Both fundamentalists and Evangelicals agree that there is a connection between the biblical promises, on the one hand, and contemporary Jews and the Land of Israel, on the other. But Evangelicals more than fundamentalists question the justice of the modern State of Israel. Some of these Evangelicals make a theological argument based on the conditions attached to the biblical promises. We will discuss these promises and their conditions in due course.

EVANGELICALS AND ISRAEL

The first eighteenth-century Evangelicals inherited from their Puritan forbears an eschatological interest in the land and people of Israel. Increase Mather and other American Puritans in the seventeenth century, for example, had predicted that Israel would be restored politically and spiritually before the millennium. Cotton Mather spent his life yearning for the restoration of the Jews.[26]

So when Jonathan Edwards (1703–1758) defended Judaism against the deists, he was drawing out lines started by others. For the first time since Marcion (d. *ca.* 160), in the eighteenth century Jews were regarded as religiously unrelated to Christians. Deists launched the attack, charging that Judaism was essentially pagan and unspiritual, and unnecessary and in fact, the source of all that was wrong with traditional Christianity.[27] Edwards argued strenuously against the deist severance of the religious link between Jews and Christians by positing one covenant binding the two religions. The Old Testament and New Testament covenants, he asserted, are different but integrally related modes of a single plan of redemption. The Old Testament covenant was the "cortex" or "shell" that "envelops" the "medulla" of the gospel or covenant of grace.

For Edwards, then, the two covenants were two phases or ways of performing the same one covenant. As Edwards put it early in his career, "The gospel was preached to the Jews under a veil."[28] The process of conversion was the same for Jews in the Old Testament as for Christians in the New. They were "convinced so much of their wickedness that they trusted to nothing but the mere mercy of God." This included the antediluvians, and indeed all those who lived since "the beginning of the world." Even the rate of conversion was the same. There were wicked and godly then, and conversions were just as frequent then as in Edwards's day (*Misc.*, 39). Christ saved the Old Testament saints just like their cohorts in the New (*Misc.*, 1283), and they believed in Christ, but under the name of the "angel of the Lord" or "messenger of the covenant" (*Controversies Notebook*, 213). In fact, Christ appeared to Old Testament Jews; Moses saw his back parts on Mt. Sinai, and he appeared in human form to the seventy elders (Exodus 24: 9–11) as well as to Joshua, Gideon and Manoah (*HWR*, 197). For that matter, every time God was said to have manifested Himself to humans in a voice or otherwise tangible form, it was always through the second person of the Trinity (*HWR*, 131).[29]

Though the two covenants had two federal heads, Adam and Christ, and one was a "dead" way but the other "living" (*Misc.*, 35), "in strictness of speech" they were not two but one. For they shared the same mediator (*Misc.*, 875), the same salvation (which means the same calling, justification, adoption, sanctification, and glory), and the same medium of salvation: the incarnation, suffering, righteousness, and intercession of Christ. The Holy Spirit was the same person applying Christ's redemption in both dispensations, and the method of obtaining salvation was the same—faith and repentance. The external means (the word of God and ordinances such as prayer and praise, sabbath and sacraments) were not different; nor were the benefits (God's Spirit by God's mere mercy and by a divine person—the angel of the Lord or mediator) and future blessings. For both, the condition was faith in the Son of God as mediator, expressed with the same spirit of repentance and humility (*Misc.*, 1353). This is why all parts of the Old Testament point to the future coming of Christ (*HWR*, 283). In sum, the religion of the church of Israel is "essentially the same religion with that of the Christian church" (*HWR*, 443).

Edwards also determined that the Jews would return to their homeland. This would happen, he reasoned, because the prophecies of land being given to them had been only partially fulfilled. It was also necessary for God to make them a "visible monument" of His grace and power at their conversion. Canaan once again would be a spiritual center of the world. Although Israel would again be a distinct nation, Christians would have free access to Jerusalem because Jews would look on Christians as their brethren.[30]

According to Arthur Hertzberg, a twentieth-century Jewish scholar, this American linkage of Jewish conversion to the millennium was why "American intellectual anti-Semitism never became as virulent as its counterparts in Europe."[31] Christians in Europe believed the End was in the indefinite future. But in America the End seemed near, and Jews were needed here and now to help usher in the return of Christ. So in the colonies, the Jewish question moved "to center stage."[32]

If Edwards was among those Americans who did not evidence an anti-Semitism as virulent as some European strains, he was nonetheless not particularly friendly to the Judaism of his day. He could never accept it on its own terms, but always demanded that it be swallowed up by the religion to which it gave birth. With arrogance he judged Jews to be proud, assuming that their reluctance to convert was obstinate refusal of the obvious.

Yet Edwards declined the invitation of the intellectual elites to minimize Christianity's debt to Judaism. If Christianity was the logical end of Judaism, its meaning could be found only through Judaism. The antitype was to be fully understood only by reference to its types. Hence tension in the Jewish-Christian relationship was a family quarrel. Edwards may have exercised hubris by claiming that his Jewish brothers and sisters were less favored by their common Father, and indeed had been disowned. But he knew they would someday be reconciled to their divine Parent, and regain their status as children in full favor.

No Evangelical thinker would ever again approach Edwards for subtlety and theological vision. But Evangelicals in the nineteenth century, particularly the newly emerging premillennial literalists, continued to look for a role for Jews to play in the end-time drama of redemption. Ariel observes that these fundamentalists were unusual in the history of Christianity: seldom had a large group assigned so much importance to Jews and their return to the land.[33] In no other case had one religious community claimed for another community a special relationship with God. And in no other field had Christian missionaries found merit in the religion whose members they were trying to convert or found authority in their scriptures.[34]

Canadian historian Paul Merkley reports that in the quarter-century that led to the creation of Israel in 1947–1948, "the sturdiest champions of the restoration of the Jews to Israel were the Evangelicals and fundamentalists. In the years when Britain was turning away from her commitments under the Balfour Declaration, and was supported in so doing by mainstream Christianity, Evangelicals sustained the Zionist cause."[35] And, according to Ashland University historian David Rausch, "the [Evangelical] movement on the whole recognized at an early date that the Holocaust was impending and believed that six million Jews had been murdered at a time when most liberal Christians were denouncing 'Jewish atrocity propaganda.'"[36]

When Israel was founded in 1948 and then prevailed through the ensuing war to establish her independence, Evangelicals and fundamentalists were ecstatic, seeing these events as the fulfillment of biblical prophecies. Mainline Protestants and Roman Catholics, however, "shifted into the ranks of those denouncing the new state."[37] While Evangelicals in the ensuing years preferred to accentuate the positive as Israel consolidated her strength, liberals tended to "dwell on the political embarrassments and the scandals and agonize about the many divisions" among Jews in Israel.[38]

The June 1967 war was a watershed in Christian attitudes toward Israel. Evangelicals saw this once again as confirmation that Jews and Israel still had a role to play in God's ordering of history. From this point on, Merkley reports, Christian Zionists were generally but not exclusively conservatives theologically while Christian anti-Zionists were generally but not exclusively theological liberals.[39] World Council of Churches (WCC) documents typically moralized about the human weakness for raising mere geography ("real estate") to a spiritual status, and "invariably" treated the creation of the State of Israel as problematic—never as the solution to a problem.[40] The National Council of Churches (NCC) denounced the 1978 Camp David Accords for allegedly ignoring the national ambitions of the Palestinian Arabs.[41] According to Merkley, the Mainline Protestant churches of the West joined the churches of the East in an attitude of resentment "shading over into active hostility."[42]

The Roman Catholic attitude was more positive, notwithstanding initial skepticism. The May 14, 1948 issue of the semi-official daily of the Vatican, *L'Osservatore Romano*, declared, "Modern Israel is not the heir to biblical Israel. The Holy Land and its sacred sites belong only to Christianity: the true Israel."[43] Yet the effect of two papal pronouncements that same year was to support the UN partition plan which did not resolve the status of Jerusalem, and to therefore resist Jordan's claim to the city. In 1967 the Vatican stopped calling for "international status" for the city and began to urge an "international statute" that would protect the rights of two peoples and three religions, and guarantee access to holy places. Vatican II's *Nostra Aetate* stated that the Church's relationship with Jews cannot be like its relationship with any other religion because of Judaism's special relationship to Christianity. Catholic seminaries angered Muslims by beginning to teach more of the Jewish context of the gospels. The Vatican negotiated its own agreements with both Israel and the Palestinian Authority in the last decade, and in 1994 under Pope John Paul II, ambassadors were exchanged between Israel and the Vatican.

Yet Rabbi Mordechai Waxman, a longtime leader in Jewish-Catholic dialogues, complained that what is missing from virtually all Church documents is the recognition of the State of Israel as the "reaffirmation of the covenant with Abraham and his descendants." To be fair, one must say that since the Holocaust both the Catholic Church and Mainline Protestant theologians have worked hard to affirm their solidarity with Jews and confidence that God's covenant with the Jewish people is ongoing. But two issues have been notably absent in most official church statements: the possibility that the restoration of the State of Israel has theological significance, and the notion of land as integral to Israel's covenant.[44]

Fundamentalists and Evangelicals, on the other hand, have generally welcomed the State of Israel as a sign that God's covenant with the Jews is ongoing. Led by Dutch theologian and Pastor Jan Willem van der Hoeven, fundamentalists and Evangelicals established the International Christian Embassy Jerusalem (ICEJ) in 1980. This organization sponsors the largest annual tourist event in Israel, a fall festival at the Feast of Tabernacles (Succoth) that in recent years has attracted an average of seven thousand visitors. It has also assisted immigrants from the former Soviet Union; by 1998 it had helped more than 40,000 and paid for fifty-one flights plus buses via Finland.

A host of fundamentalist and Evangelical organizations work to support Israelis and their state: in addition to the ICEJ are the Christian Friends of Israel (it does relief work in Israel and assists Russian

Jewish immigrants); the National Christian Leadership Conference for Israel (organizes clerics and academics to place ads in American newspapers and sponsor conferences); Voices United for Israel (works with Jewish organizations to sponsor pro-Israel conferences and statements); the Religious Roundtable (mobilizes Christians to vote for American politicians who support Israel); Christian Friends of Israeli Communities (links settlements in "Judaea, Samaria and Gaza" with American churches); Christians' Israel Public Action Campaign (claims to educate Christians on Israel as the fulfillment of biblical prophecy); and the Evangelical Sisterhood of Mary in Darmstadt, Germany (seeks to keep the memory of the Holocaust alive and urges Christians to support the State of Israel).[45] As if to underline their support for the Jewish integrity of Israel, the ICEJ and Bridges for Peace (another Evangelical group that helps immigrants to Israel) have both issued declarations that missionary efforts to Jews are not in the will of God.[46]

While most Christian fundamentalists have expressed solid support for the Zionist project and see it as the fulfillment of biblical prophecy, Evangelicals are more divided. Some prominent Evangelical leaders such as John Stott, Gary Burge, and the editors of *Sojourners* magazine flatly reject Zionism, and are more concerned with perceived Israeli injustices toward Palestinians than modern Israel's connection to biblical promises. Yet a majority of Evangelicals still see the modern State of Israel as in some sense a fulfillment of prophetic vision.[47]

FUNDAMENTALIST AND EVANGELICAL
THEOLOGY OF THE LAND

It is no wonder that so many have fought for so long over this little strip of land. Four thousand years ago people recognized its beauty and fertility. In the twentieth century BCE an Egyptian courtier who lived in Canaan wrote, "It was a good land, called Yaa. Figs were in it and grapes. It had more wine than water. Abundant was its honey, plentiful its oil. All kinds of fruit were on its trees. Barley was there and emmer, and no end of cattle of all kinds."[48] Israel's variety of climate adds to its appeal; within one hundred miles (from Jericho to Mt. Hermon) one can move from the subtropical to the subarctic. Its land forms and living conditions are almost as varied.[49]

But if the land of Israel has universal appeal, most Christians for most of the last two millennia have believed that the land has no theological importance. According to the general story line, God stopped exercising special care for Jews or their land upon the advent of the Christian church, which became the New Israel. This is what is known as "supersessionism" or "replacement theology." It first arose after the suppression of the Bar Kochba revolt in 135 CE, was promoted by second-century Christians such as Justin Martyr and Melito of Sardis, and soon became the "standard model" for understanding Judaism's relationship to Christian faith.[50]

According to Methodist theologian R. Kendall Soulen, there are three types of supersessionism:

1. Economic supersessionism, which holds that Israel's function was to prepare for the spiritual and universal form of salvation in Jesus, so that once Jesus came, Israel was unnecessary;
2. Punitive supersessionism, which argues that God abrogated Israel's covenant because she rejected Christ; and
3. Structural supersessionism, which stands for all versions of the Christian story that make the history of Israel only tangential to the narrative.

This means that every rendering of faith is supercessionist which moves from creation and fall to redemption through Christ without making Israel's story integral to the main story.[51]

Revisions to this story first appeared among the Puritans of the seventeenth century and then certain of their theological heirs such as Jonathan Edwards, who argued for a coming, literal millennium whose story featured a signal role for Jews.[52] In the late nineteenth and through the twentieth centuries premillennialists envisioned a future for Israel based on their literal reading of Old Testament prophecies. For dispensationalists, in fact, a modern Israel was necessary for the fulfillment of end-time prophecies. Jews had to return to their ancient homeland and establish a state, in order for the Antichrist to betray a pact he will make with the Jewish state, and for Christ to return to rescue God's people and restore David's throne.[53] In fact, it was only the majority Jewish rejection of Jesus that opened up the "great parenthesis" in God's plan, which in turn gave space for God to form a Christian church.[54]

Some scholars think this is oddly akin to what Paul meant when he wrote in Romans 11 that first-century Jews were "enemies of God for [Christians'] sake" (28). Since there was a "well-attested rabbinic tradition that Israel's repentance triggers the eschaton,"[55] and therefore Jewish acceptance of Jesus would bring the immediate end of the world,

God "harden[ed] . . . part of Israel" (11:25) in order to make time and space for the inclusion of Gentiles. As Charles Cosgrove puts it, "In order that Jews will not dominate gentile Christians and require them to Judaize, God has temporarily pruned the vast majority of Israelites to make what we might call 'political space' for those of other nations."[56]

After the Holocaust, a rereading of Scripture and particularly of Paul led to a new vision for Israel's future (and hence the land) among some theologians and New Testament scholars, such as Karl and Marcus Barth, C. E. B. Cranfield, Peter Stuhlmacher, and numerous Evangelical scholars. Cranfield, for example, concluded that an impartial reading of Paul's epistle to the Romans demanded a revision of supersessionism: "These three chapters [9-11] emphatically forbid us to speak of the church as having once and for all taken the place of the Jewish people."[57] Like Cranfield, scholars began to notice that Paul seemed to believe that Jewish rejection of Jesus as Messiah did not abrogate God's covenant with them, for in Romans 11 he says explicitly that "God has not rejected his people whom he foreknew" (2; NRSV). As W. D. Davies noted in his landmark work on the biblical concept of land, "Paul never calls the Church the New Israel or the Jewish people the Old Israel."[58] Elsewhere in Romans 11 Paul suggests the same theme of the continuance of the covenant: "The gifts and calling of God are irrevocable" (29); "What will their acceptance [by God] be but life from the dead?" (15); "all Israel will be saved (26) . . . [and] receive mercy" (31). Baptist theologian Craig Blaising argues that Paul bases this reading of Israel's future on Isaiah 59:20-21 where the prophet forecasts the return of divine favor on Zion and follows this promise with another, "Then all your people will be righteous; they will possess the land forever" (Is 60:21).[59]

Evangelical scholar, Thomas McComiskey, adds that this last promise of land is not dropped by Paul, even if most Jews in Paul's day were rejecting Jesus. McComiskey argues that Paul refers to the Abrahamic promises in Galatians 3:15-29, all of which (Gn 12:7; 13:15; 15:18; 17:8) refer to the land. Since Christ is the offspring to whom Paul refers ("Now the promises were made to Abraham and to his offspring . . . that is, to one person, who is Christ" 3:16), McComiskey reasons that it cannot be only justification that the offspring inherits. In other words, the promise may function differently under the new covenant, but it has not lost its territorial connotations. In this case, the land has become a world (under the dominion of Christ) but *typified* by Israel's inheritance of Palestine.[60]

If the Paul research has shown new hope for the future of Israel and its land, so too has research into the historical Jesus, with E. P. Sanders,

N. T. Wright, John P. Meier, and Ben F. Meyer among the most important scholars showing that Jesus was far more interested in Israel than
scholars had previously imagined.[61] In a recent book, Evangelical
scholar, Scot McKnight, has pushed this further by arguing that Jesus
intended to renew Israel's national covenant, not found a new religion.
He wanted to restore the twelve tribes, which would bring the Kingdom of God in and through Israel. By his death, Jesus believed the
whole Jewish nation was being nailed to the cross, and God was restoring the nation and renewing its people. Hence, salvation was first and
foremost for Israel; if the nations wanted salvation they would need to
assimilate themselves to Israel. By his claim to dispense forgiveness of
sins and create a new community of restored Israel that would inherit
the Kingdom of God, his disciples saw Jesus as the savior of Israel, as
God coming to them through Jesus, leading the nation out of exile to
regain control of the land.[62]

Roman Catholic historian Robert Wilken has observed that
"hopes of restoration and the establishment of a kingdom in Jerusalem
were not, it seems, foreign to early Christian tradition." The angel
tells Mary that "the Lord God will give to [Jesus] the throne of his
father David, and he will reign over the house of Jacob forever" (Lk
1:32–33). Jesus himself seemed to anticipate the day when Jerusalem
would welcome him: "Jerusalem, Jerusalem, I tell you, you will not
see me again until you say, 'Blessed is he who comes in the name of
the Lord'" (Mt 23:39). And, according to Wilken, the word translated
"earth" (gen) in Jesus' beatitude ("Blessed are the meek, for they shall
inherit the earth" (Mt 5:5) is the word usually translated as "land" in
the phrase "possess the land" elsewhere in the Bible.[63]

But if the Paul and Jesus scholarship has eroded support for supersessionism, most Protestant and Catholic scholars have not embraced the countervailing notion that God has a present and future
role for Jews in the land of Palestine. That is, while most Protestant
and Catholic scholars since the Holocaust fall over each other reaf-
firming God's eternal covenant with Israel, for the most part they ignore what for most Jews is absolutely integral to that covenant: the
land. Jews appreciate Roman Catholic and Mainline Protestant affirmations that God's covenant with Israel is eternal, but wonder why
they ignore or deny what they believe is an indispensable manifestation of the covenant. As the authors of Dabru Emet: A Jewish Statement on Christians and Christianity put it, "The most important
event for Jews since the Holocaust has been the reestablishment of a
Jewish state in the Promised Land." Yet most Protestant and Catholic
affirmations of the Jewish covenant ignore this central component.

A recent letter writer to the *Christian Century* complained that the editor's approach to the land of Israel "is roughly equivalent to a Jew asking a Protestant teenager: 'Hey, what's up with the resurrection thing?' A Judaism without the [covenantal] component of the land of Israel is a faith shorn of most of its power." This is in part because, as the National Council of Synagogues argues, "God wants the nations to see the redemption of Israel and be impressed. . . . They will therefore learn if they had not learned before, that the Lord, God of Israel, restores His people to His land."[64]

Catholic and Mainline Protestant theologians doing Jewish-Christian dialogue have proposed an alternative to supersessionism known as "two-covenant" theology in which Jews and Christians are related to God separately through two distinct covenants, one through Torah and the other through Jesus Christ. (This is the approach taken by the August 2002 "Reflections On Covenant And Mission," issued jointly by Jews and Roman Catholics.) Under this scheme Christian evangelism of Jews is not only unnecessary but actually an insult. Evangelicals, however, find this impossible to square with the New Testament, where Jews and Christians are in the same church and saved in the same way, Jews are evangelized by both Peter and Paul (Gal 3:6–14; Gal 3:26–29; Acts passim), Paul says the gospel concerns "the Jew first and also the Greek" (Rom 1:16), and Jesus tells his disciples, "Go nowhere among the Gentiles . . . but go rather to the lost sheep of the house of Israel" (Mt 10:5–6).[65]

Blaising notes that many of those who endorse dual covenant theology say Jesus was not the Messiah for Jews because he did not inaugurate the messianic age. But in the New Testament "the gospels uniformly present Jesus as the Messiah of Israel from the angelic pronouncement to Mary and Joseph to the sign that was nailed to the cross (Mt 27:37; Mk 15:26; Lk 23:28)." Furthermore, "the proclamation of Jesus as the Messiah of Israel is presented in the New Testament in terms of the fulfillment of Israel's covenants (Abrahamic, Mosaic, Davidic and New covenants) in the twofold manner that we commonly recognize as the present and future fulfillment of the messianic kingdom." Hence, God's riches of salvation are presented as coming not directly to individuals but as mediated by Israel. "Jesus was not promoting Gentilism as opposed to Judaism but a different kind of Judaism that belonged to the Kingdom of God."[66]

If fundamentalists and Evangelicals see a future for Jews in the Land of Israel because of their understanding of Paul and Jesus, they also see Old Testament prophecy pointing in the same direction. They take seriously God's promises in Genesis (Gn 12:7; 13:15; 15:18; 17:8) to give a land to Abraham's descendants. They cite Isaiah's vision for the renewal of Zion, especially in Isaiah 4:2–6, and for the perpetuation of a remnant. They believe that the promise of a kingdom for the new David in Isaiah 9:7 suggests a restored land, and note both Jeremiah's promise that the Jews would return to the land in chapter 32 and receive a new covenant (chapter 33), and Ezekiel's recurring theme of the ingathering of all the scattered Israelites in the land.

Furthermore, Evangelical scholars are impressed by the importance of land in Torah. Elmer Martens has remarked that land is the fourth most frequent noun or substantive in the Old Testament, repeated 2,504 times. He notes that it is more dominant statistically than the idea of covenant.[67] The *Dictionary of Biblical Imagery*, produced by one of the most respected Evangelical publishers of academic works (InterVarsity Press), contends that "next to God himself, the longing for land dominates all others [in the Old Testament]." Land is presented by Torah as a place of spiritual testing; its pollution by sin and Israel's consequent exiles are portrayed as analogous to humanity's fall from grace in Eden and consequent expulsion. Adam, formed from land, failed to protect it and therefore allowed the serpent (evil) access to it. Land also represents the human condition: "Good in principle, land is cursed as a result of humanity's sin, and people are alienated from it as well as being joined to it."[68]

Therefore enjoyment of the land is not guaranteed. With the gift of land come stipulations that must be met to continue on the land. Martens writes of the covenantal obligations God imposed on Israel as conditions for continued enjoyment of the land: cities of refuge must be established for manslaughterers, religious and moral instruction must be given and carried out, dietary rules must be followed, sabbaths and jubilees for both land and people are to be observed, and the following behaviors are proscribed: harlotry, shedding of innocent blood, child sacrifice, sexual perversion, and the remarriage of a husband to a divorced wife (Dt 19:7; 6:9; 12:20ff; Lv 19:29; 23:10–11; 25:2; 25:8ff; Nb 35:29–34; Dt 24:4; Lv 18:24–25). Disobedience would bring a curse on the land (Dt 28:15–68), and the author of Leviticus explains that the Canaanites were "vomited out" from the land because of their sins (Lv 18:24).[69] McComiskey adds that security in the land is guaranteed by Deuteronomy only by continuing obedience to God's law (Dt 5:32–33; 6:3; 8:19–20; 11:8–9, 13–15). The Psalmists, he writes, especially emphasize the necessity of obedience to remain on the land (e.g., Ps 37:27–29, 34; 85:1–2, 8–10). Proverbs sounds a similar theme, as in 2:10: "The upright will live in the land, and the blameless will remain in it." So do Isaiah (60:21; 62:4) and Jeremiah (3:16–18).[70]

Some conservative Christians, especially dispensationalists[71] and fundamentalists, tend to ignore this theme of conditionality. They suggest that Israel should never be criticized, and that no Israeli claim to land should ever be challenged.[72] But Evangelicals, particularly non-dispensationalist Evangelicals, have emphasized the conditionality of the promises. Gary Burge, New Testament scholar at Wheaton College, has noted that one line of conditions is the repeated commandment of the covenant to "love the alien as yourself." The Israelites were not to "oppress the alien," who "shall be to you as the citizen among you . . . for you were aliens in Egypt" (Lev 19:33–34).[73] Moses commanded that tithes be collected from Israelites to help poor aliens (Dt 14:29, 26:12); wages were not to be withheld from aliens (Dt 24:14); aliens were to use the same system of justice which was provided to Israelites (Dt 1:16, 24:17, 27:19).

This was remarkably demonstrated by biblical patriarchs and kings. For example, the Canaanites were not displaced when God promised the land to Abraham and his descendants. Instead Abraham and the Canaanites became neighbors and trading partners. Abraham refused to accept parcels of that land as gifts from the natives, but insisted on paying for them (Gn 23).[74]

Joshua included aliens in public recommittals to the covenant (Jo 8:33–35),[75] and kept his agreement with non-Israelites, even when that agreement had been made under false pretenses (Jo 9). Then he went so far as to risk the lives of his men to protect those non-Israelites in battle (Jo 10:6–8).[76]

David used foreigners (men from today's Lebanon, Syria, Jordan, and Turkey) as soldiers and leaders in his army. Some became his trusted advisors (2 Sm 23; 1 Chr 11:10–47). Like Abraham, he insisted on buying land even when the land had been promised to him. Ornan, a Canaanite who owned land in pre-Israelite Jerusalem when it was called Jebus, offered land to David for what was to be the site for God's temple. David refused the gift and paid Ornan 100 shekels of gold (1 Chr 21).

But King Ahab stole land and murdered its owner, Naboth. God then arranged for both Ahab and his wife Jezebel to be "executed," thus suggesting that God intervenes to avenge the defenseless (1 Kgs 21).

Burge points out that the prophets continued this refrain. Amos prophesied exile because Israelites were oppressing the poor (Amos 7:17), Jeremiah criticized the abuse of aliens (7:5–7), and Ezekiel declared that when the Jews returned from exile, they were to make provision for aliens: "They shall be allotted an inheritance among the tribes of Israel" (Ez 47:22–23).[77]

The upshot of all this is that keeping the terms of the covenant includes treating aliens with justice, indeed love. Covenant keeping is not only a matter of avoiding idolatry and treating fellow Jews with justice, but extending that justice to non-Israelites living in Israel. If Israel was disciplined for violating the covenant, some of those violations were against aliens living in the land.

Both Martens and McComiskey note the prophets' interpretation that the Israelites lost the land and were sent into exile because of disobedience to these terms of the covenant. Yet both Evangelical scholars find the prophets and other biblical authors holding to the promise of land for Israel even after Israel by disobedience has forfeited the land. Martens writes:

> Israel might and in fact did lose the land, because of failure on their part to live in the land in loyalty to Yahweh. Yet the land was inalienable in the sense that it could not be forcibly taken from Israel. Israel, however, through disobedience, forfeited the land. Prophets in the exile fell back on the inalienable right of Israel to the land, and announced a return from exile to the land, for, they said, it was rightfully theirs still (Jer 12:14–16; 16:14–15; see also Ez 36:8–15).[78]

McComiskey observes that while the prophets expanded the promised inheritance of God's people beyond the definable boundaries of Canaan to include the world, they nevertheless retained their expectation that Israel would return to the land of Palestine: "We cannot conclude that the prophets considered that promise to have been abrogated."[79] In other words, with the prophets we find new promises made for the messiah and his worldwide reign, but these new promises do not overrule the earlier promises of a particular land for a particular people. "Expansion [of the promise] is not synonymous with abrogation."[80]

The relative silence about land in the New Testament does not mean that the New Testament authors believed that the Abrahamic promises concerning land had been abrogated. McComiskey observes that Josephus was also silent about land. But Josephus deleted the theology of covenanted land because of its revolutionary implications for the messianism of the Zealots, whom he feared and despised.

Political circumstances and Josephus' purposes thus determined his presentation about the promise of the land; any claim that he did not share the Jewish view concerning the land as promised or covenanted land because of his omissions would certainly be precarious. The same is true of any argument from silence concerning the New Testament authors.[81]

McComiskey argues further that while Jesus does not speak directly in the gospels about God's promise of land to Israel; neither did the Mishnaic Tractate, *The Sayings of the Fathers*. Yet the "Fathers" were known for their belief in the promise.[82] Similarly, the Mosaic Law never included the earlier promise of Gentile inclusion, yet the earlier promise was never abrogated.[83] McComiskey links the two promises, both referring to land, typologically: they are two aspects of the promise of land in the prophets—restoration to the land of Palestine, and the rule of the world by the Messiah. The first is the earnest of the second.[84]

CONCLUDING REMARKS

I will close with two observations. First, most Jews are unaware that Evangelicals and fundamentalists have been some of their best friends—at least in the Jewish struggle for a secure homeland. Yet, as Merkley remarks, American Jews "are conditioned to look upon the conservative side of the Christian religious spectrum with loathing: these are the bible thumpers, whom everyone is permitted to despise . . . whom *not* to despise is a sign of cultural deficiency."[85] Perhaps some rethinking is in order: for Jews to acknowledge what is at least "co-belligerency," and for conservative Christians to recognize Jews as religious cousins. Fundamentalists and Evangelicals have already recognized that modern Israel is "prophetically significant," as Southern Baptist Seminary president R. Albert Mohler Jr. has put it, if not in itself the complete fulfillment of biblical prophecy that some fundamentalists have proclaimed. But they should also recognize that insofar as the state has served as a vessel of protection for the Jewish people, it is perhaps a judgment on the church and a reminder that God will protect His people even when the church will not.[86]

Second, on most of these matters most Evangelicals and fundamentalists agree. Before the second intifada there was a certain divide over where to place emphasis. Fundamentalists tended to stress more than Evangelicals the biblical promises of land and future to the Jews, while Evangelicals tended to place more emphasis on the conditionality of the promises. Hence, fundamentalists more than Evangelicals agreed with Gush Emunim supporters who defend the West Bank Jewish settlements on the grounds that the land conquered in 1967 was returned to its rightful owners. And more Evangelicals than fundamentalists would argue that while Israel has a right to *at least* its pre-

1967 borders and must be guaranteed security, Israel should not control the lives of Palestinians or prevent the establishment of a Palestinian state that is committed to peaceful coexistence. But at the same time, especially since the second *intifada*, most all fundamentalists and Evangelicals argue that the land seizures of both 1948 and 1967 occurred after wars started by Arabs to destroy the (vastly outnumbered) Jewish state, and after turning down the UN partition plan (which Jews had accepted).[87]

Many Evangelicals deny a one-to-one correspondence between the modern State of Israel and the prophetic promised return of Jews to the land—because the return is to be accompanied by widespread spiritual renewal and is not necessarily connected to expansive land claims made by some Zionists—while at the same time affirming a connection between the two. They agree with the prominent Evangelical leader Gary Burge that "God's people cannot make a religious claim to the land without exhibiting religious devotion to [the terms of] the covenant."[88]

At the same time, more and more Evangelicals are wondering if we need more humility when criticizing Israelis for how they treat Palestinians—particularly when the much-criticized fence (more popularly known as "the wall") seems to have reduced significantly the number of suicide bombings. They wonder how we would respond if we experienced a succession of 9/11-like attacks, almost monthly over several years, in a country the size of New Jersey, where nearly everyone knows someone who has been killed or maimed. More and more they see the hypocrisy of critics of Israel, who routinely excoriate Israel for alleged human rights abuses but typically ignore China, North Korea, Saudi Arabia, and other countries deemed "not free" in annual Freedom House assessments.[89] They also notice that critics of Israel regularly ignore human rights abuses against Palestinian Christians perpetrated by Palestinian Muslims and disregarded by the Palestinian Authority.[90]

No matter how Israel responds to the current political crisis, most Evangelicals and fundamentalists will continue to believe that the land of Israel is still theologically important and that the Jews still have an important role in the history of redemption. This is the contribution which conservative Protestants have made to the Christian debates about Israel: since the Enlightenment they have insisted that the Christian church has not replaced the Jews without remainder, that the old and new covenants were integrally connected in the time of Jesus and remain so today, and that if the covenant with Israel is eternal then the promise of land is also still significant.

NOTES

1. Samuel G. Freedman, "Evangelicals, Jews Build Bridges," *USA Today* (May 8, 2002), 15 A.

2. Yaakov Ariel, *Evangelizing the Chosen People: Missions to the Jews in America, 1880–2000* (Chapel Hill: University of North Carolina Press, 2000), 287.

3. Paul Charles Merkley, *The Politics of Christian Zionism 1891–1948* (London: Frank Cass, 1998), 25. Hechler (1845–1931) was an Anglican clergyman who studied theology in London and Tübingen but "retained a distinctly creedal, doctrinal, even literalist theology"; Merkley, 12.

4. Ibid., 34.

5. Ibid., 166, 191. Cyrus was the Persian king who defeated the Babylonians in 539 B.C.E. and then allowed the exiled Judeans to return home and restore the Temple in Jerusalem (Ez 1:1; 2 Chr 36:23). Second Isaiah refers to him as a divinely designated agent for the liberation of Israel. In contrast to Truman's vigorous support, President Roosevelt had only "platonic love" or "uninvolved benignancy" for Zionism, and "seemed to do nothing of substance for" Jews and the Zionist cause; Merkley, 154.

6. Gershom Gorenberg, *The End of Days: Fundamentalism and the Struggle for the Temple Mount* (New York: Free Press, 2000), 166–67.

7. Freedman, "Evangelicals, Jews Build Bridges."

8. Some of the best discussions of what Evangelicalism means in the United States are George M. Marsden, "The Evangelical Denomination," in *Evangelicalism and Modern America*, ed. Marsden (Grand Rapids, MI: Eerdmans, 1984); Marsden, *Understanding Evangelicalism and Fundamentalism* (Grand Rapids, MI: Eerdmans, 1991); Douglas A. Sweeney, "The Essential Evangelicalism Dialectic: The Historiography of the Early Neo-Evangelical Movement and the Observer-Participant Dilemma," *Church History* 60 (Mar. 1991), 70–84; Donald W. Dayton and Robert K. Johnston, eds., *The Variety of American Evangelicalism* (Knoxville: University of Tennessee Press; Downers Grove: InterVarsity Press, 1991); Mark A. Noll, *The Scandal of the Evangelical Mind* (Grand Rapids, MI: Eerdmans; Leicester, Eng: InterVarsity Press, 1994); Mark A. Noll, David W. Bebbington, George Rawlyk, eds., *Evangelicalism: Comparative Studies of Popular Protestantism in North America, the British Isles, and Beyond, 1700-1990* (New York: Oxford University Press, 1994).

9. Acts 21:8; Eph 4:11; 2 Tm 4:5.

10. I mean by this—as I will explain in what follows—an emphasis on the authority of Scripture, preaching, the cross of Christ, and conversion.

11. Alister McGrath, *Evangelicalism and the Future of Christianity* (Downers Grove, IL: InterVarsity Press, 1995), 20–22. Today in Europe it is the word used for Lutherans and Reformed who are derived theologically from the sixteenth-century Reformation.

12. For Edwards on reason, see, for example, "A Divine and Supernatural Light," in John E. Smith, Harry S. Stout, and Kenneth P. Minkema, eds., *A Jonathan Edwards Reader* (New Haven, CT: Yale University Press, 1995),

105–23; Hodge, "Introduction," in *Systematic Theology*, 3 vols. (Grand Rapids, MI: Eerdmans, 1986) 1:1–17.

13. George Hunsinger, "What Can Evangelicals and Postliberals Learn from Each Other? The Carl Henry–Hans Frei Exchange Reconsidered," in George Lindbeck, Timothy Phillips and Dennis Ockholm, eds., *The Nature of Confession: Evangelicals and Postliberals in Conversation* (Downers Grove, IL: InterVarsity Press, 1996) 134–50.

14. Martin E. Marty, "What is Fundamentalism? Theological Perspectives," in *Fundamentalism as an Ecumenical Challenge*, Hans Küng, ed. and Jürgen Moltmann, Concilium 1992/1993 (London: SCM Press, 1992), 3; R. V. Pierard, "Evangelicalism," in Walter A. Elwell, ed., *Evangelical Dictionary of Theology* (Grand Rapids, MI: Baker, 1984), 381–82.

15. For a fascinating account of a leading outpost of the "neo-Evangelical" movement, see George M. Marsden, *Reforming Fundamentalism: Fuller Seminary and the New Evangelicalism* (Grand Rapids: Eerdmans, 1987).

16. At the same time it must be noted that, as Noll has put it, Evangelicalism "has always been made up of shifting movements, temporary alliances, and the lengthened shadows of individuals." Noll, *Scandal*, 8.

17. Noll, *Scandal*, 9; "Akron Survey of Religion and Politics in America," conducted by John Green, James Guth, Lyman Kellstedt, and Corwin Smidt; cited in Noll, *Scandal*, 9n. Timothy P. Weber, *On the Road to Armageddon: How Evangelicals Became Israel's Best Friend* (Grand Rapids, MI: Baker, 2004), 9; Donald E. Wagner, "Marching to Zion: The Evangelical-Jewish Alliance," *Christian Century* (June 28, 2003), 20. Christian Smith and Michael Emerson argue that Evangelicals are prominent not because they retreat from modernity but precisely because they engage it; Smith and Emerson, *American Evangelicals: Embattled and Thriving* (Chicago: University of Chicago Press, 1998).

18. Quoted in Donald G. Bloesch, *Essentials of Evangelical Theology*, vol. 1, *God, Authority and Salvation* (San Francisco: Harper and Row, 1978), 7.

19. McGrath, *Evangelicalism and the Future of Christianity*, 53–87.

20. *Christianity and Crisis* 16 (Mar. 5, 1956), 18; Richard Fox, *Reinhold Niebuhr: A Biography* (San Francisco: Harper and Row, 1985), 265–66. Niebuhr was particularly critical of what he perceived to be Graham's use of "Madison Avenue" marketing techniques, and regarded Graham's style of evangelism as "pietistic individualism"; Fox, 266.

21. Donald Dayton discusses the historical dimensions of these patterns in his *Discovering an Evangelical Heritage* (Peabody, MA: Hendrickson, 1988).

22. Confusion often abounds, however, when people talk about literalism and fundamentalists. It is not true that fundamentalists interpret every word of the Bible in literal fashion; for example, I don't know any fundamentalists who think God is literally a rock (Ps 18:2) or Jesus a door (Jn 10:7). And even the most liberal Christians take the Bible literally when it asserts that God is one (Dt 6:4).

23. George M. Marsden, *Fundamentalism and American Culture: The Shaping of Twentieth-Century Evangelicalism: 1870–1925* (New York: Oxford

University Press, 1980), 85–93. See also Joel Carpenter, *Revive Us Again: The Reawakenings of American Fundamentalism* (New York: Oxford University Press, 1997), esp. 118, 193.

24. I should also say, however, that many fundamentalist churches (and parachurch organizations such as the Salvation Army) have provided spiritual and material uplift for the poor for well over a century.

25. For examples of this kind of dialogue, see David L. Edwards and John Stott, *Evangelical Essential Essentials: A Liberal-Evangelical Dialogue* (Downers Grove, IL: InterVarsity, 1988); Clark H. Pinnock and Delwin Brown, *Theological Crossfire: An Evangelical/Liberal Dialogue* (Eugene, OR: Wipf & Stock, 1998).

26. Frank Manuel, *The Broken Staff: Judaism Through Christian Eyes* (Cambridge, MA: Harvard University Press, 1992), 160–61; Shalom Goldman, ed., *Hebrew and the Bible in America: The First Two Centuries* (Hanover, NH: University Press of New England, 1993), xvii.

27. McDermott, *Jonathan Edwards Confronts the Gods: Christian Theology, Enlightenment Religion, and Non-Christian Faiths* (New York: Oxford University Press, 2000), 9–11, 26–28, 150–52.

28. Edwards, "Profitable Hearers of the Word," in *Sermons and Discourses, 1720–1723*, ed. Kenneth P. Minkema, vol. 14 of *The Works of Jonathan Edwards* (New Haven, CT: Yale University Press, 1997), 247.

29. The "Misc." citations in this and the following paragraphs are from Edwards's Miscellanies (private notebooks), published in the Yale edition of the Works of Jonathan Edwards, in vols. 13, 18, 20 and 23. The "HWR" citations are from History of the Work of Redemption, ed. John F. Wilson, vol. 9 of the Works of Jonathan Edwards (New Haven, CT: Yale University Press, 1989).

30. Blank Bible, Edwards Papers, Beinecke Rare Book and Manuscript Library, Yale University, 806; Edwards, *Apocalyptic Writings*, ed. Stephen J. Stein, vol. 5 of *The Works of Jonathan Edwards* (New Haven, CT: Yale University Press, 1977), 135.

31. Hertzberg, "The New England Puritans and the Jews," in Shalom Goldman, ed., *Hebrew and the Bible in America: The First Two* Centuries (Hanover, NH: New England University Press, 1993), 116.

32. Ibid. This question is not settled, however. As Avihu Zakai has recently pointed out, many English thinkers in the sixteenth and seventeenth centuries also taught an imminent millennium, and there is no clear indication that such belief reduced anti-Semitism. See Zakai, "The Poetics of History and the Destiny of Israel: The Role of the Jews in English Apocalyptic Thought During the Sixteenth and Seventeenth Centuries," *Journal of Jewish Thought and Philosophy* 5 (1996), 313–50; and Frank Felsenstein, *Anti-Semitic Stereotypes: A Paradigm of Otherness in English Popular Culture, 1660–1830* (Baltimore: Johns Hopkins University Press, 1995).

33. Yaakov Ariel, *On Behalf of Israel: American Fundamentalist Attitudes Toward Jews, Judaism, and Zionism, 1865–1945* (Brooklyn, NY: Carlson, 1991), 119.

34. Ariel, *Evangelizing the Chosen People*, 287.

35. Paul Charles Merkley, *Christian Attitudes Towards the State of Israel* (Montreal/Kingston: McGill-Queen's University Press, 2001), 219.

36. David Rausch, "Evangelical Protestant Americans," in Moshe Davis, ed., *With Eyes Toward Zion* (New York: Arno, 1977), 323–32; quoted in Merkley, *Christian Attitudes*, 219.

37. Merkley, *Christian Attitudes*, 6.

38. Merkley, *Christian Attitudes*, 24.

39. Merkley, *Christian Attitudes*, 37.

40. Merkley, *Christian Attitudes*, 49, 45. After a study of WCC documents on human rights issues, J. A. Emerson Vermaat, a Dutch journalist, says "Only rarely has the WCC criticized the human rights situation in Islamic countries in the Middle East . . . I am not aware of the issue of oppressed Jews in Arab countries ever being seriously considered by the WCC." Merkley, *Christian Attitudes*, 198.

41. Merkley, *Christian Attitudes*, 162.

42. Merkley, *Christian Attitudes*, 73. On the churches of the East, Merkley reports that Palestinian Christian contextual theology repudiates the doctrine of God's election of Israel. According to a Palestinian Christian he interviewed, "Entire generations of Palestinian Christians have grown up ignoring God's alliance with Israel and the Jewishness of Jesus, of the Madonna, of the Apostles. To them, they were all Arabs!" Merkley, *Christian Attitudes*, 76, 79. Reinhold Niebuhr was a notable exception, using the journal *Christianity and Crisis* to rally support for the Jewish State.

43. Robert Drinan, *Honor the Promise: America's Commitment to Israel* (Garden City, NY: Doubleday, 1977), 34–35; cited in Merkley, *Christian Attitudes*, 140.

44. Mordecai Waxman, "The Dialogue, Touching New Bases" in Helga Croner, *More Stepping Stones to Further Jewish-Christian Relations: An Unabridged Collection of Christian Documents* (London: Stimulus Books, 1977), 24–32; cited in Merkley, *Christian Attitudes*, 154. Catholic theologians are more willing to acknowledge Jewish concerns for the land, and some even talk about a "redemptive dimension" to the State of Israel, but there is a general reluctance to speak of land won in 1948 as connected to a fulfillment of covenantal promises. See Dr. Eugene J. Fisher and Rabbi Leon Klenicki, eds., *A Challenge Long Delayed: The Diplomatic Exchange Between the Holy See and the State of Israel* (New York: Anti-Defamation League, 1996), esp. 16–17.

45. Merkley, *Christian Attitudes*, 180–83.

46. Merkley, *Christian Attitudes*, 214. There are Evangelical dissenters from this predominant position, such as John Stott, Gary Burge, and *Sojourners* magazine. But they have not managed to divert more than a minority of Evangelicals from seeing modern Israel as a fulfillment of biblical prophecy.

47. Merkley, *Christian Attitudes*, 186-91.

48. Robert L. Wilken, *The Land Called Holy: Palestine in Christian History and Thought* (New Haven, CT: Yale University Press, 1992), 4.

49. Frank H. Epp, *Whose Land Is Palestine? The Middle East Problem in Historical Perspective* (Grand Rapids, MI: Eerdmans, 1970), 19.

50. R. Kendall Soulen, *The God of Israel and Christian Theology* (Minneapolis: Fortress Press, 1996), 19 passim.

51. Ibid., 30–34.

52. Peter Toon, *Puritans, The Millennium and the Future of Israel: Puritan Eschatology 1600 to 1660* (Cambridge: James Clarke & Co., 1970), 23–26; Christopher Hill, "Till the Conversion of the Jews," in R. H. Popkin, ed., *Millenarianism and Messianism in English Literature and Thought 1650–1800* (New York: Brill, 1988), 12–36; Zakai, "The Poetics of History and the Destiny of Israel," 313–50. On Edwards and Judaism, see McDermott, *Jonathan Edwards Confronts the Gods,* chap. 8.

53. Weber, 20–25.

54. Weber, 22–23.

55. Mark S. Kinzer, *Post-Missionary Messianic Judaism: Redefining Christian Engagement with the Jewish People* (Grand Rapids, MI: Brazos, 2005), 127.

56. Charles Cosgrove, *Elusive Israel* (Louisville, KY: Westminster John Knox Press, 1997), 87; cited in Kinzer, 128.

57. C. E. B. Cranfield, *A Critical and Exegetical Commentary on the Epistle to the Romans,* 2 vols. (Edinburgh: T&T Clark, 1979), 2:448.

58. W. D. Davies, *The Gospel and the Land: Early Christianity and Jewish Territorial Doctrine* (Berkeley: University of California Press, 1974), 182.

59. Craig A. Blaising, "The Future of Israel as a Theological Question," (paper presented to the annual meeting of the Evangelical Theological Society, November 19, 2000, Nashville, TN).

60. Thomas Edward McComiskey, *The Covenants of Promise: A Theology of Old Testament Covenants* (Grand Rapids, MI: Baker, 1985), 55, 204–05.

61. E. P. Sanders, *Jesus and Judaism* (Philadelphia: Fortress Press, 1985); N. T. Wright, *Jesus and the Victory of God* (Minneapolis: Fortress, 1996); John P. Meier, *A Marginal Jew: Rethinking the Historical Jesus,* Anchor Bible Reference Library, 3 vols. (New York: Doubleday, 1991); Ben F. Meyer, *The Aims of Jesus* (London: SCM, 1979).

62. Scot McKnight, *A New Vision for Israel: The Teachings of Jesus in National Context* (Grand Rapids, MI: Eerdmans, 1999).

63. Wilken, 49, 52, 48.

64. "*Dabru Emet*: A Jewish Statement on Christians and Christianity," *Pro Ecclesia* XI:1 (2002), 6; Jeffrey K. Salkin, *Christian Century* 119:22 (Oct. 23–Nov. 5, 2002), 52; "Reflections On Covenant And Mission," issued by the National Council of Synagogues and Delegates of the Bishops' Committee on Ecumenical and Interreligious Affairs (Aug. 12, 2002), 8.

65. Shortly after issuing "Reflections on Covenant and Mission," the Catholic bishops withdrew it. Baltimore Cardinal Keeler explained that the "Reflections" did not represent the position of the U.S. bishops, and that Jews do not have the fullness of salvation: "The faithful should be open to the action of God's grace to bring people to accept the fullness of the means of salvation which are found in the Church." *First Things* 127 (Nov. 2002), 81.

66. Blaising, 11, 12, 13, 16, 20–21.

67. Elmer A. Martens, *God's Design: A Focus on Old Testament Theology* (Grand Rapids, MI: Baker, 1981), 97–98.

68. *Dictionary of Biblical Imagery*, eds. Leland Ryken, James C. Wilhoit, Tremper Longman III (Downers Grove, IL: InterVarsity Press, 1998), 487–88.

69. Martens, 108–09.

70. McComiskey, 43, 48.

71. Dispensationalism is a system of biblical interpretation that insists on two separate covenants—one for earthly Israel and another for the church. No biblical promise for the one is to be understood as also referring to the other. Using the seventy weeks of Daniel's prophecy (Dn 9), nineteenth-century English Plymouth Brethren minister John Nelson Darby charged that Jesus' second coming was supposed to occur seven years after His resurrection. But because the Jews rejected Jesus' messianic claims, God suspended the prophetic timetable for Israel at the end of the sixty-ninth week, and permitted the "church age," which was completely unrelated to Israel's prophetic destiny. Only after the church is raptured before the Tribulation, will Israel's prophetic timetable resume, and Christ eventually return. Weber, 20–23.

72. Stephen Sizer, *Christian Zionism: Road-map to Armageddon?* (Leicester, England: InterVarsity Press, 2004), 21, 162, 182, 202; John Walvoord, *Armageddon, Oil, and the Middle East* (Grand Rapids, MI: Zondervan, 1990), for example, does not discuss conditions at all.

73. Gary M. Burge, *Who Are God's People in the Middle East?* (Grand Rapids, MI: Zondervan, 1993), 74–75.

74. Burge notes that in the Hexateuch the land is repeatedly called "Canaan" despite promises that Israel would inherit it. So Sarah "died at Kiriath Arba (that is, Hebron) in the land of Canaan" (Gn 23:2). Burge, 65.

75. When Hezekiah restored worship at the Temple, he invited foreigners to participate (2 Chr 30:25).

76. Burge points out that the analogy of modern Israel's occupation to Joshua's war against certain Canaanite cities is inappropriate. "The Canaanites promoted a religion utterly inimical to God's law. [But] modern Israel/Palestine is populated by people—Christians and Muslims—many of whom have a deep reverence for the Lord God of Abraham. In fact, Rahab's spiritual disposition was not unlike that of the Palestinians who acknowledge and worship the same God as the Jews but are not Jewish themselves"; Burge, 75.

77. These observations about aliens and the covenant are from Burge, 60–93.

78. Martens, 106.

79. McComiskey, 51.

80. Ibid., 205.

81. McComiskey, 207n. McComiskey cites B.H. Amaru, "Land Theology in Josephus," *Jewish Quarterly Review* 71 (1981), 201–29. Gary Anderson has argued similarly for Paul. "As to Paul and the fact that he does not mention the land in Romans 9, the answer is simple. Paul lived before the devastation of the Second Temple in 70 AD. The right of the Jews to their land was an inarguable commonplace in his own day." Reply to letters, *First Things* 155 (Aug./Sept. 2005), 7.

82. McComiskey cites S. Talmon and D. Flusser, "The Gospel and the Land: Early Christianity and Jewish Territorial Doctrine," *Christian News From Israel* 25 (1975), 132–39.

83. McComiskey, 208.

84. Ibid.

85. Merkley, 208.

86. R. Albert Mohler, Jr., quoted in Michael Foust, "Theologians Tackle Question of Israel and Biblical Prophecy," *Religion Today* feature story, May 6, 2002, Crosswalk.com.

87. See, for example, David Dolan, *Israel at the Crossroads: Fifty Years and Counting* (Grand Rapids, MI: Fleming Revel, 1998), 250. The "new Israeli historians" are revising this picture somewhat. They argue that Israeli troops outnumbered Arab forces at each stage of the war, and that land was sometimes taken by coercion. Benny Morris, perhaps the best known of these historians, argues that Palestinian refugees lost their homes and lands not only because Arab leaders told them to leave but also because of IDF expulsions at some sites, fear of wartime shelling, and Israeli atrocities and fear of them. Morris notes that the Arab states' invasions in May 1948, their refusal to accept proposed compromises, and their failure to absorb Palestinian refugees were also contributing factors. See Avi Schlaim, "Israel and the Arab Coalition in 1948," in Eugene Rogan and Avi Schlaim, eds., *The War for Palestine: Rewriting the History of 1948* (Cambridge: Cambridge University Press, 2001), 79–103; Benny Morris, "Revisiting the Palestinian Exodus of 1948," in Rogan and Schlaim, 37-59. More recently, Benny Morris has moved more to the right in his estimation of the 1948 war. See Ephraim Karsh, "Revisiting Israel's 'Original Sin,'" *Commentary* (Sept. 2003).

88. Burge, 118.

89. See, for example, "Are Mainline Churches Anti-Semitic?" Report documents bias against Israel that ignores worst abusers, WorldNet Daily, Sept. 30, 2004, ads.wnd.com/news/printer-friendly.asp?ARTICLE_ID=40687.

90. See Justus Reid Weiner, *Human Rights of Christians in Palestinian Society* (Jerusalem Center for Public Affairs, 2005).

9

Jews and Evangelicals—
Between Prophecy and *Mitzvot*

Yehiel Poupko

The Jewish-Evangelical relationship is as new as the Jewish-Christian relationship is old. While Evangelicals are surely heirs to all that is the Christian experience and have roots in Europe, beginning with the Reformation, the fact is that Evangelical Christianity is a uniquely American phenomenon dating back to colonial times, and as we all know, now undergoing a contemporary renaissance. As such when American Jews encounter the Roman Catholic Church and some of the Protestant churches, they meet institutions with which they have centuries and sometimes millennia of history and experience. This is not so in the Jewish-Evangelical encounter. Furthermore, the Evangelical is someone most American Jews really do not know. By and large, where there are large Jewish communities, such as the West Coast and the Northeast, there are relatively small Evangelical communities. And where there are small or no Jewish communities, there are often large Evangelical communities, such as the rural areas of America, the South, and the Southwest.

How should American Jews understand Evangelicalism? It is best to understand another faith system in the words of its practitioners and believers. The preeminent historian of American Christianity, himself a pious Evangelical Christian, Professor Mark Noll, writes:

> Evangelicalism at its best is an offensive religion. It claims that human beings cannot be reconciled to God, understand the ultimate purposes of the world, or live in a virtuous life unless they confess their sin before the living God and receive new life in Christ through

the power of the Holy Spirit. Such particularity has always been offensive, and in our multicultural, post-modern world it is more offensive than ever.[1]

This statement is at the heart of the challenge for American Jews and Israelis in their relations with Evangelical Christianity.

Many Americans see Evangelicals as coming from a lower socioeconomic class, having less education, being less cultured, and subscribing to a form of Christianity that is antimodern, unprogressive, and conservative. This impression is not accurate. The popular media play a critical role in shaping American attitudes and impressions about Evangelicals. For many Americans, the face of Evangelical Christianity is that of people such as Jerry Falwell, Pat Robertson, Ralph Reed, and Gary Bauer. In the main, most of those who identify with the Christian Right are Evangelicals, but not all Evangelicals identify with the Christian Right. The term "Christian Right" is a term of political activism. The term *Evangelical* describes a faith affirmation. Too often, the media and the public use those terms interchangeably. There are vast numbers of Evangelicals who do not identify with the political activism of the Christian Right.

On the whole, Evangelicals hold a set of positions on important social issues that are different from the positions held by the majority of, but not all, American Jews. In the main, among the core social positions of Evangelicals are: that homosexuality is a sin; that there should be no absolute right to abortion; that government aid to religious schools and "moments of silence" in the public schools are desirable, though not for the purpose of worship or religious instruction.

Events have made an improbable Jewish alliance with Evangelicals more likely. The terror war launched against Israel more than five years ago has created a paradox for the American Jewish community. The Mainline Protestants, with whom Jews are most comfortable by virtue of social, political, economic, and educational status, as well as many shared positions on domestic issues, have often turned out to be Israel's harshest critics. The Evangelicals, with whom most American Jews do not share a common set of social, political, and cultural views, have turned out to be Israel's best friends. Some American Jews find this an embarrassing irony. Most find it confusing.

There is something in Jewish experience that can aid in understanding the Evangelical experience. In the mid-eighteenth century, Hasidism emerged as a popular mysticism that promised to every Jew what heretofore had been the exclusive domain of the elite. Hasidism, which held that every Jew could have direct experience of the presence of the One God, came as a rebellion against the formalism of rabbinic scholarly high culture. Hasidism gave fulfillment to a deep longing for the simple essence of Judaism. Hasidism is taught through stories of the Hasidic masters. Those stories are sacred scripture in and of themselves because of the emphasis that Hasidism places on the individual's experience. Religious movements that place an emphasis on the personal rather than the familial or the collective experience require the testimony of personal experience to transmit their teachings. The story is the medium for the individual experience.

Evangelical Christianity has its roots in Europe, in England, and in late seventeenth-century colonial America. Like Hasidism, Evangelical Christianity seeks to broaden the individual's experience. The personal story is central in Evangelical Christianity, and Evangelical Christianity is intensely personal. As Mark A. Noll notes, "Most of Evangelicalism's early hymn writers wrote of what they had personally experienced, as did John Newton, the slave trader become Anglican priest, who wrote the lyrics: "Amazing grace! How sweet the sound/ that saved a wretch like me/I once was lost, but now am found/was blind, but now I see."[2]

When it comes to Israel, Evangelicals believe that the covenants and biblical promises made in the Torah, to the patriarchs and matriarchs and to the Jewish people, continue and are intimately bound up with, and realized in, contemporary Jewry and the State of Israel. For some Evangelicals the connection between faith and Israel begins and ends with the promise of land, and the "call to action" that comes after it, that God will bless those who bless Israel. For others, there are notions of the end of days and the return of Jews to the Promised Land. This distinction is critical.

Another way of understanding this comes from a prominent Evangelical commentator and journalist, David Neff, editor of *Christianity Today* and a contributor to this volume. A significant majority of Evangelicals, even though they do not engage in the literal application of biblical prophecy to contemporary situations and are not premillennial dispensationalists, believe that the biblical promise of land is realized in the modern State of Israel. Furthermore, geopolitical realities deepen their support for Israel, which they believe shares their democratic values and stands against regimes they find abhorrent. Nevertheless, the vast majority of Evangelicals come to their support of Israel based on a literal, plain reading of the covenant made with Abraham in Genesis 15.

In the 1970s there emerged a growing consensus that Israel in the Hebrew Bible refers to the Jewish people and that the modern State of

Israel is a fulfillment of the promise made by God to Abraham. Most Evangelicals love Israel even without a specific stated theology. Indeed all that is the drama of the Jewish people in the twentieth century—the destruction of European Jewry, the ingathering of the exiles, the establishment of sovereignty in the ancient Jewish homeland, the liberation of Soviet Jewry, and the reality of the State of Israel—in David Neff's words "figures prominently in the Evangelical imagination."[3]

There are however Evangelical intellectuals and scholars who are friends of Israel and have positive relationships with the Jewish people, but who believe it is neither in Israel's interest nor in the interest of Evangelical Christianity to unquestioningly support the government of Israel and to ignore the suffering of Palestinians. In the words of Gerald McDermott, while "most fundamentalists still endorse the Zionist project and see it as the fulfillment of Biblical prophecy, they are more divided than ever. The conflict with the Palestinians has caused many Evangelicals to question the justice of Israel's position."[4]

While many Evangelical Christians are strong supporters of Israel they present a dilemma for some in the Jewish community. Evangelicals are the only group in the United States who today work to convert Jews, vigorously and clearly asserting that without Christ there cannot be salvation, redemption, or cleansing from sin. In this regard, it is important to take note of the Lausanne Covenant, developed in 1974 at a conference attended by Evangelical Christian leaders from 150 countries. At this meeting the Lausanne Committee for World Evangelization was established. The Lausanne Covenant charges churches and Christian organizations to work together to make Jesus Christ known throughout the world. The Lausanne Covenant website also carries with it a link entitled "LC: For Jewish Evangelism." It has no such readily identifiable link for Muslims, Buddhists, or Hindus.

This presents a painful irony. On the one hand Evangelicals are great friends of Jewish national identity as expressed in Zionism and as realized in the State of Israel, and our "enemies" in the matter of the faith of the Jewish people, Judaism. Many Mainline Protestants are hardly friends of Israel as the expression of Jewish national identity, but are friendly to the religion of the Jewish people, Judaism, by virtue of the fact that they have renounced and do not practice the "mission" to the Jews. As noted above "Evangelicalism," per Professor Noll, "at its best is an offensive religion."

Gerald McDermott, in this volume, has done a comprehensive job of describing the various contemporary Evangelical Christian understandings of the return of the Jewish people to sovereignty in the Land of Israel two thousand years after the advent of Jesus of Nazareth. This remarkable event cannot but fail to capture the attention and imagination of all monotheists. It is an event of mythic and biblical proportions. It is a kind of event not even imagined in the vast and rich world of ancient pagan literatures, or Greco-Roman mythology. It is not an event about the resurrection of a god or goddess, rather an entire nation, chosen by God, given a land, exiled possibly for sin, returning two thousand years later. It leaves all who see it with a sense of abiding astonishment and no small amount of confusion. Neither the Christian nor the Jew comes well prepared to understand this return.

The Christian comes to it with only one classical religious set of ideas, the Augustinian one. The Jewish people are exiled from their land, wander the Earth in homelessness, are dispersed amongst the nations, and are lowest in God's economy and hence must suffer. They who knew the Father at Sinai should have been the first to know the Son at Calvary. Thus, the exile of the Jewish people is indispensable to the truth claim of Christianity. Every now and then theology like the rest of us must visit reality. Israel returned to the Land of Israel. The exile of the Jews is proof of what happens for the sin of rejecting Jesus Christ. But now Israel has returned to Israel. Hence, rejecting Christ is no sin. This threatens the fundamental coherence of Christianity. What is a Christian to do? The Roman Catholic Church has, in the main, developed a response, which goes something like this: the government and the State of Israel are this-worldly, secular phenomena; the Church has no theological objection to the establishment by the Jewish people of a government and a state. Indeed the Church holds that nations governing themselves in states are part of the human condition. At the same time the Church believes that whatever happens to the Jewish people is of immense theological significance for the Church. And thus while it cannot theologically explain the return of Israel to Israel, it waits patiently for that day.

For the Mainline Protestants, the response to the return of Israel to Israel has been at best benign neglect and at worst hostility. Theologically the Mainline Protestants follow the traditions of Luther who spiritualized all that is the life of ancient Israel. Israel is no longer a fleshy nation living upon a this-worldly land, with a covenant for one fleshy people, whose content is a set of carnal or material behaviors known as the *mitzvot* to be performed with the body and the other material realities of human life. Israel is only those who have come to the Christ. It is now a spiritual nation. It needs no land. It has no boundaries. Its home is grace and justification through belief in Christ. Christianity was wholly unprepared for this return, for if there is a New Israel of the New Covenant, then the Old Israel of the Old

Covenant could never possibly return. The land is part of the Old Covenant; the Old Covenant is abrogated.

Judaism and the Jewish people were no better prepared for their return to the land. In the *Tanakh*, that is, the Hebrew Bible, and in rabbinic literatures there are three epochs in Jewish history: the biblical epoch, which ends in exile; the epoch of exile, dispersal and homelessness which can only end with the coming of the Messiah; and finally the epoch of the Messianic era, in which the Messiah redeems the Jewish people and brings them back to the ancient homeland. Thus classically in Judaism only one type of return to the land is imagined and is believed. It is one brought about when God sends the Messiah. Zionism rebelled against that. But how were Jews of traditional faith to understand this development? This will be addressed toward the close of this essay. For the moment however, neither Christianity nor Judaism anticipated or were theologically prepared for this return.

Thus, there emerges a great paradox, which is not well appreciated by either Christians or Jews. Put simply it is this: for Christianity, whether Roman Catholic, Mainline Protestant, or Evangelical, the return of the Jewish people to sovereignty in the ancient homeland is an event of profound religious and theological significance. The Christian response to Zionism and the establishment of Israel is exclusively religious and theological. It either takes the form that Israel ought not to have returned due to its having rejected Christianity or that Israel's return is a sign that the Second Coming is about to happen. But what for Christians is an event of profound religious and theological significance is for the majority of Jews a secular event. The establishment of Israel after the murder in Christendom of six million European Jews is the most compelling reality and feature of contemporary Jewish existence. For most Jews this is understood secularly, for most Christians, theologically. Zionism was at its outset a distinctly secular movement. The overwhelming majority of the Orthodox believed in waiting for the Messiah to bring about the return to the Land of Israel. Approximately 75 percent of the citizens of the State of Israel view life in a secular, modern framework. Only religious Zionists view the establishment of the state as an event of religious and theological significance. The majority of the world Jewish community views it as a distinctly contemporary, modern, and secular event.

Many Evangelicals, especially those who are premillennial dispensationalists, never had the Catholic or Mainline Protestant theological problem with the Jewish return to Israel. Evangelicals always knew that Israel would return to Israel in fulfillment of biblical prophecy. However, this is a double-edged sword that only recently has been drawn from its scabbard. This double-edged sword presents a high degree of difficulty. It is already indicated by the position of certain segments of the politically active Christian Right. Central to Jewish self-understanding and Jewish reality is the fact that Israel is a modern, Western democratic state. Its decisions in matters of war and peace, its deliberations about the security of the country, its citizens' will, as a matter of democratic and Jewish conviction, are determined by the processes of a democratic society and its elected officials. This is something that some segments of the Evangelical community are not prepared to accept. This leads to the possibility of a future problem. On a visit to Washington, DC after announcing the disengagement from Gaza, then Prime Minister Ariel Sharon was told by then Speaker of the House Tom DeLay and by Pat Robertson that they could not support the plan because all of biblical Israel is God's gift to the Jews, and no government of Israel can contravene the will of God.

The Evangelical understanding of Israel has not gone unnoticed by the Mainline Protestants. The Mainline Protestants are now in a battle with the Evangelicals for the very pews of their churches, for the heart and soul of American Christianity. The tension between these groups of Protestants is perhaps nowhere more evident than on the matter of the theological meaning of the Jewish people and the State of Israel. The Mainline Protestants reject Christian support for Israel based on a theology grounded in biblical literalism, inerrancy of prophecy, and the assertion that one can look at contemporary events and know God's will. The Mainline Protestants take one more step, holding the Jewish people and Israel accountable for Evangelical support. Many Mainline Protestants in effect are saying, "How justified can Zionism and Israel be if their strongest support in the Christian community is coming from Evangelical quarters, and is meant to culminate in the conversion of the Jews?"

At the same time, the Evangelical turns to the Jewish community and in effect says, "For decades, many of you have made common cause with the Mainline Protestants, with the liberals, on a whole series of social, political, and economic issues. Yet when it comes to Israel, which we Evangelicals know matters most to you, they are not your friends, and we are."

The Jewish community finds itself caught in the middle of this feud, while Mainline Protestant attacks on Israel appear to be based not on an evaluation of the merits of the situation, but on a reflexive opposition to whatever the Evangelicals embrace.

However to be quite frank and intellectually honest, the Christian and especially the Evangelical Christian have every right to turn to those in the Jewish community who are not secularists, who are believers, and to ask them, "Since you are people of faith, how do you understand your return to your ancient homeland?" The question itself is well grounded in classical Jewish belief and thought. "I am the Lord your God who took you out of the land of *Mitzrayim*-Egypt . . . ' How do you know I am the Lord your God? I am the one who took you out of Egypt" (Ex. 20:2). God is known through God's acting in history. But how does one know which events in history and nature are part of God's plan? How does one know if any given event in history or nature is the bearer of a specific message from the one God and how is one to know the message? Who is qualified to read God's message in history and nature?

The prophet Amos (3:7) tells us "indeed my Lord God does nothing without having revealed His purpose to His servants the prophets." It is a matter of Jewish faith affirmed by Conservative, Orthodox and Reform Jews that God's direct speech to human beings ceases with the prophet Malachi. Now there is some disagreement as to when Malachi flourished, but no one thinks he flourished after the fifth century BCE. According to Judaism, there is no prophecy after that. This is one of the reasons why Jews do not accept the teachings of Jesus or the Gospel. We believe that prophecy ended five centuries earlier. So for a Jew to declare that he or she knows the specific divine message in any given event in history and nature is quite literally to blaspheme. Jews know what to do in response to events in nature and history; it is to perform *mitzvot*. However no Jew dares to assert that the recent cataclysmic tsunami is punishment from God. A Jew is obligated to do two things in response to the tsunami: first, to fulfill the *mitzvot* of saving lives and helping those who suffer, and second, to fulfill the Torah's general principle of studying nature to prevent such cataclysms in the future. Many Evangelicals, especially premillennial dispensationalists, are prepared to do what faithful Jews are unable to do as a matter of faith. Many Evangelicals are prepared to state with certainty the meaning of a given event in history or nature. A Jew may not do this.

To compound the difficulty further, Jews and Evangelicals read scripture, the *Tanakh* or Hebrew Bible, in very different ways. For the Evangelical, the entire Hebrew Bible constitutes the divinely inspired written word of God and no differentiation is made between the Torah or the Prophets and the Writings. For Judaism, that is not the case. Despite the differences in belief about the content of revelation at Sinai, Conservative, Orthodox, and Reform Jews believe that the most important section of the Bible, which contains the record of the first, last and only revelation of God, is the Torah, filled as it is with *mitzvot*. Furthermore the other sections of the *Tanakh*, the Prophets and the Writings, do not constitute divine revelation so much as they reflect divine inspiration. This leads then to another major difference between Judaism and Evangelical Christianity in reading the text of the Bible.

In the main, Judaism holds that the prophets are writing about their time. That is to say the First Temple Period in which they live. This is mainly the eighth, seventh, and sixth centuries BCE. The prophecies about the Messianic era are about the Messianic era and nothing else. Thus for the faithful Jew, the prophets do not contain predictive or determinative messages about any other period in Jewish history. While the prophets truly inspire us and deepen our sense of faith in and understanding of God, the prophetic writings do not tell us the meaning of what is happening at a given moment in history or nature. One could then argue, is not the return of Israel after two thousand years of wandering a sign that we are living in Messianic, or at the very least, pre-Messianic times? The problem with that is quite simple. Only a prophet can make that statement. A prophet is someone to whom God has spoken. There are no prophets. How then do faithful, religious Jews understand the return of the Jewish people to sovereignty in the ancient homeland?

In responding to this question there is a well known saying that goes something like this: "Christians talk theology, Jews do *mitzvot*." Jewish faith is best understood and expressed in the performance of *mitzvot* by Jews and in the study of the literature of those *mitzvot*, the Torah, the Talmud, and the codes of Jewish law. Theology is what Jews write when compelled to explain themselves to others. It appears that for faithful Jews, the meaning of our return to sovereignty in the ancient homeland demonstrates that God remains faithful to the covenant; that we the children of Abraham and Sarah, Isaac and Rebecca, Jacob, Rachel and Leah continue as the chosen family of God; that after two thousand years of exile, wandering, dispersal, homelessness and suffering culminating in the murder of six million Jews, our return and the establishment of sovereignty in the ancient homeland is a miracle wrought by God. I hasten to add miracle, yes; normative and determining reality, no. The conviction that an event in history or nature is a miracle summons one to thanksgiving, to just, righteous and holy living, to being worthy of the miracle. And that is all. The miracle brings with it no endowments and no entitlements. To be quite blunt, the establishment of the State of Israel is miraculous, but the exercise of sovereignty in the domestic and foreign affairs of the

State of Israel by any given government is a human affair for which God is hardly responsible.

Not only does Judaism believe that prophecy ceased a long time ago, the rabbis go further and tell us that since the destruction of the Temple, prophecy has been given to madmen and little children. Nevertheless, while we may not predict the future we surely ought to plan for it, or at the very least think about it. What does the future hold in store for the Evangelical-Jewish relationship? Perhaps the answer lies in the Jewish relationship with the Roman Catholic Church. With the end of World War II, the Roman Catholic Church still held on to the medieval tradition of teaching contempt for Judaism and the Jewish people and the belief that Jewish history and purpose could be explained only in light of the Jewish rejection of Jesus Christ. However, the murder of six million Jews in the heart of Christian civilization caused the Church to begin a process of self-scrutiny. At the same time the Roman Catholic Church entered into dialogue with the Jewish people. This had many results. Just as the Jewish people do not want to be told how to understand and practice their faith, the same is true for any person of faith. So it is inconsistent and presumptuous for the Jewish people to tell the Roman Catholic Church to alter its belief that all humanity needs to come to Christ. However, the Roman Catholic Church has not only called upon Catholics to understand Judaism and the Jewish people as Judaism and the Jewish people understand themselves, it has gone further. Without stating it in doctrinal fashion, the Roman Catholic Church no longer proselytizes Jews, no longer works to convert Jews to Christianity. It appears the Church has decided that given all that has happened in this sorry history, and given all the work that it has yet to do in the world, it may very well have to leave the matter of the Jewish people to God, in God's own time. Furthermore, during the past half century of dialogue, relationship development, and learning about the Jewish people through many friendships and associations, the Roman Catholic Church has come to understand and appreciate that in their life of Torah and *mitzvot*, there is justice, righteousness, holiness, and purity, and that indeed God does dwell in the midst of the Jewish people. Is it not possible to imagine that we have begun just such a process in the Jewish-Evangelical relationship?

NOTES

1. "Understanding American Evangelicals: A Conversation with Mark Noll and Jay Tolson." *Center Conversations: An Occasional Publication of the Ethics and Public Policy Center,* 29, June 2004.

2. Mark A. Noll, *American Evangelical Christianity: An Introduction* (Oxford: Blackwell Publishers Ltd., 2001), 11.

3. From a personal conversation with the author.

4. *Ethics and Public Policy Center*, www.eppc.org/programs/ecl/conferences/eventID.76,programID.31/conf_detail.ap, accessed January 3, 2006.

10

American Jews and Evangelical Christians

Anatomy of a Changing Relationship

Carl Schrag

The scene repeats itself at houses of worship across the United States: a spiritual leader recites prayers in front of packed pews, including prayers for the safety and security of Israel. It is a familiar sight in thousands of synagogues each Shabbat, but it is not limited to synagogues, and it does not happen only on Friday night and Saturday morning.

The phrases and the imagery may differ, but each Sunday morning, and at additional midweek services, thousands of Evangelical pastors, at large and small churches in every state of the Union, lead their flocks in praying for Israel. Those prayers reflect the deep-seated concern that large numbers of Evangelicals have for the Jewish State. In fact, a 2002 survey by the Tarrance Group, a Republican polling firm, found that Evangelical Christians are more likely to express support for Israel than all other ethnic or religious groups in the United States except Jews.[1] Large rallies, prayer meetings, and conventions bring hundreds or thousands of Evangelicals together to express support for Israel in communities across the country and in national gatherings in Washington, DC, San Antonio, and elsewhere.

For many American Jews who support Israel, this seemingly new source of support has caused anxiety and discomfort. Many have questioned the Evangelicals' motives and see serious hurdles to building alliances with them.

Why would any supporter of Israel reject someone else's support? What do many Jews feel is problematic about Evangelical pro-Israeli activity? Are Jews demanding that Evangelicals meet a higher standard than that expected of other groups with which they build coalitions? These questions, rather than the reasons Evangelicals support Israel, are the focus of this article.

OPPOSITES DO NOT ALWAYS ATTRACT

Why would American Jews who care about Israel and the U.S.-Israeli relationship have any qualms about accepting support regardless of its origin? What could make many of them recoil at the prospect of working together, or even being seen on the same side of an issue? Answering these questions requires considering the positions taken by American Jews and by Evangelicals on a broader array of issues.

For decades, most American Jews have been vocal supporters of liberal positions on many domestic U.S. issues. American Jews have backed abortion rights, gun control, civil rights, gay rights, strict separation of church and state, and so on. They have built many alliances with other like-minded groups to further these causes. Few of those alliances were built with Evangelical Christians, because they have been on the other side of each of these issues. (There have been notable exceptions, including coordinated efforts by Jews and Evangelicals on such shared concerns as religious freedoms and the global sex trade.)

The national director of the Anti-Defamation League (ADL), Abraham Foxman, stresses that the ADL and other organizations have been candid in telling Evangelical groups that cooperation with Jews over Israel will not affect Jewish positions on other issues. "Importantly, at no point have we heard them place any conditions on their support. There is no quid pro quo. At no point have we had to choose between our fundamental principles concerning the role of religion in America and our appreciation for their standing with Israel."[2]

There is nothing new, revolutionary, or duplicitous about this approach to coalition building. For decades, American Jewish organizations have forged alliances with other groups in American society— African Americans, Mainline Christian denominations, and countless others—on issues of shared concern; at no time has this caused American Jews to compromise their positions on other issues.

Enthusiasts stress the particular needs entailed by Israel's difficult reality since the collapse of the peace process in late 2000 and the onset of the Palestinian terror war. While Foxman maintained a distance from pro-Israeli Evangelicals in the past, he became a leading advocate of embracing their support despite the misgivings of other Jews.[3] Foxman acknowledges the concerns about the two groups' very different domestic agendas, as well as a sense among many Jews that Evangelical support for Israel is motivated by a disturbing vision of the end of days—a vision in which all Jews will have to convert to Christianity or die. Jews also cite fears about proselytizing and anti-Semitic attitudes that have long been held by many Evangelicals.[4]

Foxman, however, speaks for many American Jews when he stresses that since the Jewish faith does not accept Jesus as the messiah, Jews need not concern themselves with what Christians believe will happen in the "Second Coming." "Meanwhile," he asserts, "the very real present is one in which Evangelical leaders are educating their publics about the importance of Israel's existence, security and well-being, [something] no amount of public relations and advertising budgets could buy."[5] In other words, Jews should set aside their concerns about a distasteful eschatology when Israel, in the present, needs Evangelicals' backing. As for proselytizing, Foxman says Jews must condemn any such efforts but that they do not happen often.[6]

THE JEWISH COMMUNITY SHIFTS

Despite many hesitations, Jewish organizations have sought to embrace Evangelical support for Israel and to define parameters for forging a relationship. In its 2003 annual plenum, the Jewish Council on Public Affairs (JCPA, the umbrella organization of Jewish community relations bodies across the country) adopted a resolution on Evangelical-Jewish relations that would have been unfathomable several years earlier.

The resolution notes that American Jews have long labored to build coalitions with groups spanning the spectrum of society, and says this same approach is now being applied to Evangelical Christians. "This difficult subject takes on special importance as Evangelical Christians are often among the few significant non-Jewish communities routinely expressing support for an embattled Israel," the resolution states. "This valued support is prompting many Jews to revisit the question of relationships with Evangelical Christians on both Israel and other issues."[7] The resolution says further that cooperation on issues of shared concern should not hinder Jewish action on issues where the two communities diverge. Additionally, the resolution calls on Jewish community relations organizations to "explore opportunities to mobilize and harness the pro-Israel sentiments and activities of Evangelical Christians."[8]

Even though community relations professionals insist there is no difference between building coalitions with Evangelicals and with African Americans or any other group, the resolution represented a huge shift for American Jewry. Proponents of ties with Evangelicals emphasize, like many Israeli officials, that Israel needs all the friends it can get in these difficult times. Moreover, they insist that no quid pro quo has been demanded, or offered, on issues where Jews and Evangelicals do not see eye to eye. Nevertheless, many American Jews remain suspicious of Evangelicals' motives and uncomfortable about coordinating with them.

Writing in the *Jerusalem Report*, Stuart Schoffman takes issue with many American, Israeli, and other Jews' growing enthusiasm about Evangelical support for Israel. Although acknowledging that Evangelical backing feels welcome at a time when the world is so unsympathetic toward the Jewish State, he believes the Evangelical kind of support is not in Israel's best interest. He quotes this statement by the Reverend Pat Robertson in a speech to Evangelical pilgrims to Jerusalem in fall 2004: "I see the rise of Islam to destroy Israel and take the land from the Jews and give East Jerusalem to Yasser Arafat. I see that as Satan's plan to prevent the return of Jesus Christ the Lord. God says, 'I'm going to judge those who carve up the West Bank and Gaza Strip.'"[9] Schoffman also emphasizes that many Evangelicals support a hard-line approach to Israel's territorial issues, and view the territorial concessions that most Israelis favor in return for peace as a violation of God's plan.

Potential points of contention run the gamut from differing interpretations of Israel's best interests to a panoply of domestic issues. The ADL's Foxman addressed the latter in a 2005 address in which he warned of a well-organized effort by Evangelical leaders "to implement their Christian worldview. To Christianize America. To save us!" The fact that Evangelicals support Israel must not lead Jews to ignore what he termed "open arrogance. The arrogance comes when you believe you have the exclusive truth. And it comes if you believe God has commissioned you to change this country."[10]

Nevertheless, Israel is always on the lookout for allies, and sometimes it finds them in unexpected places. While some allies, such as the tiny island nation of Micronesia, have little to offer beyond a psychological boost, others can prove pivotal in Israel's unending battle for global public opinion. The outcome of the 2004 U.S. presidential elections highlights how important Evangelical support for Israel can be.

Polls released immediately after President Bush defeated Senator Kerry showed a striking trend: fully 21 percent of voters cited "moral values" as the key factor in casting their ballots, and 78 percent of those who cited moral values voted for Bush.[11] Suddenly, the American media focused on a huge segment of the population that had long been all but ignored by most Americans outside of that community. Following that election, American Evangelicals found themselves at center stage, weighing how best to use the newfound political capital they were deemed to have.[12]

A mere two years later, the midterm election results prompted some observers to ask whether 2004 had marked the peak of Evangelical political capital, and whether the sharp losses suffered by Republicans in political races across the country marked the beginning of a decline. Clearly, many factors contributed to the election results— factors that go far beyond the purview of this discussion—but the results have been duly noted by those who watch the shifting parameters of the church-state discussion, and by those who chronicle the influence of Evangelical Christians over public life in the United States. President Bush's former speechwriter Michael Gerson, himself an Evangelical, has posited that Evangelicals no longer respond solely to the clarion-call causes that have been associated with the Religious Right in recent years. Far from being a monolithic voting bloc, he says that many Evangelicals are looking for social issues around which to rally, and terms the shift a "head-snapping generational change."[13]

Although the Evangelical community has grown over the years— their number now estimated at 50 million to 70 million Americans— it did not appear out of nowhere. Indeed, many commentators have asked how so many non-Evangelicals could have missed this group's increasing importance. Yet, while the general American public may have been late to grasp this community's significance, Jewish friends of Israel took note earlier.

In 2002, the ADL published a series of newspaper advertisements across the country featuring a reprint of a pro-Israeli op-ed by Ralph Reed, former head of the Christian Coalition and a key Evangelical figure. The following year Reed, as a keynote speaker at the ADL's National Leadership Conference in Washington, noted that since 9/11 more Americans, and especially Evangelicals, feel a kinship with Israel. He went on to cite American Jewish concerns: "But even as those ties between our two nations strengthen, many Jews wonder: do we really want to be on the same team with these Christians? Can we really trust them? Do they come with an ulterior motive or a hidden agenda?" To dispel these concerns Reed, who cochaired Stand for Israel, the group that commissioned the 2002 Tarrance poll of attitudes toward Israel, pointed to the poll's results: "The survey confirmed my own heart. It found that 62 percent of church-going conservative Christians support Israel, and a healthy majority—56 percent—does so because of shared democratic values and God's promises to Abraham and the Jews to the land where the modern state of Israel is currently located. Only a distinct minority made any reference to the New Testament or the end times."[14]

The poll indeed provides insights into the breadth, depth, and motivations of the Evangelical support. Although 35 percent of Evangelicals said they back Israel because it is the place prophesied for the Second Coming in the New Testament, 24 percent said they support it because it is a democracy that values freedom. Another 19 percent cited Israel's being a longtime U.S. ally that works with America in the war on terror.[15]

When the pollsters pressed Evangelicals to cite their key theological reason for supporting Israel, even if they pointed to nontheological motivations, 59 percent said the Hebrew Bible's promise to bless Israel and the Jewish people (Genesis 12:3 and elsewhere) came first; 28 percent cited the end-times prophecies of the New Testament.[16]

In his remarks to the ADL leadership, Reed stressed areas of mutual concern and agreement while acknowledging that they do not annul the points of contention. "[O]ur agreement on opposition to anti-Semitism and religious bigotry in all its ugly forms, our shared support for Israel, does not mean that we should gloss over our other differences. A true friendship means speaking honestly and acknowledging differences—but we need not allow those differences to become divisions. Rather, let us agree to disagree on some issues, but work together on the many things that unite us."[17]

Reed's position is similar to that of Rabbi Yechiel Eckstein, the founder of Stand for Israel. Eckstein, who is also president of the Chicago-based International Fellowship of Christians and Jews, has been galvanizing Evangelical support for Israel since long before it was fashionable to do so. In 2005, his organization raised $48 million from Evangelicals to support bringing Jewish immigrants to Israel, funding social welfare projects there, and helping Jews in the former Soviet Union. During the summer of 2006, when Israel engaged in a prolonged conflict with Hezbollah, Eckstein's organization led the way among groups that raised $20 million from American Evangelicals to support Israel.[18] Eckstein has always been aware, however, that the shared concerns do not necessarily mean Jews and Evangelicals will agree on broader issues. His motto sums up his approach: "Cooperate whenever possible, oppose whenever necessary, and teach and sensitize at all times."[19]

OBSTACLES TO COOPERATION

Nobody disputes the fact that nearly all Jewish openness to relationship building with Evangelicals stems from concern for Israel's welfare in the difficult period since 2000. Few Jews had paid attention to Evangelicals' views of Israel before the collapse of the peace process and the descent into terror. At a time when Israel finds itself increasingly isolated on the world stage, and when there is much criticism of Israeli policies in the United States and the world, one might think American Jews would bond instantly with such an important group of pro-Israel Americans. Although some mainstream Jewish organizations like AIPAC and the ADL have indeed done so, other factors prevent a full-blown alliance from forming.

The rank and file of American Jewry has been much more hesitant about the Evangelicals than the leadership has been. The question has been highlighted in countless debates, both formal and informal, among American Jews in the past several years.

Jewish concerns about building coalitions with Evangelicals fall into three key categories, which were noted above:

1. Fear of efforts to target Jews for conversion, and the implied lack of acceptance of Jews as Jews.
2. Discomfort with Evangelical notions of "end-times" scenarios.
3. Disagreement with Evangelicals on a host of domestic policy issues ranging from abortion to church-state separation.

In many conversations with American Jews, this author has encountered countless versions of the first two objections. Both tend to be grouped under a heading of "motivation," as in, "What are the true motivations of Evangelicals who say they support Israel?"

Israeli journalist Gershom Gorenberg, who has studied Evangelical views of Israel for years, advocates caution: "Accepting the embrace of conservative Evangelicals poses problems of principle for Jews and Israel, in return for an illusory short-term payoff. Jews would do better to follow the Hebrew maxim 'Respect him and suspect him,' maintaining a polite distance and publicly delineating their differences from the Christian Right, even while at times supporting the same policy steps."[20]

Gorenberg also disputes the findings of the Tarrance poll:

> The Christian right's view of Israel derives largely from a double-edged theological position: Following a classic anti-Jewish stance, it regards the Jewish people as spiritually blind for rejecting Jesus. Yet it

says that divine promises to Jews—to bless those who bless them, to return them to their land—remain intact. Indeed, it regards Israel's existence as proof that biblical prophecies are coming true—heralding an apocalypse in which Jews will either die or accept Jesus.

He dismisses the arguments of Jews who say Israel's current needs warrant setting aside concerns about the end-times beliefs.[21] Although Gorenberg's view is shared by many American Jews, Israeli politicians have adopted the pragmatic approach being taken by so many communal leaders in the United States. Prime Minister Ehud Olmert has called Evangelicals some of Israel's best friends, as did his predecessor, Ariel Sharon.

The third concern voiced by many Jews, that Jews and Evangelicals disagree on many domestic issues, is indisputable. Many, though not all, Jews favor liberal abortion laws, while many, though not all, Evangelicals oppose them. The same can be said for a host of other issues ranging from tuition vouchers for private schools to gun control, as well as attitudes toward gays.

The JCPA acknowledges the differing views between the two communities, but urges that traditional community relations techniques be used to work with Evangelicals on matters of shared concern. No coalition is ever based on complete agreement, community relations professionals say, and the ties between Evangelicals and Jews should not be held to a different standard.

However true in theory, in practice many Jewish community activists have devoted so many years to building relationships with liberal groups that the challenge of working with conservatives catches them unprepared. What is needed is for both sides to agree to disagree on issues beyond the scope of the alliance, and for those issues to be considered off-limits.

These concerns become more interesting in light of growing evidence that the Evangelical rank-and-file may not be as focused on potentially divisive issues as their leaders. Former presidential speechwriter Gerson notes that when he asks young Evangelicals to identify Christian activist role models, most of them point to rock star and antipoverty activist Bono.[22] Surely that choice resonates with many American Jews.

However, the barrier of hesitation remains firmly in place for many American Jews, even among those who are staunchly pro-Israel. Asked about Jewish suspicion of Christian Zionists, David Brog, the author of a new book called *Standing With Israel: Why Christians Support the Jewish State*, said it remains "as widespread as falafel stands in Tel Aviv. Jews tend not to know very much about Christian theology or Christian history. As a result, they tend to lump all Christians together and hold them equally responsible for the anti-Semitic atrocities committed by Christians in the past."[23]

NOT A MONOLITH

Any discussion of how American Jews view Evangelical support for Israel is inevitably based on generalizations. It is important to note that one group, the Orthodox, views the evolving relationship differently than many others in the Jewish community. On the one hand, many Orthodox Jews place great value on cultivating non-Jewish support for Israel, and hence tend to be more welcoming of Evangelical support. This is bolstered by ideological congruence on both domestic and foreign policy; many Orthodox Jews view domestic issues such as abortion and gay rights in ways that mirror widely held Evangelical positions. Tempering the support, however, is tremendous concern about any perceived threat of proselytizing, which remains a very sensitive issue among Orthodox Jews.

Voting trends underscore the fact that no group or person speaks for all American Jews or for all American Evangelicals. Old notions about accepted "Jewish" or "Evangelical" views on various issues no longer hold sway, as growing numbers of people from each group pursue their own political paths. While exit polls indicate that 87 percent of Jewish voters voted for Democratic candidates in the midterm elections and 70 percent of white Evangelicals voted for Republicans,[24] small but increasingly vocal groups within each community have broken ranks.

Even support for Israel—the issue that lies at the heart of current coalition-building efforts—is not universal among Evangelicals. Although many Evangelical leaders are vocal advocates for Israel, the level of knowledge and understanding of Arab-Israeli issues among most of their followers is much lower.

In 2002, John Green, director of the Bliss Institute of Applied Politics at the University of Akron, conducted a study of 350 Evangelical leaders in which he found that 60 percent expressed support for Israel, a slight increase from his previous poll in 2000. Contrary to the impression of many Americans that support for Israel is paramount for tens of millions of Evangelicals, Green says that most of the rank-and-file people in the pews focus more on domestic issues than on the Middle East conflict. Even though 60–70 percent of Evangelicals may express support for Israel, some 50 percent also express support for the Palestinians, and most of them cannot answer in-depth questions about the Arab-Israeli conflict or the finer details of Israel's reality. "On a lot of questions, you will get the 'I don't know' answer," Green noted. "It is very foreign to their experience."[25]

Green's surveys yield another interesting finding. Although prominent Evangelical figures such as Robertson, former presidential candidate Gary Bauer, and syndicated radio talk-show host Janet Parshall toe a hard line against Israeli territorial concessions, Green found that most Evangelicals who have an opinion feel strongly that Israel should take steps to secure peace with the Palestinians. While finding that 60 percent of Evangelical leaders support Israel, he has also found that 52 percent of those leaders favor the establishment of a Palestinian state. Most of them say, like many Israelis who take the same position, that they will only support such a state if it does not pose a threat to Israel.[26]

In many ways, the spectrum of views on Israel found among Evangelicals mirrors the spectrum found among American Jews. It is the prominent, vocal Evangelical leaders who tend to voice the most hardline views.

CONCLUSION

American Jews continue to grapple with the question of how to regard Evangelical support for Israel. Whereas many embrace them as friends of Israel, many others shudder at the very mention of cooperation. Clearly, American Jews do not speak in one voice on this issue.

Given the paucity of pro-Israeli voices in the world today, and the new recognition of the widespread pro-Israel sympathies among Evangelicals, it seems inevitable that increasing numbers of pro-Israel Jews will reach the conclusion that Israel's interests will be served by a cautious embrace of these millions of supporters. As in all coalition building, limits must be set and issues must be defined, but it is increasingly difficult to imagine that American Jewry will veer far from the Israeli government's view. That view, which has been shared by every man who has occupied the Prime Minister's office since the mid-1990s, can best be summed up as embracing friends and emphasizing areas of shared values.

NOTES

1. The survey, commissioned by Stand for Israel, a project of the International Fellowship of Christians and Jews, polled 1,200 Americans, with an oversampling of Jews and Evangelicals. The survey found that 85 percent of

Jews expressed support for Israel, as did 62 percent of "conservative church-going Christians."

2. Abraham Foxman, "Evangelical Support for Israel Is a Good Thing," *Jewish Telegraphic Agency*, July 16, 2002.

3. Ibid.

4. Ibid.

5. Ibid.

6. Ibid.

7. 2003 JCPA Resolution on Evangelical-Jewish Relations.

8. Ibid.

9. Stuart Schoffman, "Trick or Treat," *Jerusalem Report*, Nov. 1, 2004.

10. Abraham Foxman, "Religion in America's Public Square: Are We Crossing the Line?" Excerpts from an address to the ADL National Commission, Nov. 3, 2005, www.adl.org/Religious_Freedom/religion_public_square.asp.

11. Dan Froomkin, "How Did He Do It?" *Washington Post*, Nov. 3, 2004.

12. Paul Asay, "Conservative Lobbyists Newly Energized after Votes," *Philadelphia Inquirer*, Nov. 18, 2004.

13. Michael Gerson, "A New Social Gospel," *Newsweek*, Nov. 13, 2006, www.msnbc.msn.com/id/15566389/site/newsweek.

14. Ralph Reed, remarks at ADL National Leadership Conference, Washington, DC, Apr. 29, 2003.

15. Executive Summary, Stand for Israel Survey, prepared by the Tarrance Group, Washington, DC, Oct. 9, 2002.

16. Ibid.

17. Reed, Remarks at ADL National Leadership Conference.

18. Daphna Berman, "Christians' Wartime Donations of $20 Million Went Largely Unheralded," *Ha'aretz*, undated, www.haaretz.com/hasen/spages/783410.html.

19. International Fellowship of Christians and Jews Mission Statement, www.ifcj.org. This author worked with Eckstein in 2002–2003.

20. Gershom Gorenberg, "Unorthodox Alliance," *Washington Post*, Oct. 11, 2002.

21. Ibid.

22. Michael Gerson, "A New Social Gospel," *Newsweek*, Nov. 13, 2006, www.msnbc.msn.com/id/15566389/site/newsweek.

23. Kathryn Jean Lopez, "Jews and Evangelicals Together," *National Review Online*, May 22, 2006, article.nationalreview.com/?q=ZDFiODgxY2ZkZjNhY2JmMmFjZjN2RkNDg4MTE0NGVlYzA.

24. CNN exit poll data, www.cnn.com/ELECTION/2006/pages/results/states/US/H/00/epolls.0.html.

25. Todd Hertz, "Opinion Roundup: The Evangelical View of Israel," *Christianity Today*, June 9, 2003.

26. Ibid.

⓫

Last Things

The Future of Jews and Evangelicals
in American Public Life

Mark Silk

If historians have anything to say about the future, it is only by referring to something in the past, so let me begin with a text set down near
the beginning of the conversation about Jews and Evangelicals that has
been going on since Ronald Reagan became president. It is from Nathan
and Ruth Ann Perlmutter's 1982 volume, *The Real Anti-Semitism in
America*, and it shows how far we have come since then:

> Christian-professing attitudes, in this time, in this country, are for all
> practical purposes, no more than personally held religious conceits,
> barely impacting the way in which Jews live. Their political action,
> as it relates to the security of the state of Israel, impacts us far more
> meaningfully than whether a Christian neighbor believes that his is
> the exclusive hot line to "on high."[1]

I'm inclined to doubt that any of us would contend that, at *this* time
in this country, Christian-professing attitudes are, for all practical purposes, no more than personally held religious conceits. The litany of
public issues on which such attitudes impact the way Jews live is not
short: abortion rights, gay rights, how public funding flows to faith-
based services and educational institutions, the teaching of science, to
mention just the most prominent.

Evangelical Protestants are, of course, not the only Christians ac-
tively pushing a faith-based agenda on these issues. They are, however,
the ones out front on such hot-button civil-religious struggles as the
placement of Ten Commandments plaques and monuments in and

around public institutions. More broadly, they have shown themselves less willing than other groups to play by the informal rules of religious engagement in American civil society that have been worked out over the past, let us say, sixty years. As one example, I would point to the way Franklin Graham and his evangelistic cohorts managed to take over the memorial service for the victims of the Columbine shootings in April of 1999. It did not sit well with local Jewish, Mainline Protestant, and African American Protestant leaders that, in a place which is not a stronghold of Evangelicalism, what they had every reason to expect would be an occasion for pluralistic civic mourning should have been turned into a rally for Jesus.[2]

Such civic space between government per se and private belief and practice is where much of the critical business of creating a workable religious pluralism takes place in America. What is so unsettling in the current situation is the increasing disagreement over how to negotiate that space. The imperative to proselytize, especially in places where Evangelicals feel themselves to be in control, has consequences, not least in the sphere of state institutions. The ongoing controversy over proselytization (and worse) at the Air Force Academy reflects, among other things, a generalized Evangelical desire to press sectarian views in ways that most of the rest of us think they should not be pushed—and in a manner that represents a departure from the recent past. As Anne Loveland, the leading academic authority on Evangelicals in the military, recently put it, "In the latter part of the twentieth century, military Evangelicals were never shy about asserting themselves, but they were nowhere near as brazen as today's academy faculty and administration—nor nearly as powerful."[3]

In brief, the intramural Jewish discussion of the practicalities of making alliances with Evangelicals needs to reckon with the marked changes that have occurred on the domestic scene over the past quarter-century. Or, to put it in other words, it is necessary to reevaluate the calculation that the Perlmutters, and their subsequent epigones, have urged on their coreligionists: that when considering Jewish interests, the price of acquiescing in disconcerting Evangelical attitudes on the domestic front is well worth paying in exchange for robust Evangelical support for Israel. I am not suggesting that Jews in the United States face anything like a threat to their physical security, or anything that could be termed, even by the modest standards of mid-twentieth-century America, consequential anti-Semitism. But the situation has changed, and there is no sign at the moment that we have reached a stable new status quo.

Let me now turn briefly to the nondomestic side of the equation, and again, I will begin with the Perlmutters, to wit: "We need all the friends we have to support Israel. . . . If the Messiah comes, on that day we'll consider our options. Meanwhile, let's praise the Lord and pass the ammunition." Yes, they suggest, our Evangelical friends seem to have some kind of messianic scenario in mind, but whatever it is, it's nothing for us to trouble ourselves about. What is being pointed to here is the theology of dispensational premillennialism that is presumed to underlie all Evangelical support for Israel. I don't want to spend a lot of time rehearsing that theology, which in any event Gerald McDermott and Gary Dorrien discuss in their essays in this volume. I would say that, from the Jewish standpoint, the Evangelicals' Israelism is far preferable to the British or Anglo-variety, in that it acknowledges God's ongoing covenant with the actual Jewish people, rather than postulating Anglo-Saxondom as the true Israel.

So far as I can tell, in the minds of the leaders of Evangelical politics today, it is their staunch support for Israel that is supposed to guarantee if not a full-fledged alliance with the Jews, at least an immunity from official Jewish criticism. That accounts for the cries of outrage that greet the ADL's Abraham Foxman when he raises one of his periodic alarums about Evangelical politics in America. Here, for example, is how the *Forward* described the reaction of Focus on the Family vice president Tom Minnery to Foxman's recent call for a united Jewish front against the Christian Right: Noting that the Evangelical groups Foxman cited are staunch supporters of Israel, Minnery told the *Forward*, "If you keep bullying your friends, pretty soon you won't have any."[4] But Foxman or no Foxman, what Evangelicals don't seem to grasp—or decline to recognize—is that when Christians are on the march, Jews tend to run the other way. If I may be permitted an historical analogy, just as premillennialists largely abandoned the goal of working for social uplift in reaction to the embrace of the social gospel by liberal Protestants, so it was the arrival of the Christian Right on the political scene that caused Jewish voters to end what, in the Nixon-Ford years, looked like a growing flirtation with Republicanism. It is telling indeed that, despite a policy more tied to the preferences of the Israeli government than any U.S. administration in history, George Bush was able to make only the most modest inroad into the Jewish vote in 2004.

As important as premillennialism may be in explaining Evangelical support for the State of Israel—and I do not think it is a sufficient explanation—the broader implications of a premillennialist worldview also need to be taken into account.[5] Here, it seems to me, outsiders have somewhat misjudged the thing. Specifically, there has been a tendency to believe that premillennialists, in anticipating an imminent Rapture of the Saints, give no thought to making the world a better place other than as a consequence, perhaps, of maximizing the number of the saved rounded up through evangelism. The cause of environmentalism in particular is seen as of no interest to them, since what possible reason could there be for preserving the environment if, within a short time, there is going to be no environment around to preserve? This point of view has repeatedly, and I'm afraid mistakenly, been attributed to James Watt, Secretary of the Interior in the Reagan administration.[6]

Such a position may logically follow from certain apocalyptic scenarios, though not so plausibly from a premillennialist one that envisages Christ returning after seven years of post-Rapture Tribulation to rule on earth for a thousand years. Whatever the case, and as appealing as it may be to some to be able to dismiss Evangelicals as religious wackos, actual survey data show that most Evangelicals in fact support environmental protection.[7] And as far as expecting the Rapture to come any moment now, the enthusiasm with which contemporary Evangelicals build religious institutions, send their children to college, and generally store up the goods of this world would seem to give the lie to the idea that they are a bunch of latter-day Millerites perched on hillsides waiting for the end. Indeed, it is worth arguing, but not here and now, that many Evangelicals, and especially those who come out of the broad Methodist tradition, have reconnected to their social reformist roots, reversing the so-called Great Reversal of the early twentieth century.

For the present, what I want to suggest is that, if we're interested in the social and political consequences of resurgent Evangelicalism, we would do better to focus less on what we consider the logical implications of a theology of Rapture, Tribulation, and Armageddon and instead take a look at popular examples of the premillennialist world view. These days, the best place to do that is via the fabulously successful—to the tune of 60 million copies sold, and counting—*Left Behind* series, written by Tim LaHaye and Jerry B. Jenkins. For those who may not be among the legion of readers of these novels, let me simply say that this fictionalized version of the end times does not concern itself with the good Christians who are raptured away on the twenty-first page of the first volume. Instead, as is traditional in this genre of imaginative literature, and such a genre does exist, the focus is on those who have been, well, left behind.[8] And what consumes the series is the struggle of a small band of heroes—the Tribulation Force—to combat the evil empire of the Antichrist by creating a worldwide movement known as the Christian Collective. That it is somewhat theologically irregular for some of those who are not raptured to manage to get a second chance at salvation—no Christian left behind, as it were—has been noted with asperity by some conservative theological critics of the series. My purpose here, however, is simply to suggest that the significance of *Left Behind* premillennialism in constructing the outlook of Evangelicals lies not in apocalypticism so much as in a vision of Christians, including, let it be said, anticipated Jewish converts to Christianity, constituting a beleaguered but resourceful body of warrior pilgrims, working together to defeat the powers and principalities even as they work alone on their individual salvation.

In *Fundamentalism and American Culture*, his magisterial account of the formative period of this religious tradition, George Marsden puzzles over the enthusiasm with which fundamentalists threw themselves into what he calls "hyper-American patriotic anticommunism." "How," Marsden asks, "could premillennialists, whose attention was supposed to be directed away from politics while waiting for the coming King, embrace this highly politicized gospel?" Confessing that it "is difficult to account for the phenomenon on simply rational grounds," he turns for an explanation to Richard Hofstadter's portrait of the fundamentalist mentality as "essentially Manichaean." The predilection of fundamentalists "to divide *all* reality into neat antitheses: the saved and the lost, the holy and the unsanctified, the true and the false," enabled premillennialists to align their politics with their religion, and to place both into "the framework of the conflict between the forces of God and of Satan."[9]

Evangelical politics today is nothing if not a world of us and them. It is issue-oriented politics, to be sure, but it has become, equally if not more so, partisan politics. The process by which white Evangelicals have been transformed into the most important voting bloc in the Republican Party is, it seems to me, powerful evidence of this. To cite only the most obvious example, the IRS problems of the Christian Coalition had to do with the fact that its "nonpartisan" voter guides, under the guise of comparing candidates on the basis of their stands on issues, in fact systematically skewed the comparisons to make the GOP candidates come out ahead. At the risk of stretching a point, I would even suggest that the Evangelicals' Manichaean style of American politics can be seen in the partisan regime instituted by the Republicans in the U.S. House of Representatives in the 1990s—under which, as a matter of principle, legislative majorities were never to be put together by negotiating with members of the other side.

There are, to be sure, other religious—or ethno-religious—groups whose voting patterns are highly skewed in favor of one political party or the other. Among these others, though, it is not uncommon to hear worries that this is not a good thing. Prominent African Americans and Jews from time to time make the case that their people would benefit from having staked a greater claim in the Republican Party, while in recent years the voice of Mormon authority has been raised to express concern for the lack of Democrats in the Church of Jesus Christ of Latter-day Saints. The Evangelical position, by contrast, has tended to be: the GOP or nothing. Perhaps the cold shower of the 2006 midterm election will change this, but that remains to be seen.

So what of the future of Jewish-Evangelical relations? I confess I fail to see much prospect of a new entente, heartfelt or merely pragmatic. I don't doubt that there will continue to be issues on which common cause is made. These will run from lobbying together on behalf of threatened populations, such as in the case of Darfur, to domestic efforts to secure greater support for religious liberty in the courts, as in the great Religious Freedom Restoration Act coalition of the early 1990s. On Israel, I would say that the rule is, the better it looks for a peace process that involves territorial compromise by the Israelis, the worse it will look for a united front of Jewish organizations and at least those Evangelical groups that have been most prominent in Washington in recent years. "Support for Israel" is one thing when it means standing with the Israelis against suicide bombers and worldwide criticism, quite another when it aligns itself with a truculent and marginalized settler movement against Israeli government policy.

On the domestic front, I believe we must wait for politically engaged Evangelical leaders to enunciate more clearly what it is that they would like by way of a regime of religious boundaries in American society. How much religious expression is too much in the public schools? What limits on religious expression should be observed by public officials and in public spaces? What rules should restrict government funding of religious social services? Whatever one makes of Noah Feldman's approach to solving our current church-state woes— getting stricter against material support for religious entities while allowing more latitude for public expressions of religion—the fact is that the boundary issues involving free exercise and establishment are very much up in the air, and if the most prominent voices in the Evangelical community wish to enlist the support of religious minorities, they need, for starters, to specify what they think goes beyond what the Constitution permits and what they desire.[10]

There is, I suppose, some possibility that Evangelicals will pull away from their staunch Republicanism in reaction to a discredited George W. Bush, a chastened experience with Middle East military adventurism, a discovery that fighting AIDS and securing affordable health care and combating poverty may occasionally outweigh "values" votes, and (as in the recent senatorial race in Pennsylvania) the presence of prominent Democratic candidates who seem to stand with them on at least some of the values issues. Just as heightened religious partisanship is contagious, so is reduced religious partisanship. Jews will be more likely to vote Republican—and thereby to warm up to Evangelicals—to the extent that the GOP seems less in thrall to the Christian Right. Apart from politics per se, it doesn't hurt that more moderate voices from the mainstream Evangelical community have begun to be heard above the din.

Let me emphasize that none of the above is meant to suggest that I think Evangelicals are not entitled to keep on keeping on. They have the right, and if they choose to see it that way, the duty, to carry out the Great Commission as they see fit, to violate polite ecumenical manners, to politick and lobby for as low a wall of separation as they like, and even to seek to rewrite the religion clauses of the First Amendment if that is what they want. That's what religious liberty is all about. It's just that they should not expect their devotion to Israel, however expressed, to be enough to win a *nihil obstat* or a vow of silence from American Jews.

On the Jewish side, there will doubtless continue to be the notable but marginal bodies that cultivate the Evangelical Right, such as Yechiel Eckstein's International Fellowship of Christians and Jews and Daniel Lapin's Toward Tradition. More importantly, the Orthodox minority of Jews will, as it has for some time, continue to march more in time to the Evangelical beat, and cast its votes for Republicans. The greater Orthodox sympathy for Evangelical issues, and the greater Orthodox willingness to live as strangers in a strange land, makes for easier alliances with Evangelical activists. And that is not altogether a bad thing. For their part, Jews as a whole will have to learn that the level of church-state separation that could be dreamt of a generation ago cannot be dreamt of now—at least not if they wish to live in the real world. All fights are not worth fighting, and among those not worth fighting I, like many others, would include the fight to remove "under God" from school recitation of the Pledge.

Most Jews do not live where there are a lot of Evangelicals, and vice versa. This means that the two groups are likely to view each other less as real people than as representative types, and as types represented in the news media by particular emblematic figures, be they leaders of religious organizations or celebrities of another kind. By and large, that is not a good thing. As someone who lived for nearly a decade in one of those few places where there are significant numbers of both Jews and Evangelicals—Atlanta—I would conclude by saying that I am not worried about the future of Jewish-Evangelical relations on the person-to-person level. At the playground and in the office and even on the PTA, they'll do just fine. But I do believe there is something important to be gained, on both sides, by better relations at the level of what I'll call, for lack of a better term, national communal leadership. And I wouldn't rate the prospects for that very high at the moment.

NOTES

1. Nathan Perlmutter and Ruth Ann Perlmutter, *The Real Anti-Semitism in America* (New York: Arbor House, 1982), 156.
2. Andrew Walsh, "Preaching the Word in Littleton," *Religion in the News* 2.2 (Summer, 1999).
3. Anne C. Loveland, "The God Squad," *Religion in the News* 8.2 (Fall, 2005).
4. E. J. Kessler, "ADL Urges Joint Effort Again Right," *Forward*, Nov. 11, 2005.
5. A useful book that, in my view, overstates the case for premillennialism as the cause of Evangelicals' support for Israel is Timothy P. Weber's *On the Road to Armageddon: How Evangelicals Became Israel's Best Friend* (Grand Rapids, MI: Baker Academic, 2004), esp. chapter 8.
6. See, for example, Bill Moyers, "Welcome to Doomsday," *New York Review of Books*, Mar. 24, 2005.
7. Not, to be sure, as enthusiastically as some American religious groupings, but support it they do. See surveys conducted by John Green for the Pew Center on People and the Press, 1992–2004.
8. For an extended account of the this-worldly outlook of the series, see Amy Johnson Frykholm, "What Social and Political Messages Appear in the Left Behind Books? A Literary Discussion of Millenarian Fiction," in Bruce David Forbes and Jeanne Halgren Kilde, eds., *Rapture, Revelation, and the End Times* (New York: Palgrave Macmillan, 2004), 167–95.
9. George M. Marsden, *Fundamentalism and American Culture: The Shaping of Twentieth-Century Evangelicalism 1870–1925* (New York: Oxford University Press, 1980), 210–11.
10. Noah Feldman, *Divided By God* (New York: Farrar, Straus and Giroux, 2005), 235–49.

⑫

Notes for a
Jewish-Evangelical Conversation

David Neff

In the 1970s and 1980s, Evangelicals and Jews engaged in structured conversations that were largely built around theological and religious questions. The resulting volumes[1] laid a solid foundation for future interreligious dialogue.

However, the present social and political climate in the United States has prompted a different set of questions: questions about the implications for religious minorities of Evangelical political and cultural activity and about the sense of apprehension that activism raises in the Jewish community.[2]

Q: Has the Religious Right peaked? Is the country less polarized than in the past few years?

A: Let us recognize that the polarization of the country in the past few years has been provoked by activist groups who have a stake in encouraging and maintaining the polarization. Consider first the politically premature forays into gay marriage by San Francisco Mayor Gavin Newsom and the states of Vermont and Massachusetts. Many gay activists were advising that such public events should wait until after the 2004 election. Instead, those who moved ahead gave the activist Right exactly what it needed to mobilize voters. I was present at a small gathering of Evangelical leaders at Focus on the Family headquarters when James Dobson announced in apocalyptic terms that the civilization hung on the issue of gay marriage. If memory serves, Dobson said, "If we lose this one, civilization is over."

Though the wholesale introduction of gay marriage would force American society and its conservative Christian churches to entirely rethink the relationship between civil marriage and the church, it would hardly bring the end of civilization. Nevertheless, I believe Dr. Dobson and others who reacted so strongly genuinely believed what they said.

Without the premature actions on the part of gay marriage proponents, the so-called values voters of the 2004 general election would not have been mobilized in such great numbers. And Dr. Dobson himself would not have created a separate organization (Focus Action) that allowed him to do explicitly political work that was not within the legal purview of Focus on the Family's 501(c)(3) status.

It is arguably the case that it was those who decided to push gay marriage at that particular time who nearly guaranteed George Bush's election to a second term. Now, after the 2006 mid-term election, gay marriage has been banned in the vast majority of states (either by statute or by constitutional amendment) and that issue will not give the activists on the Right anywhere near the same degree of leverage with which to organize and mobilize voters.

Recent news reports have detailed the Christian Coalition's loss of state-level chapters in Ohio, Iowa, and Alabama. According to an AP report, the organization founded by Pat Robertson is "now left with only a half-dozen strong state chapters and a weak presence in Washington."[3]

Similarly, a July poll conducted by the Pew Forum on Religion and Public Life and the Pew Research Center for the People and the Press revealed signs of disaffection with the Republican Party on the part of many Evangelicals. According to an article by the *New York Times'* Laurie Goodstein, 14 percent fewer Catholics and white Evangelical Protestants found the GOP "friendly to religion" than a year ago. (Compare this to an 8 percent decline among Americans generally.)[4] And after the 2006 elections, a Pew Forum study revealed that while 41 percent of white Evangelicals were unhappy that Democrats had won the election, 41 percent, an equal proportion, were happy with the results.[5]

These signs suggest that neither the Republican Party nor the Christian Right has a firm grip on white Evangelical voters. They will vote their consciences on key issues that matter to them, but they are not strongly partisan. The polarization is not political—though it may be moral (more on that later).

Second, consider that it was the op-ed writers in the mainstream media who after the 2004 elections discovered that "values voters" and "Evangelicals" existed in the numbers that they do. The immediate post-election writing tended to create "polarization" by telling liberal readers of the mainstream media about a new "enemy."

One of the most polarizing was Garry Wills' column "The Day the Enlightenment Went Out"[6] in which the Northwestern University historian argues (major premise) that a pluralist society whose different elements respect and live peaceably with each other is impossible without an Enlightenment spirit. He then proceeds to state (minor premise) that the key voting bloc courted by Karl Rove to give George Bush the 2004 election believes more fervently in the Virgin Birth than in evolution and is therefore anti-Enlightenment, therefore, (conclusion) we are losing our Enlightenment-based pluralism and it's all Karl Rove's fault. That may be logical (in a syllogistic sense), but it doesn't account for the fact that Evangelicals in their neighborhoods are actually quite tolerant and functionally pluralistic. Such arguments merely create a self-fulfilling prophecy of polarization.

Compare "The Dream Is Lost," James Ridgway's *Village Voice* piece, which was subtitled, "Bush Gets a Mandate for Theocracy." Ridgeway writes: "The dream of a secular, liberal democracy is lost: Christians are stronger than ever . . . "[7] This is the language of polarization which creates its own reality.

Recently, Jewish institutional leaders like Abraham Foxman,[8] James Rudin[9] and Michael Lerner[10] have similarly been identifying the enemy as the Religious Right. But their efforts (especially Foxman's) sound to these Evangelical ears like they are confusing liberal politics with Judaism in the same way that some activists on the Right confuse conservative politics with Christianity. The polarization feeds on this kind of confusion.

Third, understand that America's grassroots Evangelicals, many of whom were "values voters," really didn't change a whole lot during this period. And I suspect that before, during, and after, most of these Evangelicals were the sort described by Alan Wolfe in *The Transformation of American Religion.*[11] These were people who are committed to a particular set of biblically informed values, but who are also very tolerant of their neighbors. As long as you don't try to formally enshrine in law departures from their traditional morality, they will be neighborly to those with unorthodox lifestyles and beliefs. Unfortunately, many of these people are like those Wolfe described in *Moral Freedom*: Evangelicals who reason as individualistically and pragmatically as their secular counterparts. In *Transformation* Wolfe told the panicky Left to calm down: American religiosity, though pervasive, wasn't going to be all that dangerous. If you want dangerous religion, look to India, not Indiana.

Fourth, America's grassroots Evangelicals may vote in large numbers along the lines promoted by the Religious Right, but that does not mean that they are uncritical fans of the Religious Right. Instead, we must recognize that Evangelical Protestants broadly share the traditional values promoted by the Religious Right, but not the stridency. They believe that marriage inherently involves two sexes, and that God ordained it that way. (This is not, by the way, a view that threatens the Jewish community. The more traditional forms of Judaism also believe that marriage by definition involves two sexes and that God ordained that arrangement.)

Likewise, these Evangelical Protestant voters want to protect the free exercise of religion, and that includes the free exercise of religion in the public square. They do not see this as forcing their religion on others of different religions or of no religion. Instead, they argue that this helps to secure the free exercise of everyone's religion.

Fifth, let us ask why we are focusing so much on the Religious Right? The Religious Right is not anti-Jewish, and indeed it often works closely with Jewish activists.

But more importantly, the Religious Right is not even close to being one of the main identities that Evangelicals employ to think about themselves. From within the community, I can tell you that Evangelical Protestants think of themselves as being a biblically formed people (something they share with religious Jews). They think of themselves as fostering changed lives—often, but not exclusively, as the result of becoming a follower of Jesus. They think of themselves as people saved from sin and its power, but they are realistic about their need for that salvation. They know, personally, sin and its power, and thus they place equal emphasis on knowing Jesus and experiencing his power. While the label *Evangelical* is tricky to define, one dimension that stands out in the history of the movement is its common belief that sinners saved by grace can live transformed lives and need not be slaves to destructive behaviors. The familiar lines from John Newton's "Amazing Grace" epitomize this Evangelical self-perception as people transformed: "I once was lost, but now am found; was blind, but now I see." Newton became an antislavery activist, but his religious self-perception was always that of the saved sinner in constant need of transforming grace.

Q: What are the key issues from an Evangelical perspective regarding the Jewish community?

A: Frankly, most American Evangelicals don't spend a lot of time thinking about Jews and the Jewish community. Our populations are geographically concentrated so that most Jews have little interaction with Evangelicals, and most Evangelicals have little real interaction with Jews.

But when American Evangelicals do think about Jews, issues relating to Israel appear near the top of the list. American Evangelicals are great believers in democracy. When Yechiel Eckstein's Stand for Israel surveyed its largely Evangelical constituency, it was Israel's mitigating role as a democracy in the Middle East—and not some end-times scenario—that was most important to this cohort of active supporters of Israel.

Evangelicals are also intrigued by the existence of a Jewish community, to the extent that it represents a community of mutual obedience to the One God. We are fascinated by a community of tradition in an antitraditional era. We want to know how a community of tradition can survive in our hypermodern climate. (Let us be clear, though, that Evangelicals are probably not willing to give up their individual autonomy to achieve that. But they are interested, nevertheless.)

Evangelicals are also interested in the Jewish community because of puzzling gaps between us. We share the Hebrew Scriptures, and yet we read them very differently. We are often brought up short by the fact that we don't actually read and act on these texts in what seem to be obvious ways.

Some Evangelicals, those influenced by premillenial dispensationalism, are convinced that as part of the events of the Last Days, there will be a mass conversion of Jews to following Jesus. But even those who do not follow that particular dispensationalist scenario have to come to terms with Paul's notion in Romans 11 that there is only a "partial hardening [that] has come upon Israel, until the fullness of the Gentiles has come in." Every Evangelical Christian has to regard Paul's assertion that "as regards the gospel, they are enemies of God for your sake. But as regards election, they are beloved for the sake of their forefathers. For the gifts and the calling of God are irrevocable."[12]

Within this framework created by Paul, Jews are not for Evangelicals just one among the religious groups in the world. They are beloved of God "for the sake of their forefathers," and in God's time, he will show them the same mercy that he has shown to Gentile Christians. The continued existence of the Jewish community is a sign of that hope. To the extent that Evangelicals believe that, they want to share God's love for Jews.

This gets us into the sticky area of the evangelization of Jews. The so-called "targeting" of Jews for evangelism is controversial within Evangelical circles. Billy Graham, on the one hand, has said that he does not believe in targeting Jews for evangelism, but will evangelize them only as part of the mass of the American people. Rabbi Marc Tanenbaum applauded Graham's statements and quoted them over and over. Organizations like Jews for Jesus and Chosen People Ministries, on the other hand, will argue that they have a special calling to bring the good news about Jesus to Jewish people today. And they will point out that all evangelization, like all effective communication, needs to be framed in terms that will appeal to a particular target audience. But while Evangelicals disagree about "targeting" Jews, all will agree that it is appropriate for them to share their faith with and pray for the salvation of Jews.

What I want to stress is this: the great threat to the Jewish community today does not come from Jews for Jesus. It comes from intermarriage and cultural assimilation. Very few observant Jews who are fully integrated into a worshiping and observant community are going to be receptive to the approaches of Christian evangelists. My word to the Jewish community is not to rail against Jews for Jesus, but to shore up your own bonds of community.

Q: Have Evangelical groups, like the Southern Baptists, in recent years abandoned their historical separatist viewpoint to adopt a viewpoint similar to the Catholics? That is to say, have they traded separationism for accommodationism? How and why did it occur? What have been its consequences for the Evangelical groups, for the Religious Right, for the Jewish community, for politics, culture, and public policy?

A: American Baptists have their roots in the 1643 departure of Roger Williams from Salem, Massachusetts and his theories of complete separation. This was the historic Baptist position. Let government be government and not interfere with the church. And let the church be the church and not interfere with the government.

I would trace the change to two things (although, I'll advance my explanations as a journalist's hunches rather than as a historian's well-researched conclusions). First, in 1978, during the Carter administration, the IRS threatened the tax-exempt status of Christian schools that did not meet their standards of racial integration. Whether these were white-flight academies or something else can be debated, but the Evangelical Christian community felt this as an invasion of the government onto their constitutionally protected turf, their right to educate their own children in their own way.

Some political activists had earlier tried to mobilize conservative Christians around the abortion issue, but they had failed. It was the interference with private schools that finally allowed them to mobilize the voters. In *With God on Our Side*, William Martin recounts his interview with Paul Weyrich:

> Weyrich explained that while Christians were troubled about abortion, school prayer, and the ERA, they felt able to deal with those on a private basis. They could avoid having abortions, put their children in Christian schools, and run their families the way they wanted to, all without having to be concerned about public policy. But the IRS threat "enraged the Christian community and they looked upon it as interference from government, and it suddenly dawned on them that they were not going to be able to be left alone to teach their children as they pleased. It was at that moment that conservatives made the linkage between their opposition to government interference and the interests of the Evangelical movement, which now saw itself on the defensive and under attack by the government. That was what brought those people into the political process. It was not the other things.[13]

This helped move one particular slice of the public (in a heavily Baptist part of the country) from a strict separationism (we'll do our thing and the government can just leave us alone) to an accommodationism (government has no business restricting our free exercise, and indeed it has a positive duty to make room for, to accommodate, our practice).

The second factor pertains particularly to the Southern Baptists. Having foreseen a decline of their denomination into liberal theology, a group of key leaders plotted out a specific strategy for reclaiming their institutions—both churches and institutions of higher learning— for a more conservative theological approach. But this very successful, though bruising, approach to the internal politics of the denomination bred a similar feistiness in the public arena. The internal Southern Baptist struggles shed a certain gentlemanly approach that had once characterized their polity, and that same uncompromising desire to have their way started to make itself manifest in their public policy arm. And the theme of "reclamation" was manifested. In addition to reclaiming their denomination from a slide into theological and social liberalism, they wanted to reclaim America from a slide into social and moral liberalism. Now, you can't do that while also trying to sound like Roger Williams.

What has changed? The earlier practice of strict separationism inherited from Roger Williams and Isaac Backus protected the community during the heavy waves of Catholic immigration—Italian, Irish,
German, Polish, etc. Denying public support to Catholic schools, for
example, protected the Protestant hegemony in public education in
much of America.

That was a long time ago. But as the Christian schools became a
focal point for activism, Catholics and Baptists joined forces in seeking
not just accommodation but public funding for the dimensions of their
schools that were not strictly religious. Whereas strict separationism
served to foster nativism and anti-Catholicism, accommodationism
serves to foster religious communities in an aggressively secularist age.

**Q: Who makes policy decisions in the Evangelical community? What
is the process? How does this relate to the Jewish community? What
is meant by the phrase "the role that Jews play in the Evangelical
imagination?"**

A: Who makes policy decisions?

Evangelicals have no equivalent to a rabbinical court. Instead, we
have activists and ethicists who must be persuasive. In fact, they also
do a certain amount of political horse-trading. Behind the scenes, they
will agree that this year they will cooperate on a given issue, and then
next year they'll support someone else's issue. But ultimately, they
must persuade (or bully).

And it is also interesting to note that many of those who shape
Evangelical opinion on policy issues are not necessarily trained as
clergy. James Dobson is regularly referred to as Rev. Dobson in the
mainstream media, but he is a psychologist, not a minister. Charles
Colson is a serious student of Christian theology, but his training is as
a lawyer and his preconversion career was in politics. Pat Robertson,
who may or may not actually shape much opinion anymore, is often
referred to as a minister, but he was trained as a lawyer, and he taught
himself the business of broadcasting. He was not, to my knowledge,
formally ordained as a Christian minister.

These opinion leaders must be persuasive. The Terry Schiavo case
was one of those situations where, despite all the rhetoric, the Evangelical grassroots did not just up and follow their leaders. The lack of
factual clarity in the case, combined with the wrenching personal decisions that modern medicine brings to all of us, created a kind of ambivalent sympathy for both sides of the Schiavo family struggle. The
case didn't lend itself to activism.

Something similar can be said about research with embryonic stem cells. Most grassroots Evangelicals, like most Americans, lack the technical knowledge to evaluate the claims of researchers. But they all have family members or friends who suffer from diseases like juvenile diabetes, Alzheimer's disease, or Parkinson's, and they dream of something better for those they love. Once again, the principled opposition of the conservative Christian leadership runs into a brick wall of sympathy that clouds the issues.

Homosexuality presents another interesting area of exploration. While there is pretty solid opposition to changing the definition of marriage, there is not nearly the same level of resistance to homosexual persons—including homosexual couples. The human face of those gay coworkers or gay neighbors helps grassroots Evangelicals to distinguish between activist forces in the political arena and the persons they work with and (in my own case) play Scrabble with. I believe we will see continued growth in the number of states banning gay marriage at the same time that we will not see any growth in actual homophobia.

Now about that phrase "the role Jews play in the Evangelical imagination." I have used that phrase in several conversations and it has provoked some Jewish curiosity.

Here is what I mean by that phrase.

First, Jews have a special place in the Evangelical imagination because we share the Hebrew Scriptures, and on this particular point, Evangelicals seem to have held onto their Puritan heritage of identifying themselves with Israel. This takes two forms.

One is the idea that God has formed the church today as a covenant community that is reminiscent of ancient Israel. And along with that covenant come the blessings and curses appropriate to the obedience or disobedience of the community. There is thus a sense of destiny, but also a sense of obligation and also of judgment.

The judgment theme is illustrated, for example, in Mark Buchanan's *The Rest of God*, which is a series of Christian meditations on the Christian Sabbath.[14] The author repeatedly identifies with those with whom Jesus had his disputes over the Sabbath. He helps his readers identify with the Pharisees so that they can see how his word of judgment or correction applies to them.

This is a very old Christian trope. Indeed, it goes back to Paul's first letter to the Christians at Corinth. In chapter 10 he writes: "These things happened to them as examples and were written down as warnings for us, on whom the fulfillment of the ages has come. So, if you think you are standing firm, be careful that you don't fall!"[15] Paul asks the Jesus followers to identify with ancient Israel in its temptations as a way of guarding against unfaithfulness.

As a result of this kind of preaching and writing, many Evangelical Christians think of themselves as "spiritually" Jewish. This, in turn, lends itself to a kind of romanticism about Jews and Judaism, which is manifested in the fact that a rather large percentage of people who attend the so-called Messianic fellowships or Messianic Christian assemblies are Gentiles who find something appealing about the music and the slightly exotic mode of worship.

Second, I have already mentioned the varying degrees to which Evangelicals believe that God's covenant with Abraham means an ongoing love for the Jewish community (see Romans 11 again). Whether this is rather vague and apolitical or whether it is distilled into a fervent Christian Zionism, it is nevertheless present. And so Evangelicals feel a sense of attachment, because (in Paul's metaphor) they have been grafted onto the same tree.

Q: What are the implications of the answers to these questions? Should Jews and Evangelicals work for a greater rapport and can their relationship crystallize around something other than support for Israel? Is their relationship a purely tactical affair (on the Jewish side) or can it grow in a broader, more empathetic way?

A: We must be clear that Jews and Evangelicals are already working together in interesting ways—even on the Right. Michael Horowitz of the Hudson Institute is not a formal leader of the Jewish community, but he is someone who worked in the Reagan administration on the Campaign to Free Soviet Jewry. He has stuck out his neck politically for the international Jewish community and subsequently for imperiled Christians in Muslim and Communist lands. The tremendous push by Evangelicals over the past ten years to enhance religious freedom in places like Sudan and China would never have happened without Michael. But the grassroots support has largely come from Evangelicals.

Likewise, Evangelicals who worry about sleaze in the media have found an ally in Orthodox Jewish film critic Michael Medved. If you look at the most popular talk shows on the Salem Radio Network, the largest radio network to serve a largely Evangelical Christian listenership, two of the most popular shows are hosted by Jews: Michael Medved and Dennis Prager. There are plenty of Jews who move in conservative and neoconservative circles who are not at all upset by the accommodationist tendencies of Evangelicals.

So what should we do? Evangelicals who have a principled accommodationist stance should make it clear, whenever they can, that they are fighting for the accommodation of all legitimate religious practice. And when it means fighting for the rights of Jews in the military or in prisons or in corporations to practice their religion freely, Evangelicals should fight for those rights. Evangelicals who have a principled separationist stance should also make it clear that their separationism is precisely for the freedom of all religions.

Evangelicals need to learn how the *adversus Judaeos* tradition colors the Jewish perception of Evangelical words and actions. Yehiel Poupko has argued, and rightly so, that "medieval Christians wanted to convert Jews because they hated them, while contemporary Evangelicals want to convert Jews because they love them." What Evangelicals need to understand is that whether it is attempts at conversion or support for cultural phenomena like Mel Gibson's *The Passion of the Christ*, it is hard for Jews not to filter these words and events through a particular history.

At the same time, it seems to me, that Jews need to recognize that in contemporary American Evangelicalism, they are dealing with a completely different phenomenon than the historical Christian churches of Europe. Gibson's movie did not precipitate any fresh pogroms. And the Evangelical Christian audience that gave it such a warm remembrance fit it into their theology that it was their own sins—not the Jewish leadership—that put Jesus on the cross.

Evangelical Christians and Jews of all stripes have some fundamental differences. We will not overcome those in dialogue, nor will we get past them if we join forces to combat evils like sex trafficking or worrisome trends like the general coarsening of our mass culture. Those differences are fixed parts of our religious identities.

But, in dialogue and common action, we hope that our leaders can learn to temper their rhetoric and avoid the temptation to play to the crowd. And, we hope, many will get to know real people whose rhetoric has been open to misunderstanding, but whose heart, minds, and intentions are committed to the common good.

NOTES

1. See M. H. Tanenbaum, M.R. Wilson, and A. J. Rudin, eds., *Evangelicals and Jews in Conversation on Scripture, Theology, and History* (Grand Rapids, MI: Baker Books, 1978), 326; M. H. Tanenbaum, M. R. Wilson, and A. J. Rudin, eds., *Evangelicals and Jews in an Age of Pluralism* (Grand Rapids, MI: Baker Books, 1984), 285; and A. J. Rudin and M. R. Wilson, eds., *A Time to Speak: The Evangelical-Jewish Encounter* (Grand Rapids, MI: William B. Eerdmans Publishing Co., 1987).

2. The form of the questions addressed in this paper was developed by Nancy Isserman, Alan Mittleman, and Byron Johnson in preparation for a panel discussion at the Uneasy Allies conference, held at The Jewish Theological Seminary, Nov. 30 to Dec. 1, 2005.

3. David Crary, "Christian Coalition Losing Chapters," Associated Press, Aug. 23, 2006, news.yahoo.com/s/ap/20060823/ap_on_el_ge/christian_coalition.

4. Laurie Goodstein, "In Poll, G.O.P. Slips as a Friend of Religion," *New York Times*, Aug. 25, 2006.

5. The Pew Forum on Religion and Public Life, "Religion and the 2006 Election," pewforum.org/docs/index.php?DocID=174.

6. Garry Wills, "The Day the Enlightenment Went Out," *New York Times*, Late Edition—Final, Section A, 25, Nov. 4, 2004.

7. James Ridgway, "The Dream Is Lost: Bush Gets a Mandate for Theocracy," *The Village Voice*, Nov. 3, 2004.

8. Abraham Foxman, "Religion in America's Public Square: Are We Crossing the Line?" excerpts from an address to the ADL National Commission Meeting, Nov. 3, 2005, www.adl.org/Religious_Freedom/religion_public_square.asp.

9. James Rudin, *The Baptizing of America: The Religious Right's Plans for the Rest of Us* (New York: Thunder's Mouth Press, 2006).

10. Michael Lerner, *The Left Hand of God: Taking Back Our Country from the Religious Right* (San Francisco: HarperSanFrancisco, 2006).

11. Alan Wolfe, *The Transformation of American Religion: How We Actually Live Our Faith* (New York: Free Press, 2003).

12. Romans 11:25, 28–29.

13. William Martin, *With God on Our Side: The Rise of the Religious Right in America* (New York: Broadway Books, 1996), 173.

14. Mark Buchanan, *The Rest of God: Restoring Your Soul by Restoring Sabbath* (Nashville: W Publishing Group, 2006).

15. 1 Corinthians 10:11–12, New International Version.

13

What Makes Evangelical and Jewish Relations Uneasy?

Byron Johnson

Uneasy Allies? provides important analyses and thoughtful insights regarding the current landscape of Evangelical and Jewish relations. Drawing upon many disciplines and methodologies, Evangelical and Jewish scholars are able to offer a variety of perspectives, opinions, and data on the nature of this evolving relationship. In this way, this book makes an important and much-needed contribution to the literature and advances our knowledge in an area too often neglected by scholars.

Uneasy Allies? provides an historical and contemporary context between Evangelicals and Jews informing points of agreement as well as disagreement. In addition, scholars in this volume raise many important questions for future research. For instance, how, if at all, will Evangelical and Jewish relations be influenced by the expected rise in the number of Evangelicals over the next decade or two? Correspondingly, what will be the consequence if the predicted decline of Mainline Protestant denominations continues? Will Evangelical Christians become even more pro-Israel as their numbers increase? Will Mainline Protestant Christians become less supportive of Israel? We know that while Evangelicals tend be more conservative on political and moral issues, they are also likely to take some fairly "liberal" stances on a number of social issues (e.g. protecting the environment, the role of government in social justice related matters). What is the likelihood, therefore, that support of Israel might actually increase or erode over time among different subsets of both Evangelical and Mainline Christians?

A number of important themes emerge from virtually every chapter in *Uneasy Allies?* Perhaps the most obvious theme is Evangelical Christians tend to be some of the most ardent and vocal supporters of Israel. Multiple data sources confirm that Evangelical Christians have been and clearly remain consistently pro-Israel. Further, increasing levels of religiosity or religious commitment (e.g., higher levels of religious participation, belief, or practices) tend to be associated with even higher levels of support for Israel. What is not obvious, however, is the percentage of Jews that might embrace or be conflicted by these findings. Future research, for example, should examine different subsets of Jews to determine if views of Evangelical support for Israel vary across different subgroups of Jews. Findings from such research will likely carry considerable implications for the future of Evangelical and Jewish relations.

An equally obvious and related theme that appears throughout *Uneasy Allies?* is the observation that most Jews tend to be suspicious or, at best, ambivalent about Evangelical support of Israel. Though it may well be the case that most Jews are troubled about the unsolicited support of Evangelicals, empirical evidence supporting this notion of suspicion and ambivalence is generally lacking. In other words, we have knowledge of highly publicized remarks of Jewish leaders criticizing Evangelicals, as well as various Jewish responses to controversial Evangelical efforts like Key 73, but there remains a need to replace anecdotes with both quantitative and qualitative research confirming that these views are pervasive or representative of American Jews. In fact, as *Uneasy Allies?* demonstrates, most Jews do not know a great deal about Evangelical Christians, much less the diverse positions held by American Protestants more generally. This realization is a rude reminder of the need for careful research examining not only Jewish perceptions of Evangelicals, but other Christian groups as well. We need to determine if different subgroups of the Jewish population hold divergent perceptions of Evangelicals. Do Orthodox Jews, for example, feel the same uneasiness that more secular Jews feel about Evangelicals in general and Evangelical support of Israel in particular? It would seem to make good sense to know if and how the consternation regarding Evangelical support of Israel varies among Jews.

Another central theme expressed by the authors in *Uneasy Allies?* is that Jews are often offended, and even threatened, by Evangelicals' widely acknowledged desire to evangelize Jews. Evangelicalism surely conjures up troublesome images not only for many Jews, but for many Mainline Christians as well. However, we do not know if the evangelistic fervor and motivation of some Evangelicals is a major or minor contributor to the uneasiness of Evangelical-Jewish relations. What do we have beyond anecdotes that provide support for the notion that Evangelicals are busy trying to convert Jews? Rigorous research documenting Evangelical motivation regarding evangelism or the desire to convert Jews is lacking. Further, we do not have systematic research documenting the experiences of Jews addressing the proselytizing advances of Evangelicals. In the absence of evidence documenting Evangelical efforts to convert Jews, we are in need of research that would identify the actual basis for the threat posed by Evangelicals.

There may be as many as 100 million Evangelical Christians in America, yet remarkably, we know little about what Evangelicals think about Evangelicals. For example, recent research indicates only 15 percent of people attending Evangelical congregations identify themselves as Evangelicals.[1] We do not know if Evangelicals think Evangelicalism is synonymous with evangelism. In fact, defining Evangelicals is itself an uneasy task. For some Evangelicals it is surely the case that evangelism is fundamental to Evangelicalism. It may also be true that Evangelicalism is not primarily about evangelism. We need to know, for example, if Evangelicalism is more about proselytizing or if it is more about worship style, social activism, or adopting a worldview where one's faith informs each and every aspect of one's life—private as well as public. If the latter is true, this would help explain why many Evangelicals feel under attack by a culture that often promotes, in their eyes, a worldview very much in opposition to their own. Clearly, there is a need for solid empirical research on the makeup of contemporary Evangelicals.

In the Gospel of Matthew, Jesus gave his disciples their final instructions in what has been commonly referred to as the "Great Commission" directing the disciples to ". . . go and make disciples . . ." (Mt 28:18). No doubt many Christians, as well as Jews, recognize this passage as the Christian charge for evangelism and conversion. Is it also reasonable to assume that many Evangelicals also believe that "the Great Commission" is less about winning converts, and more about strengthening the faith of fellow Christians? We need to know if Evangelicalism is more about evangelism or more about making disciples and the process of becoming mature Christian believers. In other words, it may be possible that Evangelicals are more focused on the spiritual development of those within their ranks than they are on the conversion of non-Christians.

The chapters of this book also point to another common theme, namely, that the majority of American Jews tend to be associated with liberal political and social positions, while the majority of Evangelicals tend to be identified with conservative moral, political, and social positions. Could it be that the significant distance between the majority of Jews and Evangelicals on these core issues is the primary factor behind the uneasiness? Do politically conservative Jews find Evangelical support of Israel to be as troubling as do politically liberal Jews? If not, one wonders if it is politics more than proselytizing that makes the relationship between Evangelicals and Jews such an uneasy one.

Ironically, it is worth noting that what tends to be ignored in these discussions of Evangelical and Jewish relations is that they are quite asymmetrical on religious grounds. What superficially might seem to be a dialogue among people of faith is largely a dialogue between orthodox Christians and a contingent that includes many "cultural" Jews who may be as uncomfortable, or nearly so, with deeply committed Jews as they are with Evangelicals. Thus, a strong current of antireligiousness may distort these conversations, especially if it is framed as objections to Evangelical Christianity rather than to religion in general. This is why, for example, we need to know if it might be easier for Evangelicals to find common ground with Orthodox Jews. Similarly, would Evangelicals and "cultural" Christians feel a similar uneasiness when discussing religious issues? If so, the uneasiness would seem to be more about the divide between religious and irreligious Americans than it is between Christian and Jew. As we look to next steps in the ongoing dialogue between Evangelicals and Jews, scholars need to seriously and systematically consider the issues causing tension between these two groups. Whether it is proselytizing, politics, or even the question of religiousness, we can and should know more about the factors contributing to the uneasiness of Evangelical and Jewish relations.

NOTE

1. When asked to indicate the one term that best describes their religious identity, Evangelicals are more likely to select Bible-believing, Born Again, or Theological Conservative, than they are to select the Evangelical label. See Christopher Bader, Kevin Dougherty, Paul Froese, Byron Johnson, Carson Mencken, Jerry Park, and Rodney Stark, *American Piety in the 21st Century: New Insights to the Depths and Complexity of Religion in the U.S.*, Baylor Institute for Studies of Religion, Baylor University, 2006.

Index

9/11, 2, 92, 147, 171

abortion, 67, 79, 94, 173, 179;
    Evangelicals and, 34–36, 91, 97,
    114, 116, 132, 156, 193; Jews and,
    56, 65, 168, 174–75
ADL. See Anti-Defamation League
AIPAC. See American Israeli Public
    Affairs Committee
AJC. See American Jewish
    Committee
American Center for Law and
    Justice, 58, 114
American Family Association, 59,
    64, 113
American Israeli Public Affairs
    Committee (AIPAC), 77, 96, 173
American Jewish Committee (AJC),
    vii, ix, xi, 51–53, 56–57, 59–62,
    72n53, 89, 97, 120
Antichrist, 61, 86, 110, 139, 183
Anti-Defamation League (ADL), 66,
    80, 97; conflict with Evangelicals,
    50–51, 58–61, 64, 72n55, 78, 90,
    170, 181; cooperation with

Evangelicals, vii, xi, 52–53, 55–57,
    62, 92, 168, 171–73
antisemitism, vii, x, 27, 50, 52–53,
    55, 57, 58, 60, 61–62, 64, 91, 98,
    115, 123, 128, 135, 150n31, 169,
    175, 180
Arafat, Yasir, 91, 116, 128
Armageddon. See end times

Baptists, 7, 41, 51, 52, 104, 112,
    192–93; support for Israel, 73–74,
    80, 106, 128, 140
Barth, Karl, 130, 140
Bauer, Gary, 75, 114, 128, 156, 176
Begin, Menachem, 53, 55, 76
biblical prophecy, and Israel, 36, 37,
    51, 53, 58, 80–81, 85–86, 94,
    107–11, 128, 136, 138–46, 151n45,
    157–58, 174. See also
    dispensationalism, end times,
    premillennialism, Second Coming
Buddhism, 1–4, 6, 13, 15, 16, 17, 40,
    42, 158
Burge, Gary, 144, 147, 151n45,
    153n73, 153n75

Contributors and Editors

Yaakov Ariel, Ph.D., is a graduate of the Hebrew University of Jerusalem and the University of Chicago, where he received his doctoral degree in 1986. A professor of religious studies at the University of North Carolina at Chapel Hill, Ariel writes extensively on Jewish-Christian relations and on Christian attitudes toward the Jewish people, and the Holy Land.

Gary Dorrien, Ph.D., is the Reinhold Niebuhr Professor of Social Ethics, Union Theological Seminary and professor of religion, Columbia University. He was previously the Parfet Distinguished Professor at Kalamazoo College, where he also served as dean of Stetson Chapel. Dorrien is the author of twelve books and approximately 175 articles in the fields of modern theology, social ethics, and political philosophy. His most recent books are *Imperial Designs: Neoconservatism and the New Pax Americana* (2004) and *The Making of American Liberal Theology: Crisis, Irony, and Postmodernity* (2006).

Ethan Felson is the associate executive director of the Jewish Council for Public Affairs (JCPA) in New York City. As JCPA's Director of Domestic Concerns, Felson works with the agency's thirteen national agencies and 125 local Jewish federations and community relations councils on a range of issues including interfaith relations. He is the author of the "National Affairs" article in the *2006 American Jewish Yearbook*. Felson is a graduate of Lehigh University and the University of Connecticut School of Law.

John C. Green, Ph.D., is director of the Ray C. Bliss Institute of Applied Politics at the University of Akron, a post he has held since 1988. He is also a senior fellow at the Pew Forum on Religion & Public Life and a distinguished professor of political science at the University of Akron, where he was recognized as an outstanding faculty member in 1989 and 1994. Dr. Green has done extensive research on American religion and politics, political parties, and campaign finance. He is coauthor of *The Diminishing Divide: Religion's Changing Role in American Politics* (2000). He has also edited twelve collections of essays, the best known of which are *The State of the Parties* (1999), and the most recent is *The Values Campaign? The Christian Right in the 2004 Elections*. In addition, he has published more than sixty scholarly articles and some thirty-five essays in the popular press.

Lawrence Grossman, Ph.D., is coeditor of the *American Jewish Year Book* as well as associate director of research for the American Jewish Committee. Among his numerous publications are the annual reports on Jewish communal affairs included in the *Year Book* for the past twenty years, and, recently, essays on "Jewish Religious Denominations" (*Cambridge Companion to American Judaism*, 2005) and "Jews—Middle Atlantic and Beyond" (*Religion and Public Life in the Middle Atlantic Region*, 2006). He has also contributed articles to the *Encyclopaedia Judaica*, 2nd ed. (2005) and to the *Encyclopedia of American Jewish History* (2006). Dr. Grossman has taught courses in American Jewish history and contemporary Jewish affairs at a number of colleges.

Nancy Isserman, Ph.D., is the associate director of the Feinstein Center for American Jewish History, Temple University, a position she has held since 1992. At the Feinstein Center she has directed several successful projects including the *Challenge and Change: History of the Jews* curriculum project. She is also codirector of the Transcending Trauma Project at Council for Relationships, the Division of Couple and Family Studies, Department of Psychiatry and Human Behavior, Jefferson Medical College. The Transcending Trauma Project is a large qualitative grounded research project that has interviewed 275 survivors and three generations of family members to understand how individuals cope, adapt, and rebuild their lives after extreme trauma. Dr. Isserman recently received her Ph.D. from the Graduate Center, City University of New York. Her dissertation, "'I Harbor No Hate': A Study of Intolerance and Tolerance in Holocaust Survivors," received the Randolph S. Braham Dissertation Award 2004–2005.

Byron Johnson, Ph.D., is professor of sociology and codirector of the Baylor Institute for Studies of Religion (ISR) as well as director of the Program on Prosocial Behavior, both at Baylor University. He is a senior fellow at the Witherspoon Institute in Princeton, New Jersey. Professor Johnson's research focuses on quantifying the effectiveness of faith-based organizations to confront various social problems. Recent publications have examined the efficacy of the "faith factor" in reducing crime and delinquency among at-risk youth in urban communities, and the impact of faith-based programs on recidivism reduction and prisoner reentry. Johnson's current interests include the role of religion in fostering prosocial youth behavior, an in-depth study of American Evangelicals, and a series of empirical studies on the religions of China.

Barry A. Kosmin, Ph.D., is currently research professor, Program in Public Policy & Law and Director of the Institute for the Study of Secularism in Society & Culture at Trinity College, Hartford, Connecticut. Dr. Kosmin has directed many demographic and social surveys including: *The 1990 CJF National Jewish Population Survey*; *The CUNY 1990 National Survey of Religious Identification*; *1998 National Survey of South African Jews*; *The National Survey of South African Jews 1998*; *The CUNY American Religious Identification Survey 2001*; and *The CUNY American Jewish Identification Survey 2001*. He is joint series editor (with Dr. Sidney Goldstein) of the monograph series *American Jewish Society in the 1990s* for the State University of New York Press.

George Mamo is executive director of Stand for Israel, the advocacy initiative of the International Fellowship of Christians and Jews. Mamo has been director of a day shelter for the homeless in Atlanta; executive director of the Central Atlanta Churches coalition; and vice president of Feed The Children; and has held senior posts in the Arkansas-based Winrock International Institute for Agricultural Development. He serves on the board of the Midwest chapter of the American Red Magen David for Israel (ARMDI) and regularly speaks to major Jewish organizations about Israel advocacy and the role of Evangelicals in supporting Israel. Mamo twice has addressed the national meeting of the Jewish Council on Public Affairs, as well as the annual conference of The Israel Project.

Gerald McDermott, Ph.D., is professor of religion at Roanoke College. He has published three books on the American theologian Jonathan

Edwards, several books on cancer and theology, and two more on the Christian theology of other religions. His most recent book debates Jesus with a Mormon theologian. In addition to these interests, he has written on evangelical relations with the State of Israel. Professor McDermott is also an Episcopal priest who serves as teaching pastor in a Lutheran congregation.

Alan Mittleman, Ph.D., is director of the Louis Finkelstein Institute for Religious and Social Studies and professor of Jewish philosophy at The Jewish Theological Seminary. Dr. Mittleman is the author of three books: *Between Kant and Kabbalah* (1990), *The Politics of Torah* (1996), and *The Scepter Shall Not Depart from Judah* (2000). He is also the editor of *Jewish Polity and American Civil Society* (2002), *Jews and the American Public Square* (2002), and *Religion as a Public Good* (2003). From 2000 to 2004, he served as director of a major research project, "Jews and the American Public Square," which was initiated by The Pew Charitable Trusts. He is the recipient of an Alexander von Humboldt Foundation Research Fellowship and served as Guest Research Professor at the University of Cologne (1994 and 1996). Dr. Mittleman also received a Harry Starr Fellowship in Modern Jewish History from Harvard University's Center for Jewish Studies (1997). He has served on the Advisory Board of the Pew Forum on Religion and Public Life.

David Neff is editor of *Christianity Today* magazine and an editorial vice president of *Christianity Today International*. He also supervises the editing of *Christian History & Biography* at CTI, a company that publishes eleven print magazines and a wide variety of online resources. Mr. Neff has been at *Christianity Today* for over twenty years. Before coming to that magazine, he edited HIS, InterVarsity Christian Fellowship's magazine for college students, and taught religion and provided pastoral care at a church-related college in Washington State.

Rabbi **Yehiel E. Poupko** is the Judaic Scholar at the Jewish Federation of Metropolitan Chicago.

Carl Schrag, a former editor of the *Jerusalem Post*, studies the changing nature of relations between American Jews and Israel, as well as a wide range of grassroots pro-Israeli efforts among American Jews and Christians. Currently based in Chicago, he writes, teaches, and lectures on these topics across the United States.

Mark Silk is director of the Leonard E. Greenberg Center for the Study of Religion in Public Life and professor of religion in public life at Trinity College, Hartford. Since 1998, he has edited *Religion in the News*, a magazine published by the Center that examines how the news media handle religious subject matter. Professor Silk is the author of *Spiritual Politics: Religion and America Since World War II* and *Unsecular Media: Making News of Religion in America*. He is coeditor of *Religion by Region*, an eight-volume series on religion and public life in the United States.